Caesar's
Civil War

OXFORD APPROACHES TO
CLASSICAL LITERATURE

SERIES EDITORS
Kathleen Coleman and Richard Rutherford

OVID'S *Metamorphoses*
ELAINE FANTHAM

PLATO'S *Symposium*
RICHARD HUNTER

CAESAR'S
Civil War

WILLIAM W. BATSTONE
CYNTHIA DAMON

UNIVERSITY PRESS

2006

OXFORD
UNIVERSITY PRESS

Oxford University Press, Inc., publishes works that further
Oxford University's objective of excellence
in research, scholarship, and education.

Oxford   New York
Auckland   Cape Town   Dar es Salaam   Hong Kong   Karachi
Kuala Lumpur   Madrid   Melbourne   Mexico City   Nairobi
New Delhi   Shanghai   Taipei   Toronto

With offices in
Argentina   Austria   Brazil   Chile   Czech Republic   France   Greece
Guatemala   Hungary   Italy   Japan   Poland   Portugal   Singapore
South Korea   Switzerland   Thailand   Turkey   Ukraine   Vietnam

Copyright © 2006 by Oxford University Press, Inc.

Published by Oxford University Press, Inc.
198 Madison Avenue, New York, New York 10016

www.oup.com

Oxford is a registered trademark of Oxford University Press

All rights reserved. No part of this publication may be reproduced,
stored in a retrieval system, or transmitted, in any form or by any means,
electronic, mechanical, photocopying, recording, or otherwise,
without the prior permission of Oxford University Press.

Library of Congress Cataloging-in-Publication Data
Batstone, William Wendell.
Caesar's Civil War / William W. Batstone and Cynthia Damon
p. cm. — (Oxford approaches to classical literature)
Includes bibliographical references.
ISBN-13 978-0-19-516510-4; 978-0-19-516511-1 (pbk.)
ISBN 0-19-516510-1; 0-19-516511-X (pbk.)
1. Caesar, Julius. De bello civili.
2. Rome—History—Civil War, 49–45 B.C.—
Literature and the war   I. Damon, Cynthia, 1957–
II. Title.   III. Series.
PA6238.B3B37 2006
937'.05—dc22   2006000597

2 4 6 8 9 7 5 3 1

Printed in the United States of America
on acid-free paper

Editors' Foreword

The late twentieth and early twenty-first centuries have seen a massive expansion in courses dealing with ancient civilization and, in particular, the culture and literature of the Greek and Roman world. Never has there been such a flood of good translations available: Oxford's own World Classics, the Penguin Classics, the Hackett Library, and other series offer the English-speaking reader access to the masterpieces of classical literature from Homer to Augustine. The reader may, however, need more guidance in the interpretation and understanding of these works than can usually be provided in the relatively short introduction that prefaces a work in translation. There is a need for studies of individual works that will provide a clear, lively, and reliable account based on the most up-to-date scholarship without dwelling on minutiae that are likely to distract or confuse the reader.

It is to meet this need that the present series has been devised. The title *Oxford Approaches to Classical Literature* deliberately puts the emphasis on the literary works themselves. The volumes in this series will each be concerned with a single work (with the exception of cases where a "book" or larger collection of poems is treated as one work). These are neither biographies nor accounts of literary movements or schools. Nor are they books devoted to the total oeuvre of one author: our first volumes consider Ovid's *Metamorphoses* and Plato's *Symposium*, not the works of Ovid or Plato as a whole. This is, however, a question of emphasis, and not a straitjacket: biographical issues, literary and cultural background, and related works by the same author are discussed where they are obviously relevant. Authors have also been encouraged to consider the influence and legacy of the works in question.

As the editors of this series, we intend these volumes to be accessible to the reader who is encountering the relevant work for the first time; but we also intend that each volume should do more than simply provide the basic facts, dates, and summaries that handbooks generally supply. We would like these books to be essays in criticism and interpretation that will do justice to the subtlety and complexity of the works under discussion. With this in mind, we have invited leading scholars to offer personal assessments and appreciations of their chosen works, anchored within the mainstream of classical scholarship. We have thought it particularly important that our authors be allowed to set their own agendas and to speak in their own voices rather than repeating the *idées reçues* of conventional wisdom in neutral tones.

The title *Oxford Approaches to Classical Literature* has been chosen simply because the series is published by Oxford University Press, USA; it in no way implies a party line, either Oxonian or any other. We believe that different approaches are suited to different texts, and we expect each volume to have its own distinctive character. Advanced critical theory is neither compulsory nor excluded: what matters is whether it can be made to illuminate the text in question. The authors have been encouraged to avoid obscurity and jargon, bearing in mind the needs of the general reader; but, when important critical or narratological issues arise, they are presented to the reader as lucidly as possible.

This series was originally conceived by Professor Charles Segal, an inspiring scholar and teacher whose intellectual energy and range of interests were matched by a corresponding humility and generosity of spirit. Although he was involved in the commissioning of a number of volumes, he did not—alas—live to see any of them published. The series is intended to convey something of the excitement and pleasure to be derived from reading the extraordinarily rich and varied literature of Greco-Roman antiquity. We hope that these volumes will form a worthy monument to a dedicated classical scholar who was committed to enabling the ancient texts to speak to the widest possible audience in the contemporary world.

Kathleen Coleman, Harvard University
Richard Rutherford, Christ Church, Oxford

Acknowledgments

This book has two authors. Simple statement, complex reality: Cynthia Damon wrote the initial drafts of chapters 1 and 4, William Batstone the initial draft of chapter 2, each drafted some parts of chapters 3 and 5, and the final draft was produced in common. We remain friends.

Will Batstone would like to thank the Department of Greek and Latin at the Ohio State University for arranging a teaching schedule that freed up one quarter for work on this book and Ludwig Maximilians Universität in Munich for inviting him to speak on Caesar in the spring of 2004. Although that paper was on the manuscript tradition, the lively discussion over dinner encouraged his belief that the first book of Caesar's *Civil War* was published roughly as we have it.

For help along the way, Cynthia Damon is grateful to Caesarians and historiographers who shared their own work with her and commented on early drafts of hers: Elaine Fantham, Christina Kraus, John Marincola, Debra Nousek, Andrew Riggsby, Andreola Rossi, Geoffrey Sumi, and Tony Woodman. In their capacity as respondents to public lectures, Christopher Pelling and Geoffrey Sumi provided important challenges, as did the students in her class *Bella civilia:* The Civil Wars of Caesar and Lucan (Amherst College, fall 2004). She is grateful to David Potter and Carlos Noreña for invitations to present her work at meetings of the Association of Ancient Historians and the New England Ancient Historians Colloquium, respectively, as well as to Christina Kraus and John Marincola for an invitation to NYU for the "Past and Present" conference in honor of Tony Woodman, and to Ted Ahern for an invitation to speak about Caesar in connection with the seventy-fifth anniversary celebrations of the Graduate School of Arts and Sciences at Boston College. The lively audiences on all four occasions convinced her that people still pay attention to Caesar. She was able to pay attention to Caesar thanks to a year's sabbatical provided by Amherst College and the Mellon Foundation.

The general editors of the series, Kathleen Coleman and Richard Rutherford, helped bring our work to fruition with their well-calibrated combination of encouragement and forbearance. The Humanities editor at the press, Shannon McLachlan, neatly supervised the final stages of a project begun under the auspices of her predecessor, Elissa Morris. We are grateful to all for their part in the many-faceted endeavor that is scholarly publishing. As we are to our home institutions—specifically, to the Department of Greek and Latin at the Ohio State University and to the Dean of Faculty, Gregory Call, at Amherst College—for funding that enabled us to include the maps and the cover illustration. For the maps themselves we thank Patrick Florance, who prepared them exactly to specification and who, by his advice, improved our specifications. The cover image, plate 8 of Joan Miró's 1938 Black and Red Series, is a response to Spain's Civil War. It is included here with permission.

Contents

Editors' Foreword *v*
Preliminary Note *xiii*
Introduction *3*

1
Choices: Genre, Content, Style *8*

2
Structure as Argument in *Civil War* 1 *33*

3
Taking Sides, Making Sides *89*

4
Mastering Victory *117*

5
Writing Fighting War *143*
Epilogue: Surviving Failure *166*

Timeline of the Life of Caesar and the Civil War 173
Maps 179
Notes 185
Prominent Persons 201
Works Cited 211
Index 215

Preliminary Note

The text of Caesar and his continuators is that of Klotz. The text of Cicero's correspondence is that of Shackleton Bailey. Translations of Appian, Dio, and Plutarch are from the Loeb Classical Library, a widely accessible series of classical texts and translations; some have been lightly modernized. Other translations are our own, unless otherwise indicated. Abbreviations for the names and works of ancient authors are according to Liddell and Scott, *Greek-English Lexicon*, and the *Oxford Latin Dictionary*.

Caesar's
Civil War

Introduction

> Caesar takes hold as I write and compels me,
> hurrying though I am, to linger on him.
> —VELLEIUS PATERCULUS, *Roman History* 2.41.1

Caesar's *Civil War* is an unfinished masterpiece. It is incomplete not owing to untimely death, however, but was abandoned by an author who found himself living in a different world than that which saw the work's commencement. It might thus seem an odd candidate for a literary appreciation. But it deserves one. The *Civil War* is the story of Caesar's contest with the Pompeian party through nineteen months of civil war; it ends, after Pompey's death, amid the preliminaries to a foreign war fought to impose a Roman settlement on the kingdom of Egypt. The work shows the brilliance for which Caesar's oratory, like his generalship, was known—in the eyes of Quintilian, no mean judge, he was second only to Cicero (*Education of an Orator* 10.1.114)—and it was a political judgment that relegated the *Civil War* to the file drawer, not a literary one. The five chapters of this book explore the various components of Caesar's literary achievement in the *Civil War*. We supply here in the introduction the necessary historical background, and in the epilogue the aftermath.

When Caesar was born in 100 BCE, Rome's political system, the republic (*res publica*, literally "the public thing"), had been in place for more than four hundred years and relatively stable for nearly two hundred. By the time he was assassinated in 44, it had collapsed. The central institution of government was the Senate, which controlled the state's finances and advised magistrates on pending legislation and other matters, such as declarations of war and treaties. Sovereignty resided in the Roman People, which acting in various assemblies elected magistrates and voted on matters put to them by the magistrates with the Senate's approval. Magistrates, including the highest, the two consuls, served for one-year terms and were ineligible for further office in Rome the following year. Consuls had to wait ten years for reelection. After their year in office, the consuls and other magistrates were put in charge of tasks necessary to the administration of Rome's huge territorial empire. These tasks, or "provinces," could be geographical areas, such as North Africa, Asia Minor, or Transalpine Gaul (see map), or administrative units, such as courts, or special assignments such as the eradication of pirates from the Mediterranean or supervision of the grain supply. Provincial assignments lasted for one or more years, and most involved command of military forces, forces an ambitious commander could use to acquire territory and wealth for the state and glory and wealth for himself.

Running the empire ruined the system that won the empire. By the time of Caesar's birth, problems were evident, but the Senate, whose members were magistrates and ex-magistrates and served for life, resisted change. When reforms were proposed, often by elected representatives ("tribunes of the people") whose original function was to protect citizens from abuse by the state, they were blocked. Among the Senate's reasons, besides a disinclination to change a system in which they prospered, was the fear that the proposer of a popular reform would become too popular, too influential; oligarchy had long guaranteed stability.

One reform, however, was forced through during a rare period of danger from an external enemy, and it led eventually, perhaps inevitably, to the civil war in which the republic perished. This was the extension of eligibility for military service to propertyless citizens. Unlike the farmer-soldiers of the early republic, who returned to their farms after military campaigns in not-too-distant provinces, the soldiers of the late republic, who fought for Rome in Spain, North Africa, the Black Sea area, Syria, and further east, made the army their career and depended on the state for support (in the form of discharge bonuses of land or cash) after their retirement. But they got their bonuses only if their commander had sufficient political clout to win them from the Senate. Or if both he and his soldiers were willing to threaten military action against Rome itself. Some were.

Reforms of interest to the citizen body as a whole, to the Italian allies who fought alongside the citizen legions, and to the increasing number of provincials in the empire had still smaller prospects of successful passage. Frustration fueled violence in the streets of Rome, particularly during elections. By the late 50s, some years opened without magistrates because none had been elected, so chaotic had the political situation become.

During Caesar's lifetime the republic's problems gained in urgency. In the 80s, the general Sulla led his army against Rome not once but twice, and purged Senate and city of his political enemies. These purges were called "proscriptions" and amounted to state-sanctioned murder.[1] When Sulla was later given an extraordinary magistracy, the dictatorship, and the task of "reconstituting the republic," he strengthened the Senate (now filled with men loyal to him) and weakened the tribunes of the people, which only prolonged the stalemate. In 63, a disappointed aristocrat named Catiline mustered an army from the disaffected and the indebted and led it, too, against Rome. Cicero as consul that year organized a successful response, but only by resorting to executions without trial and by pitting Romans against Romans in the field. Later in the 60s, the army of the repeatedly successful general Pompey, returning victorious from campaigns in the eastern provinces of the empire, could have emulated Sulla's, but Pompey instead joined forces with an ambitious Caesar and tried to win satisfaction for his veterans by applying political rather than military pressure.

Caesar himself proved the biggest problem for the republic. As consul in 59, he tried to get for Pompey what he wanted from the

Senate, without success. He then turned to the assemblies of the sovereign People, which settled Pompey's demands and gave Caesar an important province for the following year(s), but not without violent clashes and unprecedented procedures. A senator named Cato was active in the resistance to Caesar both in the Senate (where his vote was that they should "abide by the existing system," Dio 38.3.1) and in the streets. In 58, the Senate declared Caesar's consular acts illegal, but by then Caesar had taken up his command (and with it legal immunity) in Gaul, where between 58 and 50 he won territory—most of modern France and Belgium—and wealth for the state, and glory and wealth for himself in campaigns that he reported to his contemporaries and recorded for posterity in his *Gallic War*. By 50, Caesar had ten loyal legions (some fifty thousand men) and two pressing needs: to avoid prosecution for his illegal acts in 59 and to obtain recognition for his military achievements in Gaul. The Senate's leaders, who included Cato, were not going to satisfy either need, and wooed Pompey—who had his own military laurels and loyal soldiers—as their champion in case Caesar should seek satisfaction as Sulla had.

This, in brief, is the background to the *Civil War*, in which Caesar tells the story of his break with the Senate and Pompey and the war that resulted. The phase of the civil war narrated by Caesar lasted from January of 49, when Caesar and one legion crossed the Rubicon river to enter Italy, to August of 48, when his forces defeated Pompey's army at Pharsalus in Greece (see timeline and maps for dates and places). Caesar's army won its first success at Corfinium, a town on the road from Ravenna to Rome, where he trapped a substantial portion of the enemy army. Pompey had already marched south with other troops and soon left Italy for Greece, where he hoped to build his military strength. Lacking ships for the Adriatic crossing, Caesar could not follow. Instead, he split his forces: some went south to Sicily and North Africa to secure Rome's grain supply, some went to the important independent port of Marseilles in the western Mediterranean, and the largest part marched with Caesar to Spain, which was Pompey's province and the base of his most reliable forces. These overlapping campaigns are narrated in interlocking panels of books 1 and 2. After victories in Spain and Marseilles and a costly defeat in North Africa, Caesar returned to Italy at the beginning of 48, stopping briefly in Rome before making a winter crossing to Greece, the site of the final phase of the fight against Pompey and the setting of most of book 3. Pompey escaped Pharsalus alive, but Caesar, following him to Alexandria, found him dead in September, assassinated by the Egyptian king. Caesar remained in Egypt to intervene militarily in a dynastic struggle between Pompey's killer, Ptolemy, and his sister/wife Cleopatra. His *Civil War* stops here.

Caesar's narrative of the war is not the only account to survive antiquity, but it is the longest. Parallel narratives exist in historical texts (Appian, Dio), historical summaries (Velleius Paterculus, cited in the epigraph), biographies (Suetonius, Plutarch), and an epic poem (Lucan). Comparisons drawn from these works, both Greek (Appian, Dio, Plutarch) and Latin (Velleius Paterculus, Suetonius, Lucan), as well as from comparable narratives from earlier and later periods, complement our discussion of Caesar's story. Our focus, however, is on Caesar's *Civil War* in its contemporary literary and historical context.

·1·

Choices: Genre, Content, Style

> ... so that knowledge of such great achievements might not be lacking ...
> —HIRTIUS, on Caesar's *commentarii*, *Gallic War* 8 preface 5

1 | *Commentarius*

The narratives that we call Caesar's *Gallic War* and *Civil War* were spoken of by his contemporaries as the "records of his achievements."[1] The term here translated as "records" is *commentarii* (its singular form is *commentarius*). The word itself contains a reference to memory (the root -men-, also present in me<u>n</u>tion, me<u>men</u>to, com<u>men</u>t and, contracted, in a<u>mn</u>esia), and our translation reflects the word's etymology.

The ancient evidence allows us to arrive at relatively good inferences about what Caesar's readers would have expected from a *commentarius*. When Caesar's officer and later continuator Aulus Hirtius, in *Gallic War* 8, refers back to *Gallic War* 7 with the phrase "it was shown in the preceding *commentarius*," "preceding *commentarius*" means something like "the record of the preceding year."[2] The *Gallic War* as Caesar published it was a set of seven *commentarii*, the records of seven annual campaigns in Gaul (58–52 BCE), not one *commentarius*, or record, of his conquest of Gaul. (After Caesar's death Hirtius added an eighth book, on which see below.) Using *commentarius* for the record of a single year emphasized the connection between the written account of Caesar's achievements and Rome's political and military calendars: the political calendar was predicated on one-year terms of office, and military campaigns, too, had an annual cycle of summer fighting and winter encampment.

The term *commentarius* was also used for written accounts in a wide variety of other forms: appropriate translations range from "notebook" (a private record of things one wants to remember: ideas, achievements, plans, excerpts from readings, notes for speeches) to "record book" (an official record of events and duties, particularly for public officials) to "treatise" or "manual" (a record of technical knowledge) and beyond.[3] In all of these uses, however, *commentarius* seems to announce a written account in which the author's effort has been expended on content rather than on literary polish. And if we look at what is said about two (lost) *commentarii* close in time to Caesar's, those of Cicero and his friend Atticus on Cicero's consulship, we can see that a style deliberately unpolished ("the unvarnished truth") was by Caesar's day expected (if not always delivered) in a public figure's record of his achievements, his *res gestae*.

What Cicero wanted recorded for posterity was 63 BCE, the year he held Rome's highest magistracy, the consulship. More specifically, it was his role as consul in suppressing a revolutionary conspiracy against the state. Atticus wrote a *commentarius* in Greek on the subject, and Cicero himself wrote (or spoke of writing) a long open letter to Pompey on his consulship, as well as an epic poem in Latin and *commentarii* in both Latin and Greek.[4] The two Greek *commentarii* were very different in style. Atticus's words were, says Cicero, "rather rough and unkempt," though "adorned by the very fact that they scorned adornment" (*Att.* 2.1.1, June 60). Of his own he says first that his aim was to write correct and cultured Greek, and that his material was "not praise but history" (*Att.* 1.19.10, March 60). Two months later, however, and with revealing ingenuousness, he tells Atticus that he has offered the account to others for "writing up," but that once they read his version they get cold feet (*Att.* 1.20.6, May 60).[5] The full confession emerges in a letter of early June in the same year: his *commentarius* "has used up the perfume cabinet of Isocrates [an orator famous for his elaborate style] along with all the little scent boxes of his pupils and some of Aristotle's paints, as well" (*Att.* 2.1.1); no wonder the authors who wanted to "write up" his consulship backed off. Cicero asks Atticus to circulate his (Cicero's) *commentarius* in Athens and other Greek cities, on the grounds that "it seems capable of bringing my affairs into the light" (ibid.).

Commentarii were by Caesar's day an established form of apologetic history, history written and published by (or for) a public figure to affirm his achievement and defend his actions. Caesar's *commentarii* on the war in Gaul, which were written as a record and justification of events in which the author played a leading role as an official of the Roman state, fit this model well: Hirtius sees manifest in them a veritable "science" on Caesar's part of knowing how to explain his plans, "explanation" being a rubric that neatly encapsulates both recording and justifying (*Gallic War* 8 preface 7). Their style was austere: Cicero calls them "naked," Hirtius "elegant."[6] It was easy to imagine that they were intended, as was Cicero's Greek *commentarius*, to serve as a basis for other narratives: Hirtius's assertion that "they were published so that knowledge of such great achievements might not be lacking to writers" echoes Cicero's comment, also on the *Gallic War*, that "[Caesar] wanted others to have ready resources upon which they could depend if they wanted to write history" (*Gallic War* 8 preface 5; Cic. *Brut.* 262). Hirtius and Cicero also agree, however, that Caesar's account was so good as to deter attempts to rewrite this history.

Caesar's three civil war *commentarii*, which we call the *Civil War* for short, although not in the end published by their author, take their start from this tradition. They concern events in which Caesar played a leading role in an official capacity: he is a provincial governor when the *Civil War* begins and later dictator and then consul. But the subject matter put pressure on the form. The correspondence between book and political calendar, for instance, is loosened in the *Civil War*.[7] And in a civil war even success is hard to "sell," while political questions are unavoidable and personalities edge in. Nevertheless, the focus stays on Caesar's public role; the *Civil War* is no more autobiographical than is the *Gallic War*.

In section 2 of this chapter, we examine the selection of material in the *Civil War* that keeps the focus public, asking what kinds of events are recorded and who the important actors are. We also make a start on the larger question of why Caesar selects material as he does, specifically, how well he answers the questions contemporaries were asking about the war. Other aspects of Caesar's selection of material are considered in subsequent chapters.

Stylistically, the *Civil War* is considerably plainer than what one imagines Cicero's perfumed and painted *commentarius* to have been. In section 3, we introduce the style of the *Civil War* by exploring what contemporary critics had in mind when they commented on the "nakedness" or "elegance" of Caesar's prose. We compare Caesar's version of a signal event—Pompey's assassination—with a version "written up" more elaborately. Style too is more fully treated later.

In both sections we touch upon essential qualities of the *Civil War*, the economy of content and style that in Caesar's *Gallic War* won him the praise of his contemporaries. But on the *Civil War* Caesar's own verdict must have been in some sense negative. The work was abandoned, the narrative of the fight for Alexandria begun but not completed. In section 4, we ask, for the first time but not the last, why.

2 | Content

In this section we look at how Caesar focuses his reader's attention by his selection of material. Looking at content separately from form (which will be treated in section 3) makes an artificial division between aspects of the work that function together, but we do so here in the interests of clarity at the outset. One further caveat: the parameters for our discussion of Caesar's material are set by what one finds in ancient military and historical narrative generally. That is, we do not comment on the fact that economic and social factors—to name just two—are given no consideration in the *Civil War*, because such factors are nowhere prominent in ancient narratives. Caesar writes about events and people, not conditions or forces or structures or populations. What we ask is, what events? and which people?

2a *Events*

Toward the end of January 49, writing from Campania where he and many of Caesar's opponents have taken temporary refuge, Cicero tells Atticus (who stayed in Rome hedging his bets) that he is eager for news about, among other things, "what Domitius is doing in the Marsian country."[8] "Domitius" is Lucius Domitius Ahenobarbus, the man sent by the Senate to replace Caesar as governor of Transalpine Gaul; "Marsian country" is the territory east of Rome near Corfinium (modern Corfinio). What Domitius is supposed to be doing is opposing Caesar's post-Rubicon march on Rome. Cicero's letters of the next few weeks are filled with news and rumors about what Domitius is doing—the topic comes up more than a dozen times between late January and early March. Other narratives of the period, as we will see below, treat Domitius's ultimately unsuccessful opposition in a rather cursory fashion, but Caesar supplies a detailed answer to Cicero's question.[9]

His account of the way he overcame Domitius occupies nearly nine paragraphs in book 1, roughly a thousand words (1.15.6–23.5). The passage is too long to reproduce here; we supply a summary with occasional supplements to give the modern reader information that a Roman reader would know without being told.

Caesar begins by recording the sizes of the opposing forces: Caesar has two legions, Domitius thirty-three cohorts (1.15.7–8). As any Roman reader would know, Domitius has the edge in raw numbers, since there were ten cohorts to a legion, but the terminology here also reflects a more important reality, namely, experience. A legion, particularly a legion of Caesar's, was ten cohorts welded by time and experience into a fighting unit with its own pride and traditions (hence he specifies that the 12th and 13th legions were with him at this time), whereas Domitius's cohorts were, as Caesar indicates, new recruits and units that had never operated together. But Caesar is not inattentive to numbers: he starts a recruitment drive of his own (1.16.1). Other preparations include a day spent collecting provisions (ibid.).

First contact occurs when five cohorts sent by Domitius to destroy a bridge three miles from his base at Corfinium are driven off by Caesar's vanguard (1.16.2). Caesar takes his legions across the still-standing bridge and establishes his camp against the walls of Corfinium (ibid.). By this point in the narrative he and his troops have shown themselves to and received the capitulation of several important towns in northern Italy (1.11–15; see sec. 3a in chap. 2); inside Corfinium is the largest force they have yet faced.

In paragraph 17, the focus shifts to Domitius. He writes to Pompey (who has two legions and some new recruits roughly 150 Roman miles away) asking for support (1.17.1–2). Meanwhile, he prepares the defense of the city: placing artillery, arranging patrols, and trying to buy the loyalty of his troops with promises of rewards from his own pocket—twenty-four acres of land to each soldier, with larger amounts in proportion to the officers (1.17.3–4).

Caesar, for his part, is not idle. He sends his legate Antony with five cohorts from the 13th legion to take the nearby town of Sulmo, which was held by his opponents (whose leaders he names) with seven cohorts (1.18.1–3). A show of Caesarian force suffices: the town and the soldiers capitulate, while the two Pompeian leaders (named again) flee. Antony and his troops return to Corfinium the same day. Caesar himself spent his first days at Corfinium fortifying the camp and mustering provisions; he was also waiting for reinforcements. The 8th legion arrives on the third day, along with twenty-two new cohorts and roughly three hundred cavalrymen from a friendly Alpine king. A new camp is made for these forces, with Curio in charge (1.18.4–6). The noose is slowly tightening.

Inside Corfinium, Domitius has had a response from Pompey (1.19.1). What it was we learn only at the end of the paragraph. At its outset, Caesar tells us instead that Domitius lied to his troops about it and made plans for his own escape (1.19.2). But, says Caesar, the deception did not, indeed could not, succeed: Domitius was under close scrutiny and the discrepancy between his confident words and timorous manner was noted, as were his secret meetings (1.19.3). For Pompey had in fact said no (1.19.4–5). Domitius's soldiers, or most of them, take matters into their own hands: Domitius is arrested and messengers are sent to tell Caesar that Corfinium and Domitius are his (1.20.1–5).

The military contest, so carefully prepared for, is thus won almost without a blow. But there are three more paragraphs to the narrative of events at Corfinium, all of them detailing how Caesar used his victory: what disposition he made for Domitius's troops (they joined his army), how he treated Domitius himself and the other notables who were with him (he let them all go), what he did with Domitius's payroll of six million sesterces—three months' pay for four legions—(he returned it to Domitius), and what happened to the townspeople (nothing). At Corfinium, says Caesar wrapping up, he spent seven days (1.23.5).

We get a sense of Caesar's purpose(s) in the selection of material for his narrative of events at Corfinium from two comparisons, one with a similar account of different events (Cicero on a military victory of his own), and one with different accounts of the same events (brief reports on Corfinium in Plutarch, Suetonius, Appian, and Dio).

Cicero's victory narrative is part of a long letter he sent from the province of Cilicia in the eastern Mediterranean, where he was proconsul, or governor, in 51–50 BCE. His addressee is Cato, an influential senator in Rome. In providing this record of his military achievements, his aim, as he makes clear, is to win Cato's support for an official commendation of his governorship. Here is his narrative of his *res gestae* at a place called Pindenissum:

> These operations concluded, I led the army to a town of the Free Cilicians, Pindenissum. Since this was a lofty and well fortified place inhabited by men who had never obeyed even kings, and since they were harboring fugitives and eagerly awaiting the arrival of the Parthians, I deemed it

important for the reputation of our empire to rein in their audacity, in the expectation that the spirits of others inimical to our empire would be broken the more easily as a result. I surrounded it with a rampart and a ditch, I set six fortified posts and a very large camp in a ring around it, I attacked with a siege ramp, siege sheds, and towers. Using much artillery, many archers, and much personal effort, without any trouble or expense to our allies, I finished the job on the fifty-seventh day, with the result that, after all parts of the city were ruined or burned, they were compelled to surrender themselves to me. (*Fam.* 15.4.10; late 51 or early 50)

Though Cicero's narrative is considerably shorter than Caesar's (131 words in the Latin), he provides Cato with many of the same kinds of information: the nature of the opponent, the preparatory fortifications, the result of the victory, the time-cost of the operation. He has more on topography; Caesar does not dwell on the presumably familiar topography of Italian towns such as Corfinium, but for operations elsewhere he regularly provides such information. In this self-contained account Cicero specifies the purpose of the operation (deterrent); Caesar's purpose at Corfinium was part of his larger purpose early in 49, namely, seizing control of as much of Italy as possible before his opponents could organize resistance. Cicero is vague as to quantities ("a very large camp," "many archers," "much personal effort") where Caesar is precise ("two legions," "twenty-two cohorts," "three miles distant," "three hundred cavalrymen," "twenty-four acres," "six million sesterces"). And of course Cicero has a battle to recount, while Caesar avoided battle at Corfinium. Caesar, on the other hand, has much more on the actions and plans and reasoning of his enemy. A civil war will yield a different kind of information than a border war: Caesar's opponents, many of whom survived the war, shared Rome with him until his assassination, while Cicero left Cilicia with relief in 50 and never returned. Caesar shows that there is more to military success than fortifications, artillery, and archers.

Different as they are, however, these two narratives agree that certain kinds of information are relevant to *res gestae*: location, troop resources, names of high-ranking personnel, purpose, preparations, strategy, outcome, cost. And the parallel with Cicero, whose quest for "the honor customarily allotted by the Senate to military achievements" (*Fam.* 15.4.13) is explicit, permits the inference that at least part of Caesar's aim, even in a civil war narrative, was similar, that he wanted to give his fellow senators an account that would enable them to evaluate and honor his military achievements. Such evaluations were a regular part of the Senate's business and the senators all had military experience of their own.

The second comparison to be made with Caesar's account will show that the events at Corfinium can be turned to other narrative purposes than documenting the merits of military achievements. The parallel accounts are all much briefer than Caesar's, and briefer, too, than Cicero on Pindenissum.

The account of Dio, himself a senator and provincial governor more than two centuries after Caesar and Cicero, is the closest in length (41.10.2, 41.11.1–3; 114 words). He specifies Caesar's purpose—"he set out next against Corfinium, because this place, being occupied by Lucius Domitius, would not join his cause"—and reports, without details, the initial phases: "after conquering in battle a few who met him, he shut up the rest and besieged them." But thereafter Caesar is virtually absent from the picture; Dio describes Domitius's decision to withdraw (presented as obedience to Pompey), his failure to win the adherence of his men (because it looked like flight), and the collapse of the resistance: "So [Domitius's soldiers] joined the invader's army, but Domitius and the other senators, after being censured by Caesar for arraying themselves against him, were allowed to go and came to Pompey" (41.11.2). According to Dio, that is, Caesar had no significant *res gestae* at Corfinium; what Dio tells is rather a story of Domitius's well-intentioned failure.

The final note in Dio's account, that Domitius, though spared by Caesar, continued to oppose him, is also present in the other parallel accounts we consider. Appian, who like Dio wrote a historical narrative of the period and had access to contemporary sources, spends seventy-seven words on Corfinium, more than half of them on Domitius's ingratitude. The rest hardly amounts to an achievement for Caesar: "At Corfinium Caesar caught up with and besieged Lucius Domitius, who had been sent to be his successor in the command in Gaul, but who did not have all of his four thousand men with him. The inhabitants of Corfinium captured [Domitius] at the gates, as he was trying to escape, and brought him to Caesar" (2.38). No worthy opponent, no preparations, no strategy; success seems to fall into Caesar's hands. Similarly in the biographer Suetonius, who allots less than a sentence to Corfinium: "When Lucius Domitius, who, having been named in the emergency as Caesar's successor, was holding Corfinium with a garrison, was captured and dismissed . . . " (*DJ* 34.1). Plutarch too points a moralizing finger—"Domitius rose up overjoyed and went to Caesar, the pledge of whose right hand he received, only to desert him and go back to Pompey"—but spends most of his seventy-two words on a fairytale anecdote about Domitius's attempted suicide, which was foiled by the physician who gave him a sleeping potion in place of poison (*Life of Caesar* 34.6–8).

For these historians and biographers, the victory at Corfinium is just a small step in a process whose outcome in Caesar's overall victory is a foregone conclusion. In such a rhetorical situation, it is the human stories of the losers and the moral pressures of civil war that are of interest, not the step-by-step achievement of military success.

Caesar's account itself has more in it than military achievements. For example, Caesar, too, mentions suicide threats at Corfinium, though without Plutarch's fairy-tale elements. In the long night that passes between the capitulation of the town (1.20.5) and Caesar's entrance (1.23.1), Publius Lentulus Spinther, the most senior of the senators with Domitius, comes out to Caesar under a flag of truce and negotiates his own security (1.22.1–6). This, he says, will offer hope in an intolerable situation: "some people in Corfinium are so utterly terrified that they feel compelled to make unduly harsh plans about their lives" (1.22.6). The commander Domitius may well be included in the "some people," but Caesar does not say so, nor does he venture beyond a euphemism for suicide ("unduly harsh plans about their lives"). Still, it is striking that other people's worries about personal matters are present in Caesar's *res gestae*. That they turn up here suggests that we need to look beyond the affirmation of military achievement in assessing Caesar's aim in writing the *Civil War*.

A substantial part of Caesar's narrative of the capture of the town shows that the worries just mentioned were baseless: nobody lost his life or his freedom there. In other words, his narrative of "the events at Corfinium" provides the answer not only to Cicero's question to Atticus about "what Domitius was doing in the Marsian country," but also to the unspoken question that accompanies it, namely, what Domitius's success or failure would mean for him (Cicero), for others who sided with Pompey, for Italy, and for the republic.[10] Caesar knew this, and in a letter that we will refer to again (*Att.* 9.7C, early March 49) he writes to friends shortly after Corfinium to speak of winning the goodwill of all and of a new style of victory. The letter was circulated at Rome and is preserved among Cicero's correspondence. More answers to the question of what Caesar's successes meant for the republic and its citizens will emerge from our discussion of book 1 in chapter 2.

2b People

The departure of Pompey and his most influential supporters from Rome in mid-January 49 initiated a rapid clarification of muddy waters in the personnel of the civil war. Pompey is reputed to have said that he would consider anyone who did not join him then as an enemy thenceforth.[11] People were agog to hear how others, particularly senators, declared themselves. The defection of Caesar's legate Labienus to Pompey was big news (*Fam.* 16.12, *Att.* 7.13a.3). Smaller fish were of interest, too; in mid-March of 49 Cicero was compiling for Atticus a list of declared Pompeians (*Att.* 9.9.4). Caesar, by contrast, avoids lists of this sort (the few exceptions will be discussed below). The men (and there are only men) mentioned in the narrative are there, at least at first glance, because they have a role in the military or political events Caesar has selected for inclusion, not as entries in a Hall of Fame (Caesarians) or Shame (Pompeians).[12]

Named individuals are equally divided between the two sides, with roughly fifty on each. On both sides the majority of those named are military officers: the magistrates, ex-magistrates, legates, and prefects who commanded large and small units of soldiers on land and sea (thirty-six and thirty-seven respectively). Coming in for individual mention in much smaller numbers are men of senatorial and equestrian status whose military role, if any, is unclear; also centurions, local notables, and soldiers (fewer than ten total in the first three categories, fewer than five in the last two). By virtue of the nature of the command structure in the Roman military, the majority of those named are senators (roughly thirty Caesarians, forty Pompeians), but status is not the predominant criterion: people are named in connection with events, not vice versa.[13]

Typical events involving names are battles, troop or ship movements, feats of military engineering, and negotiations. As an example, consider a small-scale battle in Greece reported at 3.52:

> At one moment there was fighting in two places. For Pompey had made coordinated attacks on several fortified posts in order to split up [Caesar's] troops, so that help could not arrive from nearby forces. In one place Volcacius Tullus with his three cohorts faced the attack of a legion; he drove it off. In the other, German troops that were outside our fortifications killed many of the enemy and returned to their unit unharmed.

Volcacius Tullus, who had three cohorts at his disposal to face the ten of the Pompeian legion, was from a senatorial family and may have been a senator himself at the time of the battle; his military success goes on record in Caesar's text.[14] Caesar's German auxiliaries, however, though likewise successful, had a native (and here unnamed) leader. Other legates on both sides operate on a larger scale:

> While Caesar was making these preparations and arrangements, he sent to Spain his legate Gaius Fabius with the three legions he had established for the winter in Narbo and that area. He ordered that the passes of the Pyrenees be quickly taken; at that time they were garrisoned by Pompey's legate Lucius Afranius. . . . Fabius, as ordered, moving quickly, ejected the garrison from the pass and hurried by forced marches toward Afranius's army. (1.37)

Fabius has three legions, Afranius an equal number (1.39.1); to them belong the initial phases of the war in Spain (1.39–40). Both men were senators, but their status in the narrative is defined in military, not social or political, terms, and is limited to the present occasion. Caesar omits to say, for example, that Afranius had been a subordinate of Pompey since the 70s BCE and that Fabius had conducted important campaigns for Caesar in Gaul.[15]

To another long-standing legate, Gaius Trebonius, goes the credit for building the huge works that brought Marseilles to its knees:

> While these things were being done in Spain, Gaius Trebonius, Caesar's legate, who had been left behind for the taking of Marseilles, began to build a siege ramp, siege sheds, and towers on two sides of the city. . . . To complete these works Gaius Trebonius called in a huge number of pack-animals and men from all over the province and ordered deliveries of wicker and wood. When these preparations were complete he built a siege ramp eighty feet high. (2.1)

This passage is merely a summary. Caesar devotes five paragraphs in book 2 to the tasks mentioned here. Because of the city's strength, the power of its projectiles, and the determination of its defenders, constructing the ramp and towers without exposing the men to an unacceptable level of risk required ingenuity, effort, and massive amounts of material. Rolling "galleries" made from foot-square timbers protected those transporting earth, timber, and rock for the ramp; a moveable "tortoise" sixty feet square, of equally solid construction, protected those preparing the ground in front of the ramp. The towers were feats of engineering whose construction is described from the ground up (2.9); in its detail this narrative is comparable to Caesar's (loving) description of the bridge over the Rhine that he himself supervised the building of in 55 BCE (*Gallic War* 4.17). The galleries that protected men undermining Marseilles' defenses get another chapter (2.10; see sec. 2a in chap. 5). But Caesar does not mention the fact that Trebonius was a supporter throughout the 50s.[16]

The kinds of tasks that Caesar shows subordinates engaged in find a helpful parallel in Cicero's report to Cato about his military achievements in Cilicia. In that letter he describes, besides the battle of Pindenissum, at which we looked earlier, the pacification of the region around the Amanus mountains. Here is a brief excerpt:

> I marched by night with the army in light equipment so that on 13 October, when day arrived, I was ascending into the Amanus area. Having divided up the cohorts and auxiliaries—my brother, Quintus, was in charge of some together with myself, my legate Gaius Pomptinus was in charge of others, and my legates Marcus Anneius and Lucius Tullius were in charge of the rest—we surprised and defeated them, killing or capturing them and shutting off their escape. (*Fam.* 15.4.8)

Though Cicero writes this letter to make a case for his own military laurels, he includes the names and tasks of four legates. Such reports appear to give credit to subordinates for their part in their commander's *res gestae*, and to help them on the way to their own independent *res gestae*.

If that is the case, it may seem odd that Pompey's subordinates are present in the *Civil War* in numbers comparable to Caesar's. This would be a far more striking form of generosity than Caesar's famous leniency in the treatment of opponents. A glance at a typical exploit, however, makes it clear that Caesar is capable of reporting a Pompeian achievement in such a way as to give credit with one hand while taking it away with the other.

Decimus Laelius, a Pompeian fleet commander, takes independent action at Brindisi late in the war:

> At the same time Decimus Laelius arrived at Brindisi with his fleet and, in the same way that it was done by Libo, as we showed earlier, took possession of the island at the mouth of Brindisi's port. In a similar fashion [to Antony], Vatinius, who was in charge of Brindisi, using boats that had been decked and armed, lured out Laelius's ships and captured one warship that had gone further than the rest and two smaller ships in the narrows of the port. He too began to prevent the men of the fleet from getting water, using cavalry stationed here and there. But Laelius, operating in a season more favorable for navigation, was able to supply his men with water by means of transports from Corcyra and Dyrrachium; he was not deterred from his plan. Before he got news of the battle in Thessaly [i.e., Pharsalus], neither embarrassment at the loss of his ships nor the shortage of necessities was able to drive him from the port and island. (3.100)

Laelius takes a strategic island that had been the site of a previously reported battle (3.23–24). He gets credit for being more successful than his Pompeian predecessor, Libo, who was outsmarted by Caesar's subordinate Antony and abandoned the blockade, and he picked a better time of year for carrying out his plan, but these are smallish positives. Against them Caesar sets the fact that Laelius is caught by the same trick that caught Libo, which cost him three ships. And Caesar tips the balance away from praise by referring to embarrassing losses and real hardships, and by suggesting that Laelius maintained the blockade out of stubbornness more than anything else. Moreover, neither his presence at Brindisi nor his departure had any effect on the war, which was decided in Thessaly.

Names are also recorded in the *Civil War* in connection with the conduct of negotiations. Despite the failure of all negotiations, Caesar always names the emissaries.[17] A passage in book 1 helps explain why. At 1.26, after his victory at Corfinium and the departure of the consuls from Italy, but before Pompey's own departure,

Caesar sends an emissary to one of Pompey's supporters, Lucius Scribonius Libo ("Libo" in the passage above), with the job of persuading Libo to persuade Pompey to come to terms: "If [Caesar and Pompey] could only talk together, it would be possible to lay down arms on fair terms. The praise and repute for this would come in large part to Libo, if by his authority and agency weapons were relinquished" (1.26.4). "Praise" (*laus*) and "repute" (*existimatio*) are powerful motivators for a senator, and Libo does undertake the mission to Pompey. One may compare Cicero's longing, in early March of 49, to accomplish "something worthwhile for his country" by making peace, and his satisfaction later that month in learning that a letter of his to Caesar urging peace and offering himself as its agent had been made public in Rome (*Att.* 9.11.2; *Att.* 8.9.1). Indeed he confesses to Atticus that he had given out some copies of it himself (*Att.* 8.9.1). The hope of a negotiated peace remained strong until Pompey's departure from Italy (*Att.* 8.13.1; cf. *Att.* 9.6.7, both March 49), and Caesar's record of the negotiations that did take place claims (and gives) credit for political *res gestae*.

In the passages considered so far, Caesar's selection of material seems to determine the people he mentions.[18] More precisely, the level at which he reports it determines the names recorded (officers and magistrates, not soldiers and voters), with a few interesting exceptions, such as the omission of the name of the native commanding officer of the German auxiliaries and, as we will see in chapter 4, the inclusion of the glorious deeds of centurions and ordinary soldiers. And of course having one's name recorded in Caesar's commentaries could be a dubious boon, as we saw in the case of Laelius at Brindisi. But there are a handful of passages where no task or accomplishment motivates the naming of names, passages that give us an apparent equivalent to the lists that Cicero and others were making early in 49.

For example, Caesar lists the Pompeians captured at Corfinium. Senators are named, others either identified or grouped:

> Caesar, at daybreak, orders all the senators and their children, the junior officers, and the men of equestrian rank to

be brought before him. There were fifty of them. From the senatorial order: Lucius Domitius, Publius Lentulus Spinther, Lucius Caecilius Rufus, the quaestor Sextus Quintilius Varus, Lucius Rubrius. There were, in addition, the son of Domitius, quite a few other youths, and a great number of equestrians and local notables, whom Domitius had called up from the area's towns. (1.23.2)

Later he lists the Caesarians of equestrian rank wounded on the Apsus (3.19.7: "quite a few were wounded, including Cornelius Balbus, Marcus Plotius, Lucius Tiburtius, and some centurions and soldiers") and dead at Dyrrachium: "In this one day's two battles Caesar lost 960 soldiers and the well known equestrians Tuticanus Gallus, a senator's son, Gaius Fleginas from Placentia, Aulus Granius from Puteoli, Marcus Sacrativir from Capua, along with thirty-two junior officers and centurions" (3.71.1). The two lists of victims can perhaps be explained as particularly detailed versions of the "cost-of-battle" assessments regular at the end of military narratives in Roman historiography, but the list of men captured at Corfinium remains anomalous. Its purpose becomes clear when three of those named here—Domitius, Spinther, and Quintilius Varus—reappear in the narrative on Pompey's side, convicted thereby of ingratitude for Caesar's leniency.

There are in fact two more lists that seem to exist for no other reason than to show conduct unbecoming for a Roman senator. The earlier of the two, for all its simplicity of language, gains prominence from being the beginning of the last sentence of book 2: "[Juba] himself rode into the city with an escort of a number of senators, in whose number were Servius Sulpicius and Licinius Damasippus" (2.44.3). The sight of two Roman senators in the escort of an African king cannot but have been shocking to Caesar's readers.[19] Caesar tells us nothing about the two men he names, but from other sources we learn that he had good reason to show them in an unfavorable light. Servius Sulpicius was the son of a consular who, like Cicero, hesitated long before declaring for Pompey in the spring of 49. Cicero is critical of the extent to which the father (also named Servius Sulpicius) cooperated with Caesar early on, particularly of the fact that he allowed his son to fight on Caesar's side at Brindisi.[20] We hear nothing further about the son himself until the passage just quoted, from which one must infer that he, like his father, joined the fight against Caesar.[21] His desertion may explain the negative context in which Caesar names him here. Damasippus is tarnished by his associations: he turns up again in Africa in the campaign that ended at the battle of Thapsus (April 46), in which he served as legate to Pompey's father-in-law, Metellus Scipio, a man who gets one of the most negative portraits in the *Civil War* (we get a first glimpse of him just below; see further sec. 2a in chap. 2 and sec. 4b in chap. 3).[22]

The second list comes in the preliminaries to the narrative of the battle of Pharsalus: "At that period, in their daily spats on the subject of Caesar's priesthood [i.e., on who would succeed Caesar as *pontifex maximus*], Domitius, Scipio, and Lentulus Spinther stooped to harsh and public insults, with Lentulus making much of the respect due his seniority, Domitius boasting of his influence and reputation in the city, Scipio trusting his marriage-connection with Pompey" (3.83.1–3). In preparing for the decisive battle of the war, Pompey's council of war, which includes the three consulars named here (two of them also in the Corfinium list; for the third see n. 22), discusses matters that have nothing to do with the war. Caesar drives this point home a short while later in a sentence openly critical, uncharacteristically so, of the men who opposed him: "In sum, all of them were concerned with offices or financial rewards or with getting the better of their enemies. They were not thinking about how they might win, but about how they ought to use their victory" (3.83.4). This passage is also uncharacteristically rhetorical. Caesar indulges in a totalizing generalization ("all of them") and three rhetorical figures: anaphora, in which a word is repeated at the beginning of parallel phrases ("or . . . or" is in the Latin a threefold *aut*); polyptoton, in which a word appears in different forms at the beginning of parallel phrases ("how . . . how" is in the Latin *quibus . . . quem*); and antithesis, in which contrasting concepts are juxtaposed ("win . . . use their victory").[23] All of the men in Caesar's list here died in the fight against Caesar: Domitius at Pharsalus (3.99.5), Spinther with Pompey (3.104.3), Scipio in the aftermath of the battle of Thapsus (see n. 22).

With these few but powerful exceptions, then, Caesar's selection of material can be seen as a sufficient cause to name the people mentioned in the narrative. The connection between material and personnel might seem automatic, not remarkable, except that this is a narrative of civil conflict by the winner of that conflict. What is remarkable is the extent to which Caesar refrains from rewarding or punishing in his narrative particular individuals who aided or opposed him outside of the events reported in it. This is not to say that he has no interest in the consequences of loyalty and good faith and their opposites. In fact, we will argue that the consequences of moral actions were always of interest to Caesar and became increasingly a concern in book 2, which rewards Curio's loyalty, and in book 3, where several stories can be read as exemplary of Caesarian good faith.[24] But Caesar does not set out to create a record of the loyal and the disloyal. Caesar is careful not to present himself as another Sulla, and there is no proscription list in his narrative.

Cicero is a case in point. From the copious correspondence that survives from the period covered by the *Civil War*, we know that Cicero thought hard about his role in the conflict: should he join Pompey, to whom he owed some allegiance but of whose strategy he disapproved, or should he join Caesar, who looked likely to win and who made friendly overtures; should his wife and daughter stay in Rome or retreat to a country estate; what about his son and nephew? And so on. Among the many considerations he advances in this long and agonized debate, the most difficult to answer, but the one he cared most about getting right, was the question of his reputation. What would people and posterity think about his choice? Caesar, though he cared enough about Cicero's decision to send letters and emissaries to him in the early months of 49 (*Att.* 9.6.6, 9.6A, 9.16) and to make a personal visit to him after Pompey left Italy (*Att.* 9.18), cared nothing at all about shaping Cicero's reputation via his narrative. Cicero, who eventually joined Pompey in

Greece despite Caesar's efforts, played no significant role in Italy or Greece in this period and has no place in the *Civil War*.

3 | Style

As we saw earlier, the style of *commentarii* covered a range from unkempt (Atticus's Greek *commentarius*) to plain (Caesar's *Gallic War*) to fancy (Cicero's Greek *commentarius*). Unkempt narratives are hard to find, but the difference between plain narrative and fancy narrative can be illustrated by comparing Caesar's version of events with a version where the same events are given "full-dress treatment." For a parallel passage we turn to the account of the war between Caesar and Pompey by an imperial-age Greek historian of Rome, Appian.

After the defeat at Pharsalus, Pompey sails away from Greece, eventually reaching Egypt, where he hopes to find a friendly reception owing to the assistance he once gave to the present ruler's father. But Caesar's victory destroyed Pompey's credit with his former friends throughout the empire; in Egypt the boy-king Ptolemy and his advisors set a trap, hoping to catch and kill him.

Appian's version of the story is three long paragraphs long (2.84–86); an excerpt is given here. The plotters sent a "miserable skiff" to bring Pompey from his large ship in the bay to Ptolemy, who was waiting on shore. On the skiff were the assassins, including a Roman, a former soldier of Pompey's, who invited him into the skiff:

> Pompey's suspicions were aroused by all that he observed—the marshaling of the army, the meanness of the skiff, and the fact that the king himself did not come to meet him nor send any of his high dignitaries. Nevertheless, he entered the skiff, repeating to himself these lines of Sophocles: "Whoso resorts to a tyrant becomes his slave, even if he be free when he goes."[25] While rowing to the shore all were silent, and this made him still more suspicious. Finally, either

recognizing Sempronius[26] as a Roman soldier who had served under him or guessing that he was such because he alone remained standing (for, according to military discipline, a soldier does not sit in the presence of his commander), he turned to him and said, "Do I not know you, comrade?" The other nodded and, as Pompey turned away, he immediately gave him the first stab and the others followed his example. Pompey's wife and friends who saw this at a distance cried out and, lifting their hands to heaven, invoked the gods, the avengers of violated faith. (2.85)

Further details are given in 2.86: the assassins cut off Pompey's head to save it for Caesar and bury the rest of his body in a miserable tomb. Appian quotes an inscription from the tomb and gives a history of the tomb from that day to his own, when Hadrian had it cleaned and restored. He also gives Pompey an obituary.

Caesar's version of the episode quoted from Appian is quite brief: "Having received a warm invitation from these and drawn by his acquaintance with Septimius, who had commanded a unit in Pompey's army during the war against the pirates, he climbed onto the small boat with a few of his supporters. There he was killed by Achillas and Septimius" (3.104.2–3). This version shares with Appian's the spurious welcome that lures Pompey onto the skiff, the skiff itself, and the fact that one of Pompey's assassins was a Roman and a former soldier of his. It lacks the atmosphere created by Pompey's growing suspicions, the eerie quiet, the infectiousness of guilt, and the spectators on shore and ship, as well as Pompey's words (complete with Sophoclean tag) and the parenthesis on Roman military protocol. Caesar's narrative also lacks much of the material Appian used to set the scene (2.84) and all of what he tells of the aftermath (2.86).

Spare as it is, Caesar's account of the end of the man who had been known since the age of twenty-five as Pompey the Great is effective. Not so much for what it says, or even for what it refrains from saying, but rather because it is the culmination of a project that Caesar began at the beginning of the *Civil War*: stripping Pompey of his legitimacy and his laurels. A lonely death in an Egyptian rowboat suits, indeed is almost required by, the logic of Caesar's characterization of his rival (for which see sec. 3 in chap. 3).

Setting this lean Caesar passage beside the fuller Appian version suggests how a historical event can be dressed up or down in narrative form. It is not meant to suggest that Caesar is always leaner—in section 2 we saw that he presents the events at Corfinium, for example, at considerably greater length than other writers—but to make us attentive to the variations in fullness that are manifest and important in the *Civil War*.

4 | Writing to a stop

From the passages of the *Civil War* we have looked at so far, the praise accorded the content and style of Caesar's *Gallic War* commentaries would seem to apply equally to his later work. The narrative is brief in its concentration on the war's events and people and bare in its avoidance of ornament for amplifying their political or moral significance. The overall elegance of Caesar's treatment of his chosen material is further explored in chapter 5. For our present purposes it is enough to say that the *Civil War* stands strong in a stylistic comparison with the polished and published *Gallic War*. What Caesar wrote of the civil war narrative, he wrote well. But he did not finish it.

The evidence for this lies in the text itself and in contemporary comments. The *Civil War* ends abruptly with a sentence widely considered an editorial intervention imposing closure on an incomplete narrative: "These were the initial events of the war in Alexandria" (3.112.12). That is, these are not Caesar's words but those of someone who produced an edition of the corpus of "Caesarian Wars," including not only the *Gallic* and *Civil Wars* but also the *Alexandrian*, *African*, and *Spanish Wars*.[27] None of the latter three works was written by Caesar himself, and the sentence quoted above effects the transition from Caesar's words to those of his continuators: the *Alexandrian War* follows smoothly after the *Civil War* with its opening words, "The war in Alexandria having begun . . ." (1.1).

Without the sentence quoted above, the *Civil War* does not end, it stops. The final paragraph of book 3 mentions preparations for war on both sides, preparations that only merit mention in a narrative of that war. This is not the kind of book-ending Caesar has accustomed us to over the course of seven Gallic books and the first two books of this work (on which see secs. 1b and 5 in chap. 2).

In addition to stopping in mid-narrative, Caesar refers three times to a section of book 2 that he did not include in the book 2 we have, the story of the costly defeat of his legate Gaius Antonius in Illyricum in the summer of 49.[28] Antonius and another legate had been charged with the defense of Illyricum, but when the fleet on which he depended was destroyed, Antonius was barricaded on the Adriatic island of Curicta and forced to surrender. "The capitulation of his soldiers at Curicta" was one of the setbacks, Caesar says, that he and Pompey ought to "take as a lesson and a warning to fear future eventualities" (3.10.3–6). Like the other two references to this episode (at 3.4.2 and 3.67.5), this one comes in book 3, which suggests either that Caesar wrote and then suppressed (but did not replace) the narrative of the capitulation at Curicta, or else that he intended to write it but never did; having referred to it as he does here, he cannot have intended to omit it altogether. In either case the passages in book 3 are loose ends that ought to have been dealt with in a finished work.

The internal evidence of the unfinished state of the work is supplemented by comments from contemporaries. Caesar's legate Hirtius wrote up (or planned to write up) the period "from [Caesar's] achievements in Alexandria to the end . . . of his life." Reluctant to impose himself on Caesar's text, he justified his intervention by citing the state in which Caesar left his last *commentarius*, namely, "incomplete" (*Gallic War* 8 preface 2). Since Hirtius was killed in battle just over a year after Caesar's assassination, he may not have brought his own work to its intended conclusion (though he claims in his preface to have done so); this would help explain the presence of other authors' work in the corpus (see n. 27). In any event, the *Civil War* was published in some form while men who played a leading role in the war were still alive. Another of Caesar's legates, Asinius Pollio, who wrote his own history of the conflict, criticized it for such inaccuracies as an inflated casualty count at Pharsalus; there are flaws, he says, that Caesar would have corrected, presumably had he lived to put the finishing touches on the work himself.[29]

If Caesar did not finish or publish the *Civil War*, he nevertheless brought much of the narrative into a high state of polish.[30] In book 1, the campaigns in Italy and Nearer Spain are complete and satisfying narratives supporting a powerful argument (see chap. 2). In book 2, his juxtaposition of Varro's defeat in Further Spain with Curio's defeat in North Africa is elaborate and successful (see chap. 3). As we saw above, however, book 2 lacks the narrative of the defeat at Curicta. In addition, the story of the siege of Marseilles with which book 2 begins shows incoherencies unusual for Caesar.[31] The narrative of the campaign in Greece that occupies the bulk of book 3 is another coherent whole ending with the battle of Pharsalus and, as an appendix, the death of Pompey. But the story of the fight for Alexandria is only begun. In other words, the work contains five panels complete except, perhaps, for the final fact-checking that Pollio thought was in order (Italy, Nearer Spain, Further Spain, North Africa, Greece), one panel needing further work (Marseilles), one panel projected but never put into the text (Curicta), and one well started but still incomplete (Alexandria). The importance of Caesar's project and the quality of his product—the subject matter of our chapters 2–5—make the incomplete state of the *Civil War* a puzzle. Why was it unfinished at his death?

A preliminary, and perhaps simpler, question is, when did he write it? The evidence with which to answer that question comes entirely from the work itself and has been interpreted variously. The most widely held (and in our view plausible) theory is that Caesar wrote what we have not long after the end of what Suetonius calls the "Pompeian War" (Sept. 48; *DJ* 56.1) and the initial phases of the Alexandrian War. That is, shortly after the events it relates.[32] Much of the Alexandrian war in fact consisted of waiting for reinforcements (Oct. 48–Feb. 47), and it was followed by a sojourn in a pacified Egypt (April–May 47), so there will have been time for writing. Assigning a terminal date to the period of composition is more difficult, depending, as it does, on the perceived fit between the text (with its political subtext) and the political conditions of the period 48–44. If Caesar insists in the *Civil War* that the second consulship he wanted was an office open to him, as to any other citizen, under the terms of established law (1.32.2; cf. 3.1.1), can he have done so after taking up a third consulship (for 46) that required his exemption from that law?[33] If he stresses the illegalities of his opponents' political conduct and his defense of the republic and its traditional offices (see chap. 2 passim), can he have done so while demonstrating his own scorn for tradition, as he did after Thapsus?[34] (For an example, see the Epilogue.) In effect, "as long as Caesar could write this narrative, the Republic still existed."[35] So the terminal date for its composition is the date after which one considers the republic dead. From Cicero onwards, that has been placed well before the Ides of March in 44.[36]

This brings us back briefly to the question of the work's unfinished state in 44; we will return to it in the Epilogue. The essential point for the purposes of a literary study such as this one is that the arguments advanced for the terminal date are all political arguments.[37] That is, if Caesar abandoned the work unfinished, as he seems to have done, his verdict was political, not literary. In the following four chapters we will explore both the qualities of Caesar's literary *res gestae* and the ways in which they may be seen to promote a political agenda, one whose emphasis is changing from book to book. If we are right, Caesar's *Civil War* captures the extraordinary potential of a transformative moment in history. He begins by articulating from his perspective the causes of war and projecting policies that will restore the republic to the Senate and the Roman People; he ends because those very policies have become irrelevant in a new world in which he was now coterminous with the state, the man to whom the Senate and the Roman People looked for safety or tyranny.

· 2 ·

Structure as Argument in *Civil War* 1

> ... and you say "Take account of me!"
> You, take account of us!
> —CICERO addressing Caesar, *Letters to Atticus* 7.9.4

In this chapter we argue that in book 1 of the *Civil War* Caesar uses the commentary form for a new purpose. Caesar's seven *Gallic War* commentaries have a consistent year-by-year structure and appear to function as reports to senators and others in Rome about Caesar's achievements in Gaul. They offered a picture of Caesar the general and Caesar the man who brings order and civilization to the chaotic and warring provinces, but these political and rhetorical purposes remained a function of particular scenes and of the overall picture of success toward which the *Gallic War* points but at which it never arrives, since it is Hirtius, rather than Caesar, who completes the record in book 8. The *Civil War* is different from the *Gallic War* in important ways, perhaps none so significant as the fact that its events were not news to Caesar's first readers: they had lived through and in many cases participated in those events. Thus, the primary justification of the Gallic commentaries was missing for the *Civil War*. What then was Caesar's purpose?[1]

The structure and argument of *Civil War* 1 can help us understand what Caesar may have been trying to accomplish. In this book Caesar tells the story of only a portion of the year 49.[2] By so limiting the chronological scope Caesar focuses his narrative on specific events and creates a beginning and end that, in addition to recording and reporting those events, organize and analyze them. The narrative can thus make a unified and complete argument about the causes of the civil war, the nature of the contest, and Caesar's role both in its beginnings and in the future implied by the ending of book 1. In fact, we will argue that the ending of book 1 is designed as the narrative answer to the political problems that began the war and so can be read as exemplary of how Caesar's victory will restore order and good government for Rome.

1 | Background: The *Gallic War*

For seven years, while Caesar pacified Gaul and extended the boundaries of the Roman empire—58–52 BCE—he was simultaneously creating and shaping two powerful resources for his use in the traditional Roman pursuit of fame, influence, power, and glory. One entailed power: his legions. By 52 he had ten well trained and loyal legions; some of the men were new recruits, but most were veterans whom he had tested and come to trust and who had learned to trust him. As his devastatingly fast occupation of Italy in the early months of 49 showed, they were an effective and efficient fighting machine. The other entailed influence: Caesar was writing his *Gallic War*, which would shape perceptions of his abilities and remind Romans that he would return. As we saw in chapter 1, Caesar's commentary project was in all likelihood a self-conscious elaboration of a traditional practice.

1a Ideology: Caesar representing Rome

From the beginning of Caesar's records, Caesar and his army are identified: when the army rested, he writes that "Caesar rested," and when the army completes a bridge, he writes that "Caesar completed the bridge." This is, of course, an easy metonymy (a figure of speech whereby one thing stands for another, as the part can stand for the whole), but it presages another metonymy whereby Caesar's army stands for Rome, a metonymy that becomes an important part of both Caesar's appeal to Rome and his self-aggrandizement (see further sec. 1a in chap. 5).

As Caesar is identified with his army, so he is identified with Rome's might. To a large extent this is what one expects: in the field, the general represents Roman power and interests, and just as his army is an extension of his will, so his will is or should be an extension of the power and purposes of Rome. But what might have been a normal figure of speech takes on a new power and significance in Caesar's commentaries. In both literal and symbolic ways, he is the coming of Rome. This figure of speech motivates many scenes in the *Gallic War*, which it is not our intention to explore in depth. But because the figure is also important to Caesar's self-depiction in the *Civil War*, it will be useful to see how it is introduced in the *Gallic War*.

The first book of the *Gallic War* deals with the events of 58 BCE. In the opening paragraphs, after a description of Gaul and its inhabitants and a report on the expansionist activities of the Helvetii[3] in 61 and 60 BCE, Caesar makes his entrance into the work: "When it is announced to Caesar that [the Helvetii] were trying to march through our province, he hurries to leave the city and hastens to Further Gaul by the longest possible marches and arrives at Geneva" (1.7.1). There are a couple of details worth noting here. Caesar began the *Gallic War* with the famous line that introduces a geography of Gaul, "All Gaul is divided into three parts." He then offered some political background that takes us back to 61. That is, the annalistic form that is so often mentioned in reference to Caesar's commentaries is already compromised at the outset of the work for a larger historical, ethnographical, and political purpose. Caesar is not merely recording the events of his term as proconsul; he is locating them within a history of Rome and the province and marking them as a Roman response to a larger problem of government in the provinces, in "our province." Then, when he comes to events of the year 58, the ostensible subject of *Gallic War* 1, he does not begin in annalistic fashion with the beginning of the year, but rather with his departure from Rome and arrival in Geneva. This was sometime after 28 March 58 (see timeline).

As a result, Caesar appears almost simultaneously in the narrative as the man reporting to Rome on his activities and as the man who represents and protects the interests of Rome. And he is not only the representative of Rome's immediate interests in protecting the Gauls. When the Helvetii ask to be allowed to pass through the province, he writes, "Caesar, because he held in his memory the fact that the consul Lucius Cassius had been killed and his army routed and sent under the yoke by the Helvetii, was of the view that no concessions should be made" (1.7.3). In other words, Caesar sees himself in terms of Roman history. In fact, Cassius had been killed forty years earlier, in 107 BCE (Caesar was born in 100 BCE), and, while the skeptic may believe that Caesar was forcing a fight, Caesar's rhetoric claims that he is caring for both Rome and her history. And this continues to be how Caesar presents himself.

When the Helvetii find another route against the Aedui through the territory of the Sequani (1.9), the Aedui appeal to Caesar for help: "they said that they had at all times served the Roman People well and did not deserve to see their fields destroyed . . . " (1.11.3). The Roman People, in the person of Caesar, responds accordingly: "Caesar decided that he should not wait until all the fortunes of the allies were destroyed . . . " (1.11.6). When three-quarters of the Helvetii have crossed the river Arar, Caesar attacks the remainder and kills a great number. "The name of the group was Tigurinus; for all of Helvetia is divided into four groups. This one group, when they had left their homeland, according to the memory of our fathers' generation, had killed the consul Lucius Cassius and sent his army under the yoke" (1.12.4–5). Caesar's role, by implication, has now expanded to that of history's avenger; and lest the reader miss the point, he says, "And so, whether by chance or by the plan of the gods, the part of the Helvetian population that had inflicted a notable calamity on the Roman People, these were the first to pay the penalty" (1.12.6). Caesar's touch is extraordinarily light, and yet it is clear that in his narrative he arrives as the representative of Rome, the avenger of wrongs, the protector of history, and the agent of the gods. He then adds, "In this action Caesar avenged not only national injuries but also private ones, for in the same battle in which the Tigurini had killed Cassius, they had killed Lucius Piso, a legate, the grandfather of Lucius Piso who was Caesar's father-in-law" (1.12.7). The picture of Caesar as representative of Rome and Roman virtue is completed with this detail. The quintessential Roman virtue was *pietas*, a term that referred to a man's obligations and devotion to country, gods, and family. As the avenger of Cassius and of national injuries, Caesar displays his devotion to Rome; as protector of history and participant in the plan of the gods, he displays his devotion to and alignment with the paternal deities; and as avenger of Lucius Piso, he exercises his devotion to family. From early in *Gallic War* 1 on, the coincidence of Caesar's interests and power with the interests and power of Rome and her values is implicit everywhere. It becomes explicit in the middle of book 1, when Caesar decides to oppose Ariovistus, whose aggressions against Roman allies Caesar deemed "an utter disgrace to himself and the republic" (1.33.2). "Himself and the republic"—this is a phrase we will meet again.

In the *Civil War*, we will argue, Caesar presents himself similarly as the repository of true Roman values and virtue. Just as Caesar brought Rome with her might and her institutions to the provinces, so (according to Caesar) he brings Rome home to herself by repairing failed political and social institutions and by creating on the battlefield what is lacking in the Senate.

1b Structure and closure

Before we turn to how Caesar accomplishes this task in the *Civil War*, it will be useful to consider one other aspect of Caesar's literary achievement in the *Gallic War*. This has to do with structure. We have already noted that the conventions of the commentary form, so far as we can tell, were annalistic; that is, they called for the record of events year by year. Such a record will readily correspond to the divisions of military campaigns, since ancient warfare did not generally take place year round but began in the spring and halted with the coming of winter. It will not, however, correspond to the overall trajectory of a multi-year war. Yet Caesar manages to bring his yearly commentaries to some point of satisfactory closure despite the fact that each year ends with the war in Gaul incomplete. In other words, while the war continues, each yearly narrative suggests accomplishment and closure. In fact, Caesar stops writing his *Gallic War* after the events of 52 BCE, recorded in book 7, although at the very least "mopping up" operations were still necessary and would take another two years.[4] There are, then, two questions here: How does Caesar create a formal sense of closure to his yearly narratives? And how does book 7 end—for Caesar at least—the narrative of the war in Gaul?

In general, each book of the *Gallic War* proceeds from winter encampment to winter encampment. Twice Caesar even makes clear the annalistic structure by opening a book with a reference to the consuls who entered office with the new year (4.1, 5.1). In these instances and elsewhere, he refers to his winter camps at the beginning of his narrative (2.1, 3.2, 4.1, 5.1, 6.3, 7.1) and at the end (1.54, 2.35, 3.29, 4.38, 6.44, 7.90). The return to winter camps generally signals a break in the fighting, and Caesar is careful to avoid reference to anything that would call attention to the fact that each book ends in the middle of a war. Thus, book 2 begins with rumors that the Belgae are conspiring against Caesar. This makes a good beginning, but if it had been reported chronologically, it would have appeared at the end of book 1. Book 3 begins with the unsuccessful attempt to open a route across the Alps that took place the previous year. Book 6 begins, "For many reasons Caesar was expecting a more serious revolt in Gaul," a curious assertion after the ending of book 5: ". . . and after this action Caesar found Gaul a little more tranquil." And book 7 (on 52 BCE) begins with the difficulties in Rome in 53. Thus we can see Caesar as a narrator trying to avoid reference to those events that spill over the yearly boundaries of his commentary.

He also makes use of a standard set of closural topics or themes. Winter camps, which occur at the end of all books (except book 5, in which most of the campaign takes place during the winter), are of course the easiest marker. But we also find summary statements, references to victory (books 1, 2, 7), to destruction (3, 6) and pacification (2, 5), to a return home (1, 5), and to the death of opponents (5, 6, 7). Caesar's withdrawal to winter quarters is also accompanied by details of military administration (1, 3, 6, 7) and by Caesar's administrative activities as governor (1, 6). The closural ritual of "thanksgiving" is mentioned at the end of three books (2, 4, 7).

Throughout these seven books we see Caesar's narrative imposing closure on events and dealing with the fact that events always spill over the boundaries we impose on them. In some cases, perhaps, Caesar himself thought that part of his task had been accomplished, that Gaul was pacified (book 2). In other cases, it seems clear that he wants his narrative to bring to a rest the forward momentum of events (book 5: Gaul was more tranquil), although he is quite certain that the war is not completed (book 6: Caesar was expecting a more serious revolt). We know, however, that he ended the *Gallic War* with book 7. How did he bring his account to an end?

The first thing to note is that book 7 begins with greater contextualization than we find in any book except, perhaps, for book 1; at the same time, it is more closely woven into the ending of the preceding book than is the case with any other book. Book 6 ended: "He stationed [his legions] in their winter camps, and when he had provided grain for the army he set out for Italy, as had become his custom, to complete administrative business." Book 7 begins: "When Gaul was quiet, Caesar, as had become his custom, set out to Italy to complete administrative business." He then says that the chaotic situation in Rome during 53 and the early months of 52 is the reason for rumors among the Gauls that Caesar would not join his army that spring. This encourages the Gauls to plan a campaign, to attempt to shut Caesar off from his legions, and to choose Vercingetorix as their champion. The revolt is underway. Book 7 begins, then, as an explicit continuation of book 6, but as a continuation made necessary in part by activities and enemies in Rome. Caesar's larger political purpose is muted, and perhaps ambiguous, but undeniable.

The book ends with an expansion of many of the closural features we have seen at work at the end of other books. The battle at Alesia brings about the defeat of the leader, Vercingetorix. He summons a council in which he admits defeat and offers himself to the Gauls either for death or to be handed to the Romans. Deputies are sent to Caesar, who accepts Vercingetorix and distributes prisoners as booty to his soldiers (7.89). Then, "when these matters were completed," he goes to the Aedui and "recovers that state" (*civitatem recipit*); the Arverni send legates and he requires hostages. He sends legions to winter camp, restores prisoners. The details here elaborate the turn to administration we find ending books 1 and 6 by adding the duties of the victor in administering the peace. He then gives orders to his officers and legions and sends them to various parts of the province; this takes about four sentences as he distributes seven or more legions. He himself winters at Bibracte (modern Mont Beuvray) in central Gaul. "When his dispatches are published at Rome, a public thanksgiving of twenty days is granted" (7.90.8). So ends the *Gallic War*. Again we see narrative content, the reference to the end of a campaign, the shift of focus, and a return to Rome and Roman rituals (a thanksgiving again), all facilitating a sense of closure.

Book 7, the work's longest book, seems designed to bring the *Gallic War* to an end, even though the fighting in Gaul was not over. One may argue that Alesia was both a brilliant military victory and the end of concerted revolt in Gaul; after the defeat of Vercingetorix, the battles of book 8 are minor skirmishes, troubling mopping-up operations against individual tribes. Hindsight indicates that Alesia settled the issue of Gaul, and Caesar may have both believed that that was the case and wanted others in Rome to believe it. But the point for us as we turn to the *Civil War* is that Caesar mobilized a set of themes, including victory and the administration of the peace, to create a sense of closure and accomplishment. He apparently felt that this record, ending here (although the fighting did not end here), represented his achievement. In other words, Alesia and the administrative details stand as exemplary of order and victory, even though there was more fighting to do.

Hirtius's beginning to book 8 makes it clear that the pacification of Gaul is a fiction. Despite the fact that "the whole of Gaul had been subdued," news came of plans for fresh campaigns and resistance to Rome on several fronts. On the last day of December (that is, before the end of 52), Caesar is already on the march from Bibracte to his thirteenth legion (8.2.1). After a display of might against the Bituriges, he returns to Bibracte to administer justice before marching out from his winter quarters again, this time against the Carnutes. The chaos of these details—marching out, marching back, administration in the middle of a campaign, returning to winter camps near the beginning of the narrative—is unparalleled in the Gallic commentaries and reveals by contrast Caesar's own careful selection and organization. It is that selection and organization that allows his narrative to achieve a kind of symbolic power—making Alesia the end of the Gallic war—that exceeds the literal facts. We will see something similar at the end of book 1 of the *Civil War*.

2 | Beginning *Civil War* 1

In what follows we argue that the *Civil War*, especially book 1, is an extension of the ideological and formal concerns of the *Gallic War*. We will see that once again Caesar presents himself as the repository of Roman virtue and the representative of *res publica*. The Latin term *res publica*, from which our word "republic" derives, actually means "the people's possession, the public thing." In saying that Caesar presents himself as the representative of *res publica*, then, we are implying that Caesar presents himself as the contestant in the civil war who represents the interests of the Roman People and the Roman government; the corollary to this is that his opponents are motivated by private concerns, not by the public good, that they treat the republic (*res publica*) as if it were their private possession (*res privata*). At Pharsalus, this theme colors Caesar's report of the departure of the defeated Pompey: "When our men were already inside his fortifications, Pompey grabbed a horse, tore off his general's insignia, threw himself out of the camp by the back gate, and headed for Larisa at full gallop" (3.96.3). In Caesar's view, the civil war was not a contest between "better" and "less good"

Romans; it is a contest for Rome and whether it will remain Rome, the republic, the possession of the public, protected by "our men," or become the private possession of his enemies, men who abandon Rome and throw away their insignia of office.

In order to make this argument, we will show that book 1 of the *Civil War* is a coherent and well structured "argument by narrative." We will look at how Caesar presents himself and his side, how his narrative implicitly compares his actions and purposes with those of his enemy, how he explains himself in his speeches, and how he brings the intractable problems shown at the beginning of the book to a resolution at its end. The war itself, of course, continued after the events at Ilerda that end book 1, but, as we have seen in the *Gallic War*, a sense of closure and resolution is not incompatible with the continuation of fighting, and an important battle can become exemplary and symbolic of a future victory. What makes the *Civil War* different and even unique is the fact that in its first book Caesar does not follow events to the end of the war's first year and then provide a narrative closure that coincides with the end of the fighting season. Rather, he finds the point of closure in the midst of the fighting season: the Pompeian surrender at Ilerda took place on 2 August 49. Book 2 begins with the second battle at Marseilles (mid- to late July 49) and then goes even further back to prior events in Further Spain and North Africa (see timeline). These variations on the year-by-year format are striking in two ways. Not only does the second book begin with events that precede the ending of the first, which violates strict chronology, the second book does not begin or even deal with the second year. It merely completes the story of the first year. This is so striking that some scholars have felt that books 1 and 2 were originally a single book divided by mistake at some point in the process of copying manuscripts. The manuscript tradition, however, does not support such a view, and we hope that the clarity and strength of purpose shown here in book 1 as it stands will help support the argument that Caesar meant to end book 1 where it ends in most of our manuscripts.[5]

2a Rome (1.1–6)

2A.1 THE MEETING OF THE SENATE ON 1 JANUARY 49 (1.1–2)

Caesar's civil war narrative begins abruptly with an echo of the end of *Gallic War* 7.[6] The closing words of that work (as Caesar wrote it) are, "When Caesar's letter was read at Rome, a public thanksgiving of twenty days was granted." The *Civil War* begins, "When Caesar's letter was delivered to the consuls, it was only through the greatest struggle by the tribunes of the people that it was reluctantly allowed that the letter be read in the Senate." The contrast is pointed: the man whose dispatches in 52 were gratefully received and celebrated with a public thanksgiving can barely get his letter read in 49.

There is, of course, nothing procedurally wrong with the consuls setting the agenda for discussion and refusing to address matters that others want addressed. The tribunes, although they could propose business to the Senate, had no right to preempt the consuls' decision. They were supposed to wait their turn. Therefore, when Caesar says that the tribunes did succeed through strenuous efforts in getting the letter read, there is an implication, and a reasonable one, that the tribunes succeeded by moral authority and good sense—the Senate should hear what Caesar has to say—not by procedural compulsion.[7] It is the spirit of the consuls' action that is wrong, not the letter.

When Caesar's dispatch is read, however, meaningful and substantive public discourse is thwarted by the Pompeian consuls. Caesar continues:

> But it was impossible to get them to agree to a motion about its contents. The consuls propose a general discussion about the republic. Lucius Lentulus, consul, promises the Senate that he will not fail the republic, if they are willing to speak their mind boldly and bravely; but if they keep their eye on Caesar and follow his favor, as they did on previous occa-

sions, he will take counsel for himself and will not obey the authority of the Senate. He said that he too could take refuge in the favor and friendship of Caesar. (1.1.1–3)

The portrayal of Lentulus in particular is devastating. Not only is he reluctant to have the dispatches of a general in the field read to the Senate, but his proposed "general discussion of the republic" allows him to avoid direct discussion of practical measures that would address the concerns communicated in Caesar's letter, allay the widespread fears of civil war, and move the parties toward peace; instead, he speaks in threat and innuendo. He says they should "speak their mind boldly and bravely," which of course means that they must turn their backs on the precedents of their past actions and agree with him. What, one might ask, is bold and brave about yielding to the threats of the consul? But the most devastating remark is the last: if they yield to Caesar's point of view (which Lentulus will not allow to be discussed), then Lentulus himself, Caesar's enemy, will also ingratiate himself with Caesar and avoid danger ("take refuge," he says).

The open duplicity in Lentulus's proposal is stunning. Bold speech means agreeing with the consul. Speaking their mind means changing their mind. Meanwhile, the consul threatens to turn his back on the republic and admits that he could become a false friend to Caesar. But there is a fundamental lack of logic as well. If the senators agree with Caesar, Lentulus says, then he will disobey the Senate—but how can his favoring of Caesar (however duplicitous) be disobedient to a Caesar-favoring Senate? Impossible. Lentulus's lack of logic indicates that his words are meant to threaten and coerce. "Disobeying the Senate" means simply that their interests, whatever they might be, will have no influence upon him; he will look after his private interests, not the republic. Caesar presents this consul as beyond responsibility and account.

Next, we hear from Metellus Scipio, Pompey's father-in-law: "Scipio speaks to the same point, saying that Pompey has it in mind not to fail the republic, if the Senate follows; but if they hesitate and act too leniently, they will beg in vain for his help, should they want it afterward" (1.1.4). The point is essentially the same as Lentulus's point and similarly illogical, although sharpened and more cruel. Scipio conjures a vision of senators imploring Pompey for help against a cruel Caesar, and Pompey remaining aloof. But this is ridiculous. If the Senate does not follow Pompey or reaches a compromise with Caesar, then presumably Caesar will have no reason to brutalize the senators. That would be self-defeating. In fact, the words barely disguise Pompey's own penchant for cruelty, since it is cruelty he seems to be asking for from the senators when he threatens them "if they hesitate and act too leniently," and cruelty that he offers if they are too lenient. Lest one imagine that this representation of Pompey is Scipio's invention, Caesar adds: "this speech of Scipio seemed to be issued from the mouth of Pompey" (1.2.1).[8]

There are two noteworthy aspects to this presentation. First, Pompey appears as one who demands not just obedience but obedience with the proper display of alacrity. This means that as the Pompeians talk of "the authority of the Senate" they are simultaneously taking that authority away. Twice already they have characterized senators as followers: "if they follow Caesar's favor," "if the Senate follows [Pompey]." Second, the implication of Metellus Scipio's rejection of lenient and measured action has a context that the modern reader might not be aware of. Leniency (*lenitas*, along with forms of the adjective *lenis*) is associated in the *Civil War* with Caesar: 1.1.4 (here), 1.5.5, 1.74.7, 2.24.3, 3.25.2, and 3.98.2. It is also a term Caesar uses of himself in a letter preserved in Cicero's correspondence: "I had decided on my own to present myself with as much leniency as possible [*quam lenissimum*] and to work toward reconciliation with Pompey" (*Att.* 9.7C.6, early March 49). Furthermore, the opposite of leniency is harshness or cruelty, something Pompeians seem to value. We have already seen cruelty in the image of a helpless Senate vainly imploring Pompey. And "cruelty" is exactly the term Caesar will associate with the Pompeians a few sentences hence, concluding his narrative of the day's discussion thus: "Severe proposals were made; as each man spoke most harshly and most cruelly, so each was praised most warmly by the enemies of Caesar" (1.2.8).

It is important to remember that Caesar is not reminding or telling his audience what various people said, or summarizing the debate. He is creating a scene in which Pompeian speech is threatening and duplicitous while Caesarian speech is silenced, where leniency is threatened, cruelty is rewarded, and nonsense hides violence. Debate founders on allegiances and obedience, instead of examining alternatives. How can you debate with Scipio's ventriloquized Pompey? How can you counter Lentulus's confused and duplicitous logic? How can you deliberate when all disagreement with these words-from-elsewhere is silenced? It is a scene in which action seems to be directed by the hand and character of Pompey as much as it is directed in the interests of Pompey.

In the second paragraph, Caesar becomes more precise about the policy failure that this threatening and illogical posture entails. He records the proposals made by three senators, pointedly calling each "a more lenient view" (1.2.2, *leniorem sententiam*). Again, the positions Caesar records are designed to create an argument about Pompeian policy. First, Marcus Claudius Marcellus, a Pompeian, proposes that armies should be raised before the Senate takes any action. He says that this is necessary so that under the protection of the army the Senate can deliberate "safely and freely" (1.2.2), terms that seem cynical and sinister in this context of threats and coercion. One must wonder whether the armies will protect the Senate's safe and free deliberations or apply coercion to what the Pompeians will call "safe and free" deliberations. It is quite possible that when Marcellus speaks of "safe and free" speech, he really wants to surround the Senate with an even larger army, a form of protection that would ensure the Senate's vote against Caesar. This may sound cynical, but what sense is there in a literal reading? That Marcellus wanted the Senate surrounded by an even larger army, a Pompeian army of course, so that they could engage in free debate? Not likely. What is more likely is that Marcellus did not want a vote to go against Caesar until the Pompeian side felt secure and protected by an even larger army. This is Pompeian freedom. In other words, Marcellus was not protecting debate, which was already being coerced; he was protecting the Pompeians who were coercing debate and he was preparing for the civil war that this coercion would make inevitable.

Still, Marcellus is making a substantive point about strategy: Pompey had two legions at Capua, but they were legions that had formerly served under Caesar in Gaul, and his other forces were two newly conscripted legions. Given that Caesar's army amounted to at least nine veteran legions, Marcellus's proposal is prudential.[9] In fact, throughout the early days of the civil war Pompey's undue confidence in his forces is a matter of public concern and condemnation (see sec. 1 in chap. 3). By the time the aristocracy in Rome had a chance to read Caesar's narrative, he had clearly demonstrated in the field his speed and determination against Pompey's ineffective troops and in the process shown that, for all his cynical abuse of process, Marcellus was right to think that Pompey needed more men. Cicero himself complains in January that Pompey has too much confidence in his armies (*Att.* 7.13.2). The failure of Marcellus's suggestion, despite its apparent duplicity, amounts to a failure by the Pompeians to take effective action in their own best military interests. Before long Caesar will have another Pompeian make this charge directly (Cato at 1.30.5).

The second proposal comes from Marcus Calidius, a leading orator. Eventually he sided with Caesar, but at this time he, like the majority of his fellow senators, seems to be trying to balance competing interests and avoid war; his proposal addresses equity. He proposes that Pompey should go to his provinces so that there would be no reason for war, thus voicing the Caesarian claim that Pompey's presence in Italy is provocative (1.2.3). He explains that Caesar is afraid that the two legions Pompey "stripped" from him are being held in Italy as a danger to him. Calidius's proposal (reduce troops in Italy) is the opposite of Marcellus's (increase troops in Italy). But both are rejected. It is more important to the Pompeians to force immediate action against Caesar than it is to be prudent or equitable.[10]

The third speaker is Marcus Caelius Rufus (best known by his family name Caelius), a Caesarian at the time, who supports Calidius's proposal. Since Caesar is not comprehensive in his report of the

Senate's deliberations, one may wonder why he bothers to say that Caelius "followed the view of Calidius with some few matters modified." There is almost no content to this report, but the fact that Caelius was a Caesarian adds to the consideration of equity the clear suggestion that there was a practical compromise acceptable both to uncommitted senators like Calidius and to Caesarians like Caelius. These three proposals, in addition to what their respective failures reveal of the duplicity and irrationality of Pompeian actions and the resulting political impasse, amount to an argument that there were prudential, equitable, and practical alternatives to the rush to war.

The proposals fail because the response of the Pompeians, as Caesar reports it, is swift and violent:

> All of these men were <u>scolded and attacked</u> by <u>abuse</u> from the consul Lucius Lentulus. Lentulus utterly refused to put Calidius's view to a vote; Marcellus was <u>terrified</u> by the <u>abuse</u> and withdrew from his position. And so, <u>because of</u> the consul's declarations, <u>because of</u> the <u>terror</u> created by the army that was present, <u>because of</u> the <u>threats</u> of Pompey's friends, the majority under <u>compulsion, unwillingly and coerced</u>, followed the view of Scipio. (1.2.4–6; for the Latin see note)[11]

In chapter 1 we had much to say about Caesar's plain style, but in the passage just quoted we find an uncharacteristic use of repetition, expansion, and parallelism (see underlined words) to make vivid the violence and coercion of the vote. Then, with an extraordinary sense of stylistic contrast, Caesar follows this turmoil with the unadorned citation of the Senate's decree against him, the sober report of the tribune's intercession on his behalf, and the referral of their intercession to the Senate for censure (1.2.6–7). The paragraph ends with a summary of Pompeian actions, quoted above, that brings out the ethical critique that underlies the opening of the book: "Severe views are expressed; as each man spoke most harshly and most cruelly, so he was praised most warmly by the enemies of Caesar" (1.2.8).

In the opening two paragraphs of book 1, Caesar introduces themes that will recur throughout the *Civil War*: the implied contrast between Caesarian leniency and Pompeian cruelty; the Pompeian tendency toward verbal abuse, coercion, and duplicity; their refusal to allow debate; their rashness and lack of logic and strategy; their disregard for the constitutional rights of the tribunes. Caesar depicts government in Rome under the eye and direction of Pompey as the destruction of senatorial government. This is important, because Caesar's actions in response to the Senate's decree will make him an "enemy of the republic." If the Senate, however, does not represent the republic, "the public thing," then Caesar may claim to be acting against the private interests of those who oppose him, interests that his narrative suggests are in fact destroying the republic.

2A.II The evening meeting and the motives of the Pompeians (1.3–4)

The second event of Caesar's *Civil War* reinforces and intensifies the claims of the first while developing the petty and personal dimension of this Pompeian failure in government. "The Senate was dismissed toward evening and all its members were summoned by Pompey" (1.3.1). This second (unofficial) gathering of senators, outside the city at night and in response to Pompey's call, can be seen to represent the real nature of Pompeian government as well as its illegitimacy. The Latin word for "were summoned," *evocantur*, suggests that Pompey treats the senators as soldiers who have been asked to reenlist, who are called *evocati*. In fact, one might say that the very term "summoned, called up, enlisted" develops the implications of "if the Senate follows." And lest we miss the implications of Pompey's summons, Caesar repeats the term in the next sentence: former soldiers are being summoned and reenlisted by Pompey (1.3.2, *evocantur*). When in the next sentence after that Caesar describes the city as filled with "[military] tribunes, centurions, and *evocati*," the term is both a technical term for reenlisted soldiers and a description of all who were under Pompey's summons. Caesar says that they fill the city and the Comitium, the place for public meetings (1.3.3); what began with terror, coercion, and threats has now become a gathering army at the heart of civil life.

Caesar pictures Pompey as a general who treats the senators as enlisted men: he praises, encourages, chastises, and goads (1.3.1). Then, in a repetition of the way the legitimate meeting of the Senate ended, this nighttime Senate filled with Pompey's friends and Caesar's enemies conducts business: "By their declarations and their numbers the uncertain are terrified, the hesitant are made bold, and the power of free deliberation is stolen from the majority" (1.3.5). Lentulus had earlier spoken of "bold and brave" speech, Marcellus had sought to enlist a larger army to protect the Senate's ability to deliberate "freely," but in Caesar's narrative it comes to this: Pompeian government means the loss of the Senate's power of free deliberation.

As if to reinforce his point, Caesar then records that Lucius Piso and Lucius Roscius, both of them office-holders in 49, asked for six days in which to inform Caesar of the Senate's decision, and that other senators asked that a legation be sent. "*All of them* were resisted, *all of them* opposed by the consul [Lentulus], Scipio, and Cato" (1.4.1). The repetition of "all of them"—Caesar's Latin uses anaphora of *omnibus*—suggests a thorough silencing of dissident voices in the Senate.

Having shown that government, deliberation, and the Senate's decision were not free and were not representative of "the public thing," Caesar now takes the opportunity constructed by his narrative to give the reasons for opposition by the three men listed above (1.4.1-3). Cato, he says, had long been an enemy and was resentful because he had lost a recent election. In other words, his opposition is motivated by personal enmity and his own failure in the republican process of election. Lentulus was deeply in debt and wanted to take advantage of the financial opportunities that come to one who has an army and a province. For this Pompeian, private wealth is more important than the commonwealth. And Caesar adds that Lentulus bragged that he was going to be "a second Sulla," an allusion to one of the bloodiest periods of recent Roman history and therefore to Pompeian cruelty (see further sec. 1a in chap. 3).

Finally, Metellus Scipio, too, Caesar says, is motivated by his hope for provinces and armies—but also by his marriage ties to Pompey, his fear of prosecution, his love of ostentation, and his adulation of the powerful. Private considerations all.

Capping the list, Caesar turns to Pompey. In some ways, his handling of Pompey is restrained: "Pompey himself was incited by the enemies of Caesar . . ."; but what might seem to excuse Pompey becomes evidence of his willingness to put personal prestige above the public good—"he did not want anyone to equal his public standing." His concern with his standing makes him malleable, and his malleability leads to betrayal: "he had turned away utterly from Caesar's friendship and had ingratiated himself with their common enemies, most of whom he had inflicted on Caesar at the time of their marriage connection."[12] He has, moreover, a bad conscience: "he was disturbed by the scandal of the two legions that he had turned away from their march to Asia and Syria for the purposes of his own power and dominance" (1.4.4). In this sketch, Pompey becomes a pawn of others and of his own emotions, incapable of competing for public standing with Caesar and incapable of honoring friendship and family connections. If one recalls Caesar's self-portrait at the beginning of the *Gallic War* as one who filled his obligations to country, gods, and family, this picture of Pompey, who turns Roman legions to his personal advantage, who turns against old friends and family connections, and who will shortly take money from temples (1.6.8), is a picture of failed Roman virtue. The fact that he diverts two legions from their appointed task is emblematic of his willingness to put his own "power and dominance" ahead of the republic. This passage ends with what seems a simple assessment: "he was eager to bring the matter to a fight" (1.4.5).

2A.III THE *senatus consultum ultimum*, OR "FINAL DECREE" (1.5)

This picture of Pompey and the Pompeians in Rome is a foil for the contrasting picture of Caesar in Ravenna that ends the next paragraph. But before we get there, Caesar reports the events that lead to the senatorial decree of 7 January, a period in which "everything was done in haste and confusion" (1.5.1). He has taken four paragraphs to outline the events of one day and one evening; now, without any temporal articulation, he covers several days of meetings under the heading of "haste and confusion." Caesar's relatives are not allowed to inform him of the Senate's decision and the tribunes are not allowed to oppose the danger to themselves or to exercise their "last" right of intercession (1.5.1). This is unprecedented, he says, even in response to "the most turbulent tribunes" of times past (1.5.2). The Senate then "races down" to "that last and final" senatorial decree, something that before only happened in the midst of "a virtual conflagration of the city": desperation about law and order, reckless legislators (1.5.3). The decree, Caesar says, concerns both Caesar's command and the tribunes, men "of the highest public importance." The decree itself is "extremely oppressive and harsh." "Immediately, the tribunes leave the city and take themselves to Caesar. He was at that time in Ravenna, and he was hoping for a response to his most lenient demands [*lenissimis postulatis*], if by some human equity the matter could be brought to peace" (1.5.4–5).

It is important to notice the superlatives, the metaphors, and the emotional appeals here, which gain in force and effectiveness by virtue of their context and the contrast with Caesar's typically plain style.[13] In fact, Caesar's narrative itself becomes hasty and (as we will see) confused about chronological detail as it represents the putative confusion of these events. The fact that the Senate did not meet on several available meeting days (1.5.4) suggests that things were not so hasty and confused as Caesar would like his readers to believe (or recall, since many of his readers would have participated in these events). But Caesar's commentaries are not recording events so much as analyzing them and representing through them larger political issues. As, for example, in the formal parallelism of the contrasting phrases about Pompey, eager for the matter to be brought to war (*rem ad arma deduci*), and Caesar, hoping that the matter could be brought to peace (*res ad otium deduci*).

2A.IV Pompeian government (1.6)

Like the preceding paragraph, Caesar's description of the events following the "final decree" is rapid, partisan, and at times confused. The point of the description, however, is clear. We begin with a Senate meeting outside the city. Although such a venue was legal, provided that the Senate met within one mile of the city walls and that the place was both public and consecrated, there was no reason to meet outside the city—unless Pompey wanted to be present (see n. 8). When Pompey then repeats what he had already had Scipio say, his role as instigator of the impasse is clear. Not only that, but this repetition participates in the same mocking irony that led Lentulus to ask the senators to be bold and brave. Pompey warmly praises their "manliness and consistency" (1.6.1). Now the Latin word for "manliness," *virtus*, comes into English as the word "virtue," but in Latin it is a specific kind of manly virtue (*vir* = "man"), and in Caesar it always refers to the manly virtue of military men. So, when Pompey praises the senators' manliness, he is simultaneously marking them as "his soldiers" and mocking their terrified and desperate acquiescence to the threats of his henchmen. This becomes clearer when he mentions their "consistency" (*constantiam*); for, as Lentulus had just noted, in recent times they had sided with Caesar. Furthermore, in the proceedings that follow, Caesar describes the senatorial decrees in the passive voice: beginning with the introduction of business in 1.6.3, we find sixteen passive verbs in five sentences.[14] This does two things: first, it undermines Pompey's rhetoric of "manly senators" and supports Caesar's implied claim that the Senate was coerced; second, it makes it possible for Caesar to avoid naming senators who opposed him. We will return to the value of this silence in our discussion of Caesar's audience in chapter 3; for now it is enough to note the passivity and even inevitability that Caesar's language implies.

Complementing the arrogance with which he treats the Senate, Pompey displays an unwarranted confidence in his forces. He claims to have ten legions fully prepared (1.6.2), and other evidence seems to confirm that eventually he did raise as many troops as this.

The problem, however, is that at the time it was not true in any meaningful way: Pompey's six best legions were in Spain, while the others were two legions that he had "stripped" from Caesar, and possibly two legions of fresh recruits. The issue is not just the quality of the legions but their proximity and placement. These are strategic matters that should affect planning. No wonder, then, that in about two weeks Cicero will complain: "I see no garrison, the reason that [Pompey] was kept near Rome, and I see no place to put a garrison. All of our hope lies in two legions that were kept here by a trick and practically belong to somebody else" (*Att.* 7.13.2; 22 January 49). Pompey also claims that he "has discovered and found out" that Caesar's troops will not follow him, surely one of the grossest miscalculations of the war. Caesar calls attention to Pompey's arrogant pride with the unparalleled doublet "discovered and found out."

The end of the paragraph recounts the steps taken by the Senate. What little opposition there was is defeated (1.6.3–4). Unprecedented actions are taken: provinces are assigned to "private citizens," bypassing two legitimate governors "by private agreement." The consuls then set out from Rome without taking the auspices, "a thing that had never happened before that time," and "contrary to all precedent" private citizens had public attendants throughout the city and on the Capitoline (1.6.5–6).[15] Under Pompeian control the "public thing" is becoming a "private thing." The paragraph comes to a close with a flurry of activity: "Throughout all of Italy, levies are held, weapons are requisitioned, monies are exacted from towns and stolen from temples, and all divine and human laws are overturned" (1.6.8).

The rhetoric is powerful and effective. It is also, however, misleading. There is, for instance, no record of money being stolen from temples; in fact, the funds in the public treasury in the Forum temple of Saturn were left behind for Caesar to take (1.14.1). Furthermore, the levies that Caesar mentions twice and that participate in his picture of Pompey as a man as eager to gather and enlist armies as to strip legions from Caesar, were, as Cicero notes above ("no garrison"), mainly a failure. But, more importantly, the chaotic events that Caesar summarizes with such speed here include the departure of the consuls from Rome on the night of 17 January and the panic that followed on 18 and 19 January. These events, however, took place after Caesar had crossed the Rubicon (10 or 11 January—not mentioned in the *Civil War*), after the fall of four towns south of the Rubicon (by 16 January, 1.11.4), and after Pompey himself had left Rome (17 January, 1.14.3). Yet when Caesar begins paragraph 1.7 with a reference to them—"when Caesar learned of these things"—he turns the consequences of his invasion into one of the reasons for his decision to march. Selection and organization here tell a story of Pompeian failure, violence, and cowardice that may be emotionally true (Cicero and others were appalled by Pompey's flight from Rome) but is chronologically untrue. It was Caesar's march into Italy that created the chaos, not the chaos that provoked Caesar's march.

The phrase that ends this first narrative unit of the *Civil War*, "all divine and human laws are overturned," is a common one for political chaos in the late Republic: Cicero uses it of Caesar, "who perverted all things divine and human," and the historian Sallust uses it of the general decline in the late Republic, "which overturned everything human and divine" (*Off.* 1.26; *Jug.* 5.2). If there is a difference in Caesar's expression it is the specification of laws, which helps to position Caesar not just as a moral authority but as a defender of law and order. This is, perhaps, one of the reasons for the distortion of chronology discussed above. For, if Caesar presented himself as deciding to enter Italy in response to the complaints of the tribunes who fled Rome on the night of 7/8 January (1.5.5) and came to Caesar in Ravenna, he would appear as the defender of tribunician rights. A good thing, certainly, but intervention seems even more justifiable when "all divine and human laws are overturned" and when the general who marches to Rome in response to widespread chaos is in a position to appear as the return of good government and republican values.

2b Caesar (1.7–11)

In the first section of *Civil War* 1 Caesar presents the situation in Rome as it degenerates through terror, coercion, and threats into a destruction of public interest, the gathering of armies, political and moral chaos, and the inevitability of civil war. The next section justifies Caesar's entrance into Italy. It has two major movements. In the first, Caesar, addressing his troops, emphasizes the need for defense, specifically against the "injuries" done to himself (his "dignity" or "standing") and those done to the tribunes. The second argues the practical impossibility of any settlement with the Pompeians because of their "lack of equity," "unfair conditions," and duplicity. The speech and the soldiers' response to it refute Pompey's delusional belief that Caesar's troops will desert him.

2B.1 Caesar's speech to his troops (1.7)

Caesar's speech is a neatly organized mini-oration.[16] It has three parts and, like all but one of Caesar's utterances in his commentaries, is quoted indirectly (on indirect discourse, or paraphrase, see sec. 2c in chap. 5). The first part establishes Caesar's complaint on grounds of "injustices," which are stressed through the amplification of doublets: "He recalled the injustices of his enemies at all times, and complained that Pompey had been <u>duped and twisted</u> by the <u>malice and envy</u> caused by Caesar's renown, though he himself had always <u>supported and promoted</u> Pompey's <u>honor and status</u>" (1.7.1; for the Latin see note).[17] In the second part, 1.7.2–6, Caesar turns to the legal issue of tribunician rights but does not treat it as a narrowly legal matter. Instead, he uses the politically charged term "new" to describe the actions of the Pompeians: they have gone beyond Sulla in muzzling the tribunes of the people, and used the "final decree" in unprecedented circumstances. Joining the oppression of tribunician rights with the attack on himself (something he did earlier, as well) is a kind of sleight of hand, since the "final decree" was passed to authorize military action against Caesar, while overruling the tribunes' veto was simply a necessary preliminary. In the third section of the speech (1.7.7) he turns to his "reputation and standing." This allows him to point out that he and his soldiers have been successful for eight years—he calls this "managing the public thing" (*rem publicam . . . gesserint*)—and that they have won many battles, have pacified Gaul and Germany. This list is also, in the context of Pompey's boasts, a reminder of the effectiveness and cohesiveness of Caesar's army. The soldiers shout their approval and the paragraph ends with them saying that they are ready "to defend against the injustices done their general and the tribunes of the people" (1.7.8). Thus, Caesar presents his attack on Rome and defiance of the Senate as a defense of traditional and constitutional rights and a defense against personal and public injustices. He mentions the republic three times. The last word of his reported speech is "defend" and the last word the soldiers shout in support is also "defend."

2B.II PRIVATE AND PUBLIC (1.8–10)

"Having discovered his soldiers' feelings, he sets forth to Ariminum and there meets the tribunes who had fled to him. He summons the rest of his legions from their winter quarters and orders them to follow" (1.8.1). The unassuming beginning of this paragraph has some details worth unpacking. The march from Ravenna to Ariminum took place on the night of 10 or 11 January. It was on this march that Caesar crossed the Rubicon, leaving his province with an army under arms in violation of his commission as a general. It seems clear that Caesar wants to avoid calling attention to his legal status at this juncture. Secondly, we have already noted that throughout the *Gallic War* Caesar begins his yearly account by leaving his winter quarters. The recollection of that norm here marks the event not just as the beginning of the campaign season but as the beginning of a military commentary. In other words, this is the beginning of war.

Caesar's march, however, is immediately interrupted. One Lucius Caesar, "whose father was an officer of Caesar's," arrives with "a commission regarding private business" from Pompey (1.8.2). The fact that Caesar starts only to stop for negotiations portrays his willingness to bring matters to peace. On the other hand, it is invidious to characterize Lucius Caesar's commission from Pompey as "private business." Of course, it recalls the portrait of Pompeians turning the republic into a private possession, but it also undercuts the public themes of Pompey's message before we hear them. Pompey says that he wants to clear himself with Caesar and stop Caesar from interpreting actions undertaken for the republic as personal attacks. He says that he always considered the republic's advantage more important than his own private interests, and that Caesar too should set aside his passion and anger for the sake of the republic and not harm the republic. Caesar has Pompey mention the republic four times in three sentences. But he also draws attention to the private channels Pompey employs: "[Lucius Caesar] added a few things of the same kind along with excuses for Pompey. The praetor Roscius discussed with Caesar nearly the same things in the same words, and he noted that Pompey had mentioned them to him" (1.8.4). It all sounds a little shady: excuses, go-betweens, rehearsed speeches, private business.

Responding to Pompey provides Caesar with another opportunity to lay out his case (1.9). Since the mission itself was private and not well known, he is relatively free from the constraints of veracity; there is (and was) no check on the accuracy of what he writes. He speaks again of "injuries," of his "honor" and his "standing," and of his "political enemies," all of which we have heard before. But he also broadens issues and adds some new ones. Addressing the army, he had said that the tribunes' right of intercession should be "free"; now he says Italy should be "free of fear" and the republic should have "free" elections. He asks that the republic be given back to the Senate and People, and asserts that the republic is the principle for which he will endure anything. To that end he suggests that armies be dismissed and levies halted, and that Pompey leave for his provinces.

The power of Caesar's language here and its implications as an analysis of the causes of civil war depend almost entirely on the preceding chapters. It is because we have seen debate silenced that we understand Caesar's concluding proposal for "discussions" (*colloquia*; 1.9.6) to be an effort to restore the basic principles of civil government. Moreover, the simple fairness of asking those who bring Pompey's words to him to carry back his to Pompey creates a kind of argument by contrast (1.9.1). In this paragraph he moves from a relatively narrow focus on the damage done to his honor and standing if he was denied the special election arrangements voted him by the Roman People, to larger issues of the republic. Almost imperceptibly Caesar joins his own political interests to this larger context: "<u>free elections and the entire republic</u> should be handed back to the Senate and the Roman People" (1.9.5). The election of Caesar to his second consulship is inextricable from the interests of the republic.[18]

2B.III IMPASSE (1.10–11)

Pompey does not accept or debate Caesar's overtures. His talk of putting the republic before his private interests is reduced to a series of orders issued to Caesar: "Let him return to Gaul, and leave Ariminum, and dismiss his armies" (1.10.2). This is followed by the promise that, under those conditions, Pompey would go to Spain; otherwise, the consuls and Pompey would not stop levying troops.

In the next paragraph Caesar brings his introductory section to a close with some brief editorializing. This time the rubric under which he gathers the events that lead to what he calls "a great despair of peace" is simply "unfair conditions" (1.11.3; 1.11.1). And the unfair conditions themselves amount to two related contingencies: Pompey will not leave Rome and will not dismiss his armies, but Caesar must leave Italy and must dismiss his armies. But had not Caesar said that he would suffer anything for the sake of the republic? His actions here would contradict his avowed willingness to suffer anything for the republic (1.9.5) if he had not tied his defense of his honor to his defense of the tribunes, and his defense of the republic to the free elections that would serve his own political interests. As Caesar tells it, the personal losses Pompey would like him to suffer are not really, or not only, personal losses; they are intolerably implicated in a larger and more important loss: the loss of the republic to private interests. Thus, with no opportunity given for discussions, Caesar despairs of peace. He sends Antony to Arretium and begins himself, for the first time, to hold levies around Ariminum (1.11.4).

2c Summary and overview

In the opening chapters of the *Civil War* Caesar constructs an argument by narrative that portrays the civil war as the result of Pompeian failures. These failures may have their personal elements, but Caesar is not so much concerned to denigrate the character of the Pompeians as to show the effect of their actions and inaction upon government at Rome, which he variously terms "the republic," the "civil state," "the Senate and the Roman People." Fundamental to the Pompeian failure is their tendency to put private interests above "the public thing": their failures in the electoral process, their debts, their personal ambitions, and their fears and hatreds lead to the destruction of debate, of reason, and of sound policy, just as they lead to the gathering of armies and a great desperation about peace. Pompeian cruelty, terror, and coercion, along with a tendency to intransigent extremes, are contrasted with Caesarian leniency and reason and patience. Caesar had decided by the time of Corfinium that he would not rule like Sulla. Before 11 March 49, he wrote to his friends Oppius and Balbus about his leniency at Corfinium and his efforts to win a reconciliation with Pompey: "Let us see if we can recover the goodwill of all in this way and enjoy a lasting victory, since others were not able to avoid hatred or to hold on to victory longer by using cruelty.... Let this be our new policy for maintaining the victory: to strengthen our position with mercy and generosity" (*Att.* 9.7C.1). And so, when Caesar, as was mentioned above, portrays the senatorial actions that culminate in the "final decree" in five sentences and sixteen passive verbs, and when he speaks of terror and coercion and an unwilling and unfree Senate, he is picturing a loss of "the public thing" that his war must restore.

3 | Developing the argument

The position that Caesar lays out in the opening paragraphs has a certain clarity owing to its structure: six paragraphs on the action of the Pompeians in Rome and the flight of the tribunes, five paragraphs on Caesar's response. The Roman narrative moves from Pompeian-instigated turmoil in the Senate and the passage of the "final decree," to the meeting of the Senate outside of Rome that Pompey attended, to the allotment of provinces, levying of troops, and requisitioning of money. The Caesarian narrative gives Caesar's response first in a speech to his troops, then as a reaction to some overtures from Pompey himself, and finally in a brief summary of the reasons he rejected Pompey's counter-response. This makes for a coherent picture of actors, causes, and political impasse, albeit one that violates chronology and ignores the fundamental illegality of Caesar's crossing the Rubicon. Another chronological distortion helps him suggest that the abandonment of Rome reflected a general mistrust of Pompeian leadership.

3a Sequence: The goodwill of Italy (1.12–15)

A brief summary of the course of events will help us see the argument built into Caesar's narrative in the next panel of book 1. Caesar crossed the Rubicon on the night of 10 or 11 January, and occupied Pisaurum, Fanum, and Ancona during 12–14 January. Lucius Roscius met Caesar at Ariminum (17 or 18 January), at the same time that the consuls fled Rome, and took Caesar's reply to Pompey on 23 January. The Senate and Pompey met at Capua and replied to Caesar on 25 January, and he rejected the terms of this reply on 28 January.

Caesar orders these events differently. He recounts his rejection of terms on the 28th at 1.11. But then at 1.12 he tells of the capitulation of Iguvium, which he had taken on around 21 January, and at 1.13 of Auximum, which he also took before 28 January. Caesar then says at 1.14 that Pompey and the consuls fled Rome upon receiving news of his occupation of Auximum (28 January), when in fact Pompey had fled Rome on 17 January and the consuls on 18 January.

The chronological distortion here allows Caesar to place the abandonment of Rome within a context of similar events. An analysis of how Caesar does this illustrates one of the ways in which his narrative creates implications about the course of events. The fact that a sequence of events suggests causation or similarity is, of course, one basic reason to keep the sequence accurate if you are trying to tell the truth, and to change it if you are trying to distort something more than the details.[19]

In the opening chapters we saw that the Pompeians were duplicitous and hasty, abusive and overconfident. As soon as Caesar despairs of peace (1.11.3), he sends Antony to Arretium and occupies Pisaurum, Fanum, and Ancona himself. He then sends Curio to Iguvium (1.12). The narrative of the town's capitulation is short and has a clear theme: Caesar, learning of the goodwill (*voluntas*) of the people of Iguvium, sends Curio; the Pompeian in charge, Thermus, distrusting the goodwill of the town, flees; Pompeian soldiers desert; the town receives Curio with goodwill. There is nothing particularly remarkable about this story: it is in Caesar's interest to construe the outcome of events as evidence of the goodwill of the townspeople (rather than as the result of fear); the flight of Thermus shows a lack of self-confidence and strategy; the desertion of troops looks back at Pompey's over-confidence in his legions (and will become a theme). The story portrays Caesar's cohorts as liberators and justifies Caesar's subsequent "confidence in the goodwill of Italian towns" (1.12.3).

Auximum, held by Attius Varus, is the next Italian town to open its gates to Caesar. Varus learns of his arrival; the townspeople take Caesar's side and tell Varus that he is in danger; Varus is frightened; he tries to flee and, forced to join battle, is deserted by his soldiers; Caesar thanks the townspeople of Auximum (1.13). In isolation, this story is no more remarkable than the story of Iguvium. What is remarkable is that it seems to be another version of the same story: Caesar, trusting in the goodwill of the men of Iguvium, liberates the town; Caesar, trusting in the goodwill of Italian towns, liberates

Auximum. The change from the goodwill of the single town Iguvium to the goodwill of Italian towns, moreover, suggests that Caesar sees his stories as making a general point about Pompeian occupation, Italian resistance to it, and Caesarian liberation from it.

In paragraph 1.15 Caesar recounts how he overran Picenum. The whole district received him most willingly (1.15.1); Cingulum promised to help most eagerly (1.15.2; on this episode see sec. 4a in chap. 3). At Asculum the Pompeian Spinther learns of the arrival of Caesar; he flees from the town; a large part of his soldiers desert (1.15.3). Same story.

Now, if we return to the chronological distortion we were considering, we find that the story of events in Rome (17/18 January; 1.14) is narrated so that it takes place between Auximum (28 January; 1.13) and Asculum (1 February; 1.15). In Caesar's narrative, news of his actions at Auximum arrives in Rome; one consul is terrified and flees the city. Then there are reports that Caesar is about to arrive; the other consul and a number of magistrates flee; Pompey flees and goes to the legions he had stripped from Caesar (1.14.3); the consul Lentulus arms gladiators belonging to Caesar (1.14.4).

Caesar did not, at this time, go to Rome. However, in the context of the stories just considered, we have a narrative in which news of Caesar's imminent arrival is followed by the fear and flight of Pompeians. Although he does not say that Pompeian soldiers deserted at this juncture, the narrative sequence just described suggests that the Pompeians cannot or will not fight and that they are surrounded by citizens (this time in Rome itself) and soldiers (both legionaries and gladiators) that they cannot or should not trust.

This overview of the narrative from paragraphs 12 to 15 shows again how Caesar at the beginning of the *Civil War* uses sequence, parallelism, and contrast to suggest underlying realities. Here, the argument is that the Pompeians operate in bad faith, that they coerce the Italian towns (and Rome) whose real desire is to be under Caesar's protection, and that they abandon what they take but cannot hold.

3b Contrast: Corfinium (1.15–23)

The events at Corfinium, the next major episode of the first book, continue to develop the picture of Caesar the statesman and liberator by means of a contrast with the Pompeian Lucius Domitius Ahenobarbus, the man chosen by a cowed Senate to replace Caesar in Gaul. This is a story about a duplicitous and distrusted general who betrays his men and is betrayed by them as well as by Pompey.

As Caesar's narrative turns away from Rome to the battlefield, one would expect a change of emphasis, and to some extent one gets it. Caesar likes to describe the gathering and alignment of troops, troop movements and strategies, the building of fortifications, and siege machinery. And, as any good Roman general and politician would, he shows that he is worthy of honor and office by demonstrating his abilities on the battlefield. The parallel between military and civic achievements will be made explicit later in the book, when Caesar will say to the Senate that "as he had been eager to be superior in achievements, so he wished to be the victor in justice and equity" (1.32.9). At Corfinium the military and the domestic virtues are interwoven.

3B.1 POMPEIAN DISSIMULATION AND FAILURE

A key element is the presentation of Caesar's Pompeian opponent, Domitius. As Caesar's legions gather around Corfinium, Domitius, aware of his danger, sends a message to Pompey asking for help. From the beginning something is amiss: Domitius's letter to Pompey "begs and prays that he help him" (1.17.1, *petant atque orent* [sc.] *litterae*). Caesar does not use this desperate doublet elsewhere. When Pompey, as we saw in chapter 1, refuses, Domitius repeats the typical Pompeian failures in character and government (1.19). He dissembles and lies; he holds discussions, but they are private, held in secret with a few close familiars. Domitius's soldiers notice this behavior—"Domitius's face does not match his words" (1.19.3)—and have their own discussions (1.20). They point out that they had stayed because of hope and trust in their leader, but that he was making plans for his own safety. This mini-critique of Pompeian methods, of the Pompeian tendency to turn "the public thing" into a matter of private concerns and personal safety, is all the more powerful from the mouth of Pompeian soldiers. But, for our interest in the larger governmental issues that Caesar likes to address, the next development is devastating. Soldiers from "the Marsian country" disagree with the nascent mutiny and try to remain faithful to the faithless Domitius. The result is a mini–civil war (1.20.3): "such a disagreement arose between them that they tried to engage in battle and fight it out with arms." When the suspicions about Domitius's duplicity are confirmed, however, the mini-war comes to an end, and "<u>all</u> the soldiers <u>with a single plan</u> surround Domitius and bring him out in <u>public</u>" (1.20.5). Unity, unanimity, and the public realm—these are the things that Pompeian methods of duplicity and poor strategy destroy and that are repaired by resistance to the Pompeians. At this point, Domitius's soldiers send a deputation to Caesar saying that "they are prepared to open the city gates and to do whatever he commands and to hand over Domitius alive into Caesar's power" (1.20.5). The word "alive" sets the stage for Caesar's response.

3B.II Caesar victorious

The battle for Corfinium ended without a fight, not simply because of Caesar's strategy, speed, and superior forces, but also because of Pompeian duplicity, fear, and self-serving secret discussions. Caesar's reaction (1.21) to the offered surrender takes a form that allows him to present not just his thoughts but himself as a thoughtful and foresightful general. Let us see what he thinks about (for the form see sec. 2b in chap. 5).

"When these things were known, Caesar, although he was of the opinion that it was of great importance to take possession of the city and to transfer the cohorts to his army and camp . . . " His first thought is strategic and military: he should secure the victory as soon as possible. This, of course, makes sense, and Caesar makes sure that his reader is aware of its "great importance." Indeed, he interrupts his sentence at this point to explain why this strategic concern is so important: "... lest any change of heart come about because of bribery or improvement of morale or false news ..." These fears did not need to be outlined if Caesar's purpose was to recount events or to glorify his victory. Instead, they illustrate the range of Caesar's considerations, and in that regard what is remarkable is their variety: he does not imagine only one mechanism of influence, nor does he limit himself to intentional acts. He knows that soldiers and conquered towns can change their minds about surrender for any number of reasons, including false news. And before the sentence comes to the main clause and to Caesar's decision, he adds another explanation: "... because it is often the case in war that from small changes great events come about ... " Again, the purpose of the clause is in large part to present Caesar as an experienced general, one who knows war and has observed how unpredictable it can be (for more on this aspect of Caesar's self-portrait see sec. 2 in chap. 4).

In the main body of the sentence Caesar comes to his countervailing concern: "... nevertheless, fearing that with the entry of the soldiers and the license of nighttime the town would be torn to pieces, he warmly praises the men who had come to him. He then sends them back to the city and orders the gates and walls to be watched." Caesar's "warm praise" for the soldiers who had surrendered to him recalls (by repeating the verb *conlaudare*) earlier scenes. First, it recalls and repeats the warm praise Caesar offered Attius Varus's soldiers when they deserted to him at Auximum (1.13.5). Second, it recalls two instances of Pompeian praise. In the first, men are praised for cruelty: "as each man spoke most harshly and most cruelly, so he was praised most warmly by the enemies of Caesar" (1.2.8); and in the second, decisions that, as we saw earlier, arose from fear and cowardice are praised as virtues: "Pompey warmly praised the manliness and consistency of the Senate" (1.6.1). The contrast is striking: Caesar praises those who join him and entrusts them with the protection of the town; Pompeians praise cruelty and cowardice.

In the second movement of this episode, as we saw in chapter 1, Spinther asks for a discussion with Caesar during the last watch of the night. He is concerned about his own safety, a typical Pompeian concern. But Caesar interrupts the plea Spinther bases on Caesar's past services to him, insisting that "he had not left his province to cause trouble but to defend himself from the insults of his enemies, to restore the tribunes who had been expelled from the state to their position of honor, to vindicate his own freedom and that of the Roman People from oppression by a faction of the few" (1.22.5). These arguments, which convince Spinther (correctly) that his safety is assured, we have heard before. But the reference to defense against "insults of his enemies" links the Corfinium episode, in which Caesar will protect those who have capitulated "from the insults of the soldiers" (1.23.3), to the opening chapters of the book, where he reports both insults to his standing and instances of verbal attack on the senators. Where the Pompeians use insults, Caesar protects against them.

The final disposition at Corfinium is played out against the background of the general principles involved in the Pompeian abuse of power—verbal aggression (threats, insults), coercion, self-interest—all of which are addressed here. Senators and their sons, army officers, and other Romans of high status are brought forth from the city, shielded, as we have seen, from the soldiers' insults. After Caesar points out that they have not shown gratitude for his favors—the case of Spinther is particularly salient here—he dismisses them and they are safe. He returns money to Domitius, despite the fact that it was public funding provided to Pompey for soldiers: "he did not want to seem more restrained in regard to human life than in regard to money" (1.23.4; cf. "alive" at 1.20.5). In other words, he offers safety even to opponents and a disposition of resources (both human and financial) that looks beyond his personal profit and satisfaction. The passage shows political virtues in action and presents Caesar as the answer to the problems that the Pompeians have created.

Among those captured and pardoned at Corfinium is a Pompeian officer named Numerius Magius. Showing yet another political virtue in action, Caesar sends him to Pompey with a request for a discussion (1.24.5); he speaks of the republic and the common safety and the need to discuss the terms of peace. The narrative of Corfinium supports this overture.

3c Silence: Brindisi (1.24–28)

The siege at Brindisi is represented in the *Civil War* as the last opportunity for peace, a goal that Caesar continued to pursue despite the intractability of Pompey and the Senate and despite Pompey's apparent indifference. While en route to Brindisi, Caesar sent Numerius Magius to Pompey with an invitation to discuss peace. In the meantime, Caesar begins elaborate works to blockade the entrance and facilities of the port, in order, he says, to ensure Pompey's departure from Italy (1.25.4). (The consuls, with the larger half of the army, have already crossed to Greece.) However, he also, he says, "administered the war in such a way as not to conclude that terms of peace had to be abandoned" and made numerous attempts at opening discussions even though they hindered his own operations (1.26.2). When nothing is heard from Numerius Magius, Caesar sends another messenger to encourage a meeting about peace. This time word does come back: Pompey said he could not discuss peace without the consuls being present (1.26.2–5).

Clearly the picture Caesar wants his reader to have is one of Caesar the statesman willing to postpone effective hostilities for a chance at peace and of Caesar the general confident that even a hampered effort will be sufficient to secure his military objective. He wants us to see that, while he did everything possible for peace, the Pompeians insisted on war, a point he has made before. Once again, however, letters preserved in Cicero's correspondence allow us to see that Caesar's argument has overruled his accuracy. One letter of March 49 reports that Pompey sent Magius back with a counteroffer "concerning peace" and that Caesar responded (*Att.* 9.13A.1). Caesar himself wrote that letter. As he did the one that shows that he was intent on forcing the issue, not holding back. The comment of Cicero, who quotes Caesar's letter, is to the point:

"Where is that peace about which Balbus wrote that he was tortured with expectation?" (*Att.* 9.14.1–2, 24 or 25 March 49). So the fact that in the *Civil War* Caesar tells us that he sent Magius to Pompey but not that Pompey replied, and claims to have delayed and even held back his military efforts (if that is what "administered the war in such a way" means) while he was in fact forcing Pompey's departure from Italy, makes it clear that establishing Pompeian responsibility for the war is a major burden of his narrative, even if not all of the evidence he offers for that argument is reliable.

As he makes his overtures for peace through Magius, we hear again the terms that focus Caesar's analysis of what is going wrong. He emphasizes the need for discussion (forms and derivatives of *colloquium* at 1.24.5, 1.26.3, 1.26.5), the importance of the republic and the common safety (1.24.5), the need for terms of peace that are fair (1.24.5, 1.26.2 and 3), the need to disarm (1.26.4). This is a synopsis of what was argued in the opening paragraphs, where the Pompeians would not allow open or free discussion, put private interests above the public interest, had no regard for equity and fairness, and gathered armies while insisting that Caesar disarm. It creates a powerful image of Pompeian failure when Caesar summarizes and recounts these impasses at the very moment that Pompey is about to abandon Italy. Here, Caesar plays to a sense many had at the time that Pompey's abandonment first of Rome and then of Italy was an abandonment of the republic, a diplomatic as well as a military failure (see sec. 1 in chap. 3).

Caesar joins these representations of Pompey's refusal to negotiate with a sinister image of his preparations for departure from Italy. The picture recalls themes we saw in the narrative of Caesar's entry into Italy: the Pompeians are an occupying force hated for their arrogance, insults, and lack of fairness (1.28.1). When they flee the city, the townspeople are eager to help Caesar and his men (1.28.2). And, although Pompey and his troops do escape, Caesar's men still manage to capture two ships (1.28.4). Interwoven into this story, moreover, is a description of Pompey's desperate attempt to protect his abandonment of Italy through treachery and deception. We have seen the Pompeians deceive and coerce before, in the Senate and outside Rome. Now Caesar gives a military version of treachery and deception. The Pompeians dig trenches across the streets in Brindisi and place sharpened stakes in the trenches. Then they cover them over with wickerwork and earth. To be sure, war is war, and Caesar had done the same thing at the siege of Alesia (*Gallic War* 7.73), but there the enemy were Gauls and Caesar was not escaping. The townspeople of Brindisi help Caesar by warning him of the concealed stakes.

4 | Recapitulation

When Pompey flees Italy, Caesar decides not to pursue him. The story we have been reviewing up to this point is remarkable in two ways. First, although we are almost one-third of the way through the book, there has not been a single pitched battle. The Pompeians have fled, deserted, or capitulated, but Caesar has not been forced to kill a single Roman or Italian. All this will change when Caesar goes to Spain—and yet even there his manner of waging war will minimize casualties. Second, the momentum of events since the passage of the "final decree" has been toward Pompey's abandonment of Italy, while the individual events themselves repeat a basic pattern of failed Pompeian control in the towns and failed peace negotiations. This narrative inertia supports Caesar's analysis of the war. In fact, Pompey's abandonment of Italy is itself another instance of the narrative pattern according to which Pompeians hear of Caesar's arrival, mistrust themselves and their armies, and flee. At Rome, when Caesar addresses the Senate, he will recount his version of cause and blame for almost the last time in the first book of the *Civil War* (1.32). Only during his speech at Ilerda (1.85) will he return to this wider justification of the war.

4a Pompeian government (1.30–31)

Before we get to Rome, however, Caesar quickly recounts the movements of his officers Valerius and Curio in Sardinia and Sicily, where they face the Pompeians Cotta and Cato. He then follows the senatorial governor, Tubero, to North Africa. We know from Cicero's letters that Curio did not set out for Sicily until mid-April, while Caesar met the Senate in Rome on 1–3 April, so once again we have a chronological distortion, and once again the distortion seems purposeful, since Caesar begins the chapter on events in Rome by insisting on this very chronological distortion: "when he had dealt with these matters" (1.32.1). What is the effect of recounting the events in Sardinia, Sicily, and Africa before Caesar's self-justification to the Senate?

With these events reported before the meeting of the Senate, Caesar's narrative can proceed directly from Rome to Marseilles, where he places his officers Decimus Brutus and Gaius Trebonius in charge of a siege, and from there to Spain for the fight against Pompey's most experienced forces, commanded by Afranius and Petreius. But the chronological inversion does more than permit a clear narrative line tracking Caesar's movements. The events in Sardinia, Sicily, and Africa also set the stage for his meeting with the Senate by recalling earlier narratives of Pompeian government.

In Sardinia, we hear a tale familiar from Caesar's march through northern Italy. The people of Caralis hear that the Caesarian Valerius is being deployed against them. They eject the Pompeian Cotta from their city; he is terrified because he knows the entire province is opposed to him; he flees to Africa.

In Sicily, we have a variation on this tale, one that also recalls Pompeian actions in Rome. Cato is gathering troops, indeed compelling Roman citizens to enlist. He hears of the arrival of Curio. But this time, in place of a general revolt by the citizens, we get a speech: Cato complains that he was abandoned and betrayed by Pompey, that the war was not necessary, that the Pompeians were not prepared although Pompey said that everything was ready. Then Cato flees.

Finally, we follow Tubero, who had been given the governorship of North Africa by lot—the normal procedure, not one of the Pompeian "strange new" methods. He arrives in his province to find that the Pompeian Varus—who abandoned Auximum back at

1.13.2, as Caesar reminds us here (1.31.2)—has assumed the governorship since there was no one else in control. Like Cato, Varus has been conscripting troops. But instead of following the authority of the Senate and handing the province over to Tubero, Varus will not even allow Tubero to come to land. Caesar adds that he did this despite the fact that Tubero's son was on board and was very sick.

These stories are a narrative recapitulation of Pompeian attitudes and principles. The Pompeians may be busy making armies, but they flee because they are hated by the people they govern and because they are betrayed and abandoned by their own leader, Pompey; and they use their positions for personal self-aggrandizement without any regard for legality, senatorial decree, or even common humanity.

4b Caesar in the Senate (1.32–33)

The chronological distortion that puts these illustrations of Pompeian government before the report of Caesar's first appearance in the Senate in a decade provides an effective background against which Caesar may represent his own concern for the republic. But the effect of paragraphs 32–33 also depends on Caesar's presentation of the Senate meetings dominated by Pompeians at the beginning of the book (1.1–6). We are at the end of a climactic structure that began with Pompeian threats and coercion in the Senate and with the refusal to send a legation to Caesar, all of which blocked the pursuit of a peaceful resolution. At the April meeting, even though Pompey has abandoned Italy and Caesar has come to address the Senate, the Pompeians continue their obstructionist activities. "Lucius Metellus, a tribune of the people, was put up by Caesar's enemies to disrupt this business [sending a legation, about which more below] and impede any other business [Caesar] tried to enact" (1.33.3). Metellus's intractability so frustrates Caesar's efforts that he leaves for Gaul and Spain after three days without progress. Compounding his difficulty in getting the Senate to act is the familiar problem of Pompeian threats and senatorial fears: "The Senate agreed to send legates [to Pompey], but they could not find anyone to send, and the chief reason everyone refused to serve on the embassy was fear for personal safety" (1.33.1).

There is an implicit contrast here between how Caesar handles the Senate and how the Pompeians acted under similar circumstances. While the Senate was earlier cowed by Pompeian threats and insults, Caesar punctuates his own address with verbs of debate: "he recalled" (*commemorat*, a historical present, as are the following verbs), "he pointed out" (*docet*), "he laid out" (*proponit*), "he emphasized" (*praedicat*), "he urged and pleaded" (*hortatur ac postulat*). We may recall that Lentulus and Metellus Scipio offered the Senate alternatives. Lentulus said that "he would not fail the Senate and the republic, if they would speak boldly and bravely, but if they looked to Caesar . . . he would take counsel for himself and would not obey the Senate's authority" (1.1.2), and Scipio said that "Pompey would not fail the Senate if they followed; but if they hesitated and acted too leniently, the Senate would implore his aid in vain, should they want it later" (1.1.4). In contrast, Caesar "urged and pleaded that they take up and administer the republic together with him. But if they balked in fear, he would not fail the task and would administer the republic by himself" (1.32.7).[20] The word we have translated here as "fail" is used by all three speakers, and it is surely pointed that Pompeians imagine senatorial failure as an excuse to turn their backs on the Senate, while Caesar imagines the same kind of failure as requiring him to take up the reins of government himself. One might say that in reality the difference is merely rhetorical, but that is the point: Caesar's rhetoric creates a difference.

At the end of Caesar's speech the contrast becomes explicit. Unlike the Pompeians, he urges that a legation be sent to Pompey, and in doing so he takes an opportunity to refute and critique Pompey: "He was not afraid of what Pompey had said in the Senate a little earlier, that authority accrued to those to whom legates were sent and that the fear of those who sent them was made manifest. This seemed to be the mark of a shallow and weak spirit. He, for his part, as he had been eager to be superior in achievements, so he wished to be the victor in justice and equity" (1.32.8–9).

Just as this address brings full circle the events that began in Rome in early January, so it brings to an end Caesar's litany of injustices and his overtures for peace. We hear of the Senate, the republic, and the People for the last time until the end of the book. Caesar also speaks for the last time until the end of the book of the loss of his standing, and of the chaos of Rome at the time of the "final decree"—he repeats the political slogan for chaos ("to mix everything up," 1.6.8, 1.32.5) that he used earlier. From this point on, it will be war, and the terms that refer to governmental processes are, for the most part, abandoned. However, the consequences of Pompeian political failings will have their parallels in the last two-thirds of the book, just as they have already led to failures in Italy.

Caesar's narrative ultimately uses these parallels to create a strong sense of closure at the end of book 1. In fact, Caesar's speech at Rome lays the groundwork for seeing the parallel between Pompeian administrators and Pompeian generals. When Caesar asks the Senate to join him in governing the republic, the term he uses is "to administer" (*administrare*). This term is used by Caesar eight times of conducting war and four times of governing the republic;[21] we saw it at 1.25.3 of Caesar's siege operations at Brindisi. The parallel between military action and political action underlies his return, in the closing chapters of the book, to issues addressed at the beginning: there, he will speak again of injustices and of his enemies; he will struggle with Pompeians again over open discussions and will speak of peace terms. He will both illustrate and decry the Pompeians' cruelty and harshness and their refusal to dismiss their troops. But, at the end of the book, in word and in deed Caesar, because of his victory at Ilerda, will be able to effect a momentary peace. Troops will be dismissed. Controversies will be settled. Property will be restored. Terror will be ended. There will be talk of peace and good faith. We will hear again of leniency, and for the first time we will hear of joy. We turn now to those closing scenes to show how the first book of the *Civil War* makes a coherent and unified argument about Caesar and the possibilities of good government for Rome.

5 | Closure: The problem

So far our discussion has shown that Caesar's narrative, through repetition and contrast, selection and sequence, presents a consistent argument about the causes of the civil war and who bears the ultimate responsibility for it. We have tried to show that Caesar's argument points to Pompeian failures that are not just a matter of personal viciousness or institutional difficulties, but that entail postures and abuses that negate the very terms of Roman republican government. The Pompeians destroy the possibility of open and free discussion; they substitute the private for the public; they destroy honor and standing; they gather and hold armies to secure and protect their injustices. From Caesar's point of view this is not a struggle between Romans for the control of Rome but, more crucially, a struggle for the very existence of Rome and the republic.

In order to develop the commentary form in book 1 as the vehicle not just for the occasional analysis of Pompeian failures but for a coherent argument about Rome and his role in Roman government, Caesar must give the book a sense of closure, a sense that the problems that he has illustrated, and that have led to war, have been or can be solved. There are two major difficulties, however, in doing this: first, a year-by-year report of events does not readily lend itself to closure; and second, the civil war was far from over at the end of 49, where the first book of a commentary on the war would typically end.

Caesar addresses both problems by varying for the first time the annalistic structure of the commentary. We saw in our discussion of the *Gallic War* that Caesar could create a sense of closure to his individual books by concluding with a final battle, sending his troops to winter camps, and turning to administrative tasks. This was often accompanied by a shift of focus—for example, a return to events in Rome and Roman rituals such as the "thanksgivings" for Caesar's accomplishments. The events of 49 do not lend themselves to this type of closure: the last campaign of the year was the defeat of Caesar's officer Curio in North Africa, and Caesar himself, although "administering the republic" in Rome in December, was directing his efforts to his future consulship (for 48) and the coming campaign against Pompey.[22] This is opening material, not closural—and Caesar opens book 3 with it. But the battle of Ilerda, which ended on 2 August 49, could provide a kind of narrative or "natural" closure. Events omitted from book 1 would have to be covered in a second book. As they are (see timeline).

5a Narrative closure

The relatively natural closure provided by the ending of a major battle is reinforced in Caesar's narrative in two ways: the conclusion follows a tale of suspense and interruption, and it deploys closural themes. The beginning of the end seems to be marked at the beginning of paragraph 84: "At last," Caesar writes. The story is so seamlessly told that it is hard to draw a clear line of demarcation between preliminary and concluding events in Spain. Nevertheless, if we begin at paragraph 59, when Caesar in Spain hears of Decimus Brutus's success at Marseilles and when "at the same time the bridge was nearly completed and fortune was changing," we can see how Caesar gives special prominence to the coming battle. The completion of the bridge in paragraph 59 makes it possible for the first time for Caesar's cavalry to disrupt the attempts by Afranius's and Petreius's men to gather food. There is an immediate change in both morale and material conditions. Local inhabitants send Caesar delegations, provide supplies, ally themselves with him; in addition, a Pompeian auxiliary cohort deserts to Caesar's side (1.60.4). Afranius and Petreius become afraid and decide to change the theater of the fighting to Celtiberia and "to prolong the war until winter" (1.61.4).

With one obstacle overcome, Caesar now faces another, and it is precisely how to bring the war to an end, how to avoid prolonging the fighting. In other words, the situation can be read as an allegory or emblem of the civil war: the Pompeians attempt to find ways to prolong the war, while Caesar tries to shorten the war and to make it as bloodless as possible. Caesar makes this explicit. When Caesar's soldiers saw the Pompeians trying to escape, "All over the camp the soldiers met in groups and regretted the fact that the enemy was slipping from their hands, that the war was being drawn out longer than necessary" (1.64.2). They then ask to be allowed to ford the river where the cavalry had crossed. This is a good story about the willingness of Caesar's men to face any obstacle and their eagerness for victory, but Caesar is careful to cast it in terms of bringing the war to an end. The soldiers succeed in crossing the Segre and by the middle of the afternoon they have caught up with the enemy (1.64.4–7).

In the following paragraphs, Caesar and the Pompeians race for a mountainous area where the Pompeians feel they will have an advantage. As usual, Caesar's men find themselves on the more difficult terrain, march harder, go farther, and "help each other along" (1.68.2). Caesar's skill in "administering war" is evident in the alacrity with which his soldiers act. And Caesar reminds his readers once again that the end is at stake: "But no one refused this labor because they thought that it was going to be <u>the end of all their labors,</u> if they could cut the enemy off from the Ebro river and prevent him from getting food" (1.68.3).

Caesar also reminds his readers of some by now familiar Pompeian characteristics. As his men take a circuitous route to cut off the Pompeians, their march looks to the Afranian army like a retreat. Consequently, the Pompeians believe that they have succeeded. They run from the camp and jeer at Caesar's men: "they were attacking our men with insults and shouts" (1.69.1). It is a scene that reminds one of the Pompeians in Rome—arrogant and mistaken. "But when they saw the column gradually turn back to the right and noticed that already the head of the column was beyond their camp, no one was so dull or slow that he didn't conclude that they had to leave the camp immediately and engage the enemy" (1.69.3). "Engagement" is what Caesar was aiming at.

Now the race is on again. Afranius has few good options: if he marches ahead, he will be separated from his supplies; he is pursued by the cavalry from behind and sees Caesar's army in battle formation ahead. He halts on a hill and sends his cavalry to take a mountain. They are attacked by Caesar's men and killed to a man in sight of both armies. But just when the tide is about to turn decisively, another interruption: Caesar's commanders come to him and urge that he join battle; it is time to fight, and "every soldier is more than ready for it" (1.71.2). But Caesar responds in high-minded fashion: he wants to bring the matter to a conclusion (again, the closural term) without bloodshed. He is concerned for his own men and does not want to tempt fortune. He is also concerned for his fellow citizens fighting on the other side (we have not heard of Roman citizens or of the Roman state since paragraph 32) and would prefer to obtain his object while keeping them safe (1.72.2–3). That is, as soon as the practical obstacle to success is removed, the statesman general appears, simultaneously concerned for victory and for his fellow citizens, and introduces ethical and political obstacles. Caesar decides to allow Afranius and Petreius to retreat. He begins a siege.

What follows is a scene that confirms the wisdom of Caesar's position. Afranius and Petreius go to inspect their fortifications, and their soldiers take advantage of the opportunity to meet with Caesar's soldiers (1.74). The two camps become like one. Friends and acquaintances find each other. There is joy and congratulation. For a moment, the war is over. But it is over only because the Pompeian leaders are absent. As soon as Petreius hears of what is happening, he comes rushing back to camp (1.75.2). Again, we are caught in a suspenseful movement: the stated goal (to end the war, to keep from dragging it out unnecessarily, to spare the lives of fellow citizens and soldiers) is almost at hand when it is interrupted. This both confirms the projected closure (as desirable and possible) and suspends it.

The scene of interruption (1.75–76), furthermore, replays the beginning of book 1: Petreius arms slaves, his praetorian cohort, and some barbarian cavalry; he interrupts the open discussions of the soldiers; he drives "our men" out of the camp; he kills any he can catch. Caesar's men are terrified by the danger and retreat to his camp. Then Petreius forces his army to swear a loyalty oath and turn over for execution any Caesarians they have with them. Many of his men disobey and sneak the Caesarians out at night. Caesar ends this part of his narrative with phrases and clauses that recall the events in Rome as he had described them in paragraphs 1–6: "And so the <u>terror</u> imposed by the leaders, the <u>cruelty</u> displayed in the punishments, the <u>strange new</u> sanction of the oath <u>removed any hope</u> of immediate surrender and changed the minds of the soldiers and <u>drove the matter back to the original state of war</u>" (1.76.5). In terms of narrative, we overcame Caesar's practical obstacles to victory, then we glimpsed the political and ethical value of a bloodless victory, only to have it interrupted by Pompeian terror and cruelty.

The war of harassment is renewed: "progress was slow and gradual," and there were frequent desertions to Caesar (1.80.1). But "Caesar's columns keep pressing on them and all together threaten an attack" (1.80.5). The Pompeians' movement grinds to a halt: "Then, indeed, without any opportunity to look for a suitable place for a camp or to proceed further, they stop because they have to" (1.81.1), and they are confined within their camp. Caesar draws up his cavalry in a battle line, but refuses to initiate an attack. Soon, two battle lines face each other, neither making a move: "the confrontation was prolonged and they were held in battle lines until the setting of the sun" (1.83.2). In terms of the narrative, this interruption serves to set off the final conclusion, which comes immediately, as both a separate event and a repetition of the earlier fraternization of camps. The conclusion is marked as such: "<u>At last</u>, cut off from all supplies, with their animals kept in camp without food now for four days, suffering from a lack of water, wood, and grain, [the Pompeians] seek a discussion [*colloquium*]" (1.84.1).

The fact that the Pompeians seek a discussion is thematic and significant. Since the opening chapters of the *Civil War* Pompeians have been destroying discussion and offering in its place declarations and threats. Caesar here joins the narrative of events with the thematic critique, not without, however, a final reminder of Pompeian duplicity: the discussion that they seek is a private one, in some place removed from the soldiers (1.84.1). Caesar of course refuses, and the public negotiations that end book 1 take place. We will discuss them in some detail below. Here it is important to note that with the tactical problem (Caesar's need for supplies and a way to cut off the Pompeian escape) solved, the ethical problem (the desire for a bloodless victory) solved, and the political problem (forcing the Pompeians to capitulate, and opening public discussions) solved, Caesar administers the peace with such equity and fairness that even Pompeian soldiers come to him for a resolution of disputes (1.87.2). Thus, we have the familiar return to administration that signaled closure in the *Gallic War*. This is coupled with the deployment of troops, the dismissal of armies, and a march from Spain to the Var, the river that marks the eastern boundary of Transalpine Gaul. The last word of book 1 is both closural in its natural reference and a closural solution to the problem that began the civil war: "and there the rest of the army was dismissed" (1.87.5).

5b Argumentative closure

All that has been said about the natural or narrative closure created by the ending of a battle and dismissal of troops would have little political force if it were not reinforced by argumentative closure. By this we mean that, if Caesar's narrative has intellectual and argumentative coherence, then its closure must provide a solution to the problems it has analyzed and exposed. This returns us to the basic problem of closure in an incomplete narrative of civil war. The civil war did not end at Ilerda, and the battle could be considered just another Caesarian victory, albeit an important one. We examine now the extent to which Ilerda not only recalls the Caesarian critique of Pompeian tactics but also offers Caesar's response as an exemplary solution to the problems the Pompeians have created. In the interests of space, we will treat paragraphs 74–87 together as an elaboration and response to the problems presented in the opening paragraphs, 1–11.

A quick review of how in Caesar's narrative the civil war begins will set the terms for our discussion. When Caesar writes to the Senate, Pompeian obstruction moves matters quickly from difficulty to impossibility. The situation deteriorates because of threatening Pompeian innuendos and duplicity, faulty logic, and bad policy. The consuls threaten the unwilling (1.2.4–6, 1.3.5), oppose leniency with cruelty and harshness (1.2.2, 1.2.8, 1.5.4, 1.5.5), and take away tribunician rights (1.7.3–4). The result of their tactics is the destruction of open discussions (1.2.5, 1.3.5, 1.11.3) and the inability to resolve controversies (1.9.6). Public offices are given to private men by private agreements (1.6.5). Levies are held, armies are summoned or retained, veterans are called up (1.3.1–3, 1.4.5, 1.9.5, 1.11.1). There is in all of this a general attack on constitutional norms: "favor" and "friendship" become code terms for partisanship; "strange new" precedents are introduced. Caesar asks that "free elections and the entire republic be handed back to the Senate and the People," but is rebuffed. Caesar hopes for peace, while Pompey is eager for war.

Turning to Ilerda, we find that these are the very issues Caesar recalls and addresses again. The movement from difficulty to impossibility is reversed, literally: the march that had ground to a halt becomes the happy return of soldiers to home. Here, for the first time, with the departure of Afranius and Petreius, the soldiers get an opportunity for open discussion (1.74.1), which they willingly take. Caesar's policy of leniency and his efforts to bring things to an end without bloodshed seem to bear fruit and are generally approved (1.74.6). This is all interrupted by the return of Petreius, but the opportunity we see in paragraph 74 returns in the very last paragraph when the Pompeian soldiers "of their own free will" go to Caesar for the resolution of controversies.

In place of threats and duplicity, we find among the soldiers openness and trust, and in place of division we find unity and community. The Pompeian soldiers are "thankful" that they have been spared; they ask about Caesar's "good faith"; they speak of what is "correct and proper" (1.74.2). With the return of Petreius, discussions are interrupted and, since war has resumed, the captured Caesarians are killed (1.75.3). As was mentioned above, the return of Pompeian tactics brings with it the language that described the Pompeians at the opening of the book (1.76.5, quoted above). Some Pompeian soldiers desert of their own accord, and Caesar treats them with respect, "restores" them to their former status and rank (1.77.2). And then, in the final scene, Caesar reestablishes openness: he refuses private negotiations and demands open discussions (1.84.2). Issues are debated on both sides (1.86.3), and no one is forced to take an oath (1.86.4). In place of threats and terror, we find an arrangement that is "welcome and pleasing" (1.86.1) to the soldiers.

Take another instance: the opening debate in the Senate foundered, and the senators could not decide on a policy that was prudential (get more armies) or equitable (send both Pompey and Caesar to their provinces) or practical (accept the Caesarian support for the second proposal). In place of this chaos, Caesar offers the scene we recounted above in which his own legates, centurions, and tribunes urge war upon him. Their arguments are practical: the soldiers are ready, the Pompeians are afraid and would soon be forced to look for water (1.71.2–4). Caesar responds first with a general's concerns: why lose more men? why get deserving soldiers wounded? why tempt fortune? Then he considers larger issues of statesmanship: it is good to win through strategy; he felt pity for his fellow citizens (1.72.1–3). "Most of the soldiers did not approve of Caesar's plan; in fact, they openly talked among themselves, saying that, since such an opportunity for victory was being lost, they were not going to fight even if Caesar wanted them to" (1.72.4). It is important in the story Caesar tells that his men do not agree with him. If we contrast this with the senators in Rome, we may see that Pompeians respond to the disagreement of senators and peers with threats and abuse, while Caesar responds to the disagreement of his soldiers with quiet perseverance.

The dismissal of armies, the talk of peace, the resolution of controversies, the Caesarian insistence on open discussions and freedom from fear, on pity for fellow citizens and respect for soldiers, on the return of property to its rightful owners and the provision for fair restitution—all of this brings to a close Caesar's argument about who bears the blame for the civil war and the political implications of Pompeian behavior. In a sense, Caesar is here making an argument coherent with his self-presentation in the *Gallic War*, namely, that he represents Rome and her best traditions. He is the civilizing force.

5c Aesthetic or formal closure

Impossible as it is to separate cleanly formal closure (which depends upon repetition and variation of elements in formal patterns) from narrative closure, it will be useful for our assessment of Caesar's literary achievement in the *Civil War* to see how purely formal elements complement the narrative and argumentative movements, examined above, toward the solution of a problem.

Beginning with paragraph 74, the narrative we have described has an A-B-A structure. That is, there is a movement toward a peaceful resolution that is interrupted and then restored. When Afranius and Petreius leave their camp, the two camps join together as if they were one, looking for friends and kinsmen. Just when it looks as if the battle would end without bloodshed, news of what is happening is reported to Petreius, who returns to camp, breaks up the fraternization, and reestablishes a state of war. When Caesar's strategy at last succeeds and the Pompeians are cut off from supplies, they admit defeat; Caesar then speaks again of peace (1.85.2).

Book 1 overall has this same A-B-A structure. This is, of course, the structure of any successful narrative: a project or goal is established that is interrupted or thwarted until a final resolution is reached. Thus, in the *Civil War*, we begin with Caesar's efforts to negotiate a peaceful settlement, to find some way to open discussions, to dismiss armies, to restore equity and justice. This is met with Pompeian resistance, terror, threats, and finally armies, until Ilerda provides a temporary but symbolic and exemplary solution. Within this large-scale structure, the narrative of obstruction and battle (the B part of the A-B-A structure) is interrupted by Corfinium (1.19–24), where Caesar will offer safety, liberty, discussion, dismissal of troops, and concern for the republic, and by the events in Rome (1.32–33), where Caesar will again speak of patience, injury, peace, open discussion, justice, and the republic. In other words, the narrative is a complex movement: A (attempts to establish peace) interrupted by B (military action) leading to A (attempts to establish peace), with the B segment itself interrupted: B = b (occupation of Italian towns) a (clemency at Corfinium) b (siege at Brindisi) a (speech in Rome) b (march to Ilerda). The whole can be represented as A-babab-A.

For a structure like this to work, it is necessary that the initial A elements project a point of closure and that the final A elements return to that point. This is sometimes referred to as "ring-composition." All it means in narrative is that the ending must in some sense be present in the beginning and the beginning corrected or restored in the end. We have been arguing that the ending present in the beginning of the *Civil War* has to do with an analysis of the political and administrative problems that resulted in war. This is, of course, created by the author's rhetoric and analysis and is not a feature of events themselves: the passages of narrative that we have called "A" (or "a") share thematic terms, as a quick survey of Caesar's vocabulary shows.[23] Certain terms are found only at those places we would designate as "A" (or "a"). These include words for cruelty, bitterness, honor, peace, dismissal, discussion, injustice, safety, insults, and the whole class of superlatives (on which see sec. 1b in chap. 5). But, perhaps more striking, other words occur only at the beginning and at the end. These include the Latin terms for controversy, leniency, pity, unwillingness, oaths, the strange and new, the restoration of losses, terror, and finality. In fact, it is at the end that "that last and final decree of the Senate" meets with Caesar's refusal to exact "the final punishment" from Afranius and his own "single and last condition for peace," that "they should leave the provinces and dismiss their army" (1.85.11). "In accordance with his instructions, the march was made from Spain to the river Var, and there the rest of the army was dismissed."

Appendix:
Structure and Word Distribution in Book I

The following table and graph show the distribution of terms important to the argument and structure of *Civil War* 1, by episode. For discussion see section 5.

Appendix Table

Episodes	Opening	Italy	Corfinium	Italy	Rome	Massilia	Afranius/Petreius	Massilia	March to Ilerda	Ilerda
Chapters	1–11	12–18	19–24	25–31	32–33	34–36	37–55	56–58	59–71	72–87
controversy (*controvers-*)	9, 9									86, 87
leniency (*lenis*)	1, 2, 5									74
pity (*miser-*)										72, 84, 85, 85
unwilling (*invite*)	2									86
laws (*iura*)	6									85, 85
oath (*iura, sacramentum*)										76, 76, 76
strange new (*novus*)	7									76, 85
restore losses (*amis-, restit-*)	7									87
terror (*terr-*)	2, 3	14								76, 79
final (*extrem-*)	5, 5									85
cruel (*crudel-*)	2				32					
bitter (*acerb-*)	2, 5				32					76, 85
honor (*honor-*)	7, 8				32, 32					77, 77, 85

peace (*pax*)	11		26, 26							74, 85
dismiss (*dimitt-*)	2, 9, 10, 11									85, 85, 86
discussions (*conloq-*)	9, 11		19, 19, 20, 22, 24	26	32					74, 75, 77, 84, 84, 85, 85
injustice (*iniur-*)	7, 7, 9			28	32, 32	36				85
safety (*salut-*)	5, 5		20, 22, 22, 24							74
to summon (*evocare*)	3, 3, 3, 7, 8	17	23	27		35	39			74, 74, 85
gratitude (*grat-*)	1, 1, 4	13, 18	23				53			74, 74
good faith (*fid-*)	10		20			34		56		74, 74, 84, 86
patience (*patient-*)				26	32					85
conditions (*condic-*)	9, 11		24, 24	26, 26	32					85, 85
insults (*contumel-*)	8, 9		22, 23	28					69	
abuse (*convic-*)	2, 2		23							
consulship (*consul-*)	5, 11		22		32					85
superlatives	2, 2, 5, 5, 5, 5, 7	15, 15			32					84, 84, 85, 85
Total words/paragraphs	54/11	6/7	17/6	11/7	12/2	3/3	3/19	1/3	1/13	55/16

This information can be graphed as a function of the number of occurrences per section of these thematic words or as a function of the frequency per paragraph in the different sections. The second series eliminates disparities caused by unusually long or unusually short sections.

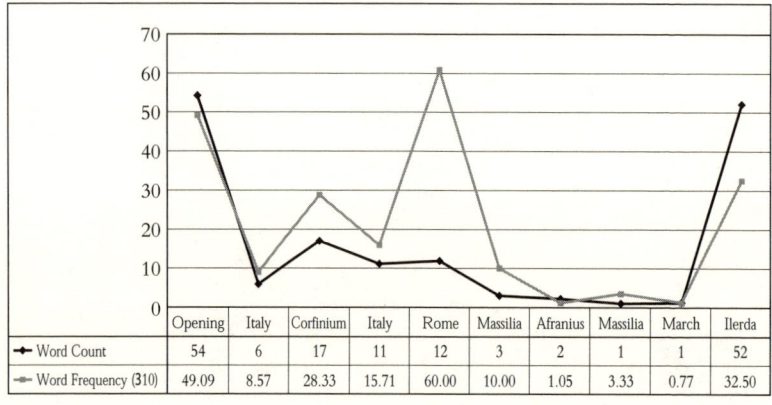

	Opening	Italy	Corfinium	Italy	Rome	Massilia	Afranius	Massilia	March	Ilerda
◆ Word Count	54	6	17	11	12	3	2	1	1	52
■ Word Frequency (310)	49.09	8.57	28.33	15.71	60.00	10.00	1.05	3.33	0.77	32.50

· 3 ·

Taking Sides, Making Sides

> For them and me to continue to act
> in character—that's all I want.
> —CAESAR, quoted by Cicero, *Letters to Atticus* 9.16.2

Characterization in a civil war narrative is more important, and more difficult, than it is in a colonial narrative, such as the *Gallic War*, of "us" against "them." When the principal combatants are all Roman and all members of the governing elite, the difference between "us" and "them" needs careful delineation. But drawing the lines is complicated when the composition of the two parties shifts over time, as it did in dramatic fashion after the battle of Pharsalus in August of 48. Men who had joined Pompey at the outset of the conflict, in January of 49, or in the course of the ensuing months, faced a choice after his military defeat: to continue resisting Caesar, to withdraw from the contest, or to join Caesar. Those who chose the last moved from "them" to "us," and the neutrals might still, it could be hoped, so realign themselves. Only the first group (and those who died at Pharsalus) remained in the category of "them."

We saw in chapter 1 how important a constituent of Caesar's narrative the personnel of Roman war and politics are, in chapter 2 how the issues of this war and of postwar politics are presented in book 1. In this chapter we focus on books 2 and 3 as we look at Caesar's characterization of participants in the civil war, and at what the various characterizations offer to survivors with their varied histories on and between sides.

1 | Audience

In developing a sense of the *Civil War*'s implied audience—that is, the kinds of people and the kinds of interests that would have been gratified to have a narrative like this—we cannot apply the model of the *Gallic War*. In the earlier work, Caesar provides information to Rome about his accomplishments in Gaul, which no one but his officers and soldiers had witnessed. In the *Civil War*, however, he is writing of events that many in his audience participated in. Some are among the recipients, authors, and subjects of Cicero's surviving correspondence, where they give us an independent view of some of the *War*'s crucial events—as we saw in chapter 2, it is because we have Cicero's letters that we can occasionally uncover a chronological distortion in Caesar's narrative.[1] Why would Caesar write a version of events that others would have their own view of?

Much of this independent perspective on the civil war is lost to us, but from what survives in Cicero's correspondence it is clear that in the *Civil War* Caesar addresses many of the issues that concerned Cicero and (one may infer) the senators who in large numbers opposed Caesar, voted for the "final decree," fled Rome with Pompey, and often continued to resist even after Caesar had captured and pardoned them. A review of these issues will help us understand Caesar's audience, particularly the important segment represented by the men, public figures all, from whom Caesar needed cooperation in administering the postwar state, and who needed from Caesar a narrative of the war that facilitated their cooperation.[2]

We begin with issues contemporary with the events narrated in the *Civil War*. Issues attested in the post-Pharsalus correspondence are treated in the chapter's final section.

1a Contemporary issues

Warmongering: We saw in the discussion of book 1 that Caesar presents the Pompeians as eager for war. This is an image that would have had resonance with contemporary readers. In December of 50 Cicero reports that Pompey and the Pompeians need to be urged in private to consider peace (9 Dec. 50, *Att.* 7.3.5), while Pompey speaks with Cicero as if war was inevitable and says nothing about peace (10 Dec. 50, *Att.* 7.4.2). Shortly thereafter Cicero says that Pompey does not even want peace; in fact, he seems to fear it (25 or 26 Dec. 50, *Att.* 7.8.4–5). And many regarded Pompey's actions as deliberately provocative. Apropos of Pompey's trip to Campania to take command of the two legions that Caesar complains so bitterly about at the beginning of the *Civil War*, for instance, Cicero reports: "You can't believe how many Roman knights, how many senators, I saw who very bitterly condemn the general handling of affairs and especially this trip of Pompey's. Peace is what we need!" (mid-Dec. 50, *Att.* 7.5.4).

Of course, there were those who believed that Caesar, too, wanted a fight, but Cicero, as late as December, thought it unlikely: "The only comfort I take in this is the fact that I do not think that Caesar . . . will be so mad as to bring all this to a crisis" (c. 13 Dec. 50, *Att.* 7.4.3). And Cicero's view of both parties is the same after the fighting has begun. While Caesar is racing Pompey to Brindisi, for example, Cicero expects that he will offer conditions for peace that will be either ignored or refused: "I do not think that they will meet and, if they meet, I do not think Pompey will agree to any conditions for peace" (3 March 49, *Att.* 8.15.3).

Threats: Caesar, as we saw, complains that the Senate was coerced by Pompeian threats. While Cicero's picture is not as precise as Caesar's, one still gets from him a sense that the threat of violence was readily associated with Pompeians. When Cicero tells Atticus that, when asked his opinion in the Senate, he will not say what he really thinks—namely, that everything must be done to avoid conflict—but instead will say that he agrees with Pompey

(c. 18 Dec. 50, *Att.* 7.6.2), he implies that he feels coerced. The kind of pressure Pompey could apply is vividly illustrated in a letter in which Cicero contemplates advocating peace, but hesitates: "I am afraid of troubling Pompey, afraid that he will turn on me 'that most terrible Gorgon-look'" (13 March 49, *Att.* 9.7.3, quoting Homer, *Od.* 11.634). Months after the fact Cicero remembers the threats before Pompey left Italy: "What threats he made to the townspeople, what threats he made by name to men on our side, and finally what threats he issued to all who remained at Rome!" (18 March 49, *Att.* 9.10.2). And after Pharsalus he remarks that Pompey counted all who remained in Italy as enemies (27 Nov. 48, *Att.* 11.6.6).

Overconfidence and betrayal: As we saw in the discussion of book 1, Caesar treats Pompeian threats and obstruction as elements of a chaotic public policy, one that destroys discussion, fails to deal with the facts, and in the end is forced into retreat and flight. Of course, Caesar knew the outcome when he wrote book 1, but the picture he presents there of unwarranted confidence followed by a sense of betrayal also emerges from letters contemporary with events. Before the war begins, Cicero is pleased with Pompey's confidence: "he is extremely contemptuous of [Caesar] and utterly confident in his own and in the republic's forces" (25 Dec. 49, *Att.* 7.8.4). But by the time Pompey has fled Rome, things seem different: "I am so confounded by the rashness of this utterly mad proceeding. . . . So far, unless I am crazy, everything has clearly been stupid and reckless" (18 Jan. 50, *Att.* 7.10.1). Pompey's failure to prepare adequately to face Caesar seemed particularly reckless, prompting Cicero to exclaim, in late January, "it is certain that either we have acted or our leader has acted so that we have left port without a rudder and handed ourselves over to the whirlwind" (23 Jan. 49, *Att.* 7.13.2). Later Cicero will say that nothing was done with wisdom or courage (18 Feb. 49, *Att.* 8.3.3), and that the republic's cause was handled without bravery or principle (6 March 49, *Att.* 9.1.4). Even after Caesar's invasion of Italy, Pompey gets much of the blame for the situation in which senators found themselves. On 10 March Cicero tells Atticus of a fellow senator's complaints about "Pompey's criminal negligence, and the Senate's fickleness and stupidity," and he himself, angered by Pompey's "recklessness," blames Pompey more than Caesar: "I am feeling more unfriendly to him than to Caesar" (*Att.* 9.5.1–2).

The net result was that Pompey gained a reputation for duplicity and faithlessness. Cicero, while not himself charging Pompey on these grounds, provides evidence that that was being done by the end of February: "the one is considered the savior of his enemies, the other the deserter of his friends" (25 Feb. 49, *Att.* 8.9a.1).

Cruelty: The association of Pompey and the Pompeians with cruelty is less explicit in Cicero than in Caesar. In fact, in Cicero's letters cruelty seems to be a feature of civil war in general. In his long letter of 18 March reviewing the current circumstances, for instance, he calls civil war "a type of war most cruel and vast" (*Att.* 9.10.2) and victory in civil war "cruel and deathly" (*Att.* 9.10.3). It is perhaps in this context that we should understand his complaint that "Pompey undertook a cruel and destructive war" (11 March 49, *Att.* 9.6.7) and the later charge that Caesar's blockade of Pompey at Brindisi was cruel (25 March 49, *Att.* 9.14.2).

In this same letter of 25 March we get a glimpse of the fear that lies behind the description of civil war as cruel when Cicero mentions the victims of "cruel Sulla" (*Att.* 9.14.2). Sulla, when Caesar and Cicero were young men, marched his troops into Rome twice and eliminated his opponents by outright slaughter and by posting lists of proscribed citizens who could be (and were) killed with impunity and whose property was confiscated by the state and used to reward his partisans. Early in the *Civil War*, Caesar draws a connection between the Pompeians and Sulla: "Lentulus . . . boasted among his friends that he would be a second Sulla, to whom supreme command would return" (1.4.1; cf. 1.7.2–4). And the Sullan precedent was indeed on people's minds as civil war loomed. As early as 18 December 50, we find Cicero worrying that Caesar will be no more restrained than Sulla (*Att.* 7.7.7). At this point Cicero sees both Caesar and Pompey as potential tyrants—"Victory will produce much suffering and, to be sure, a tyrant" (17 Dec. 50, *Att.* 7.5.4)—and when Cicero first hears of Caesar's clemency at Corfinium, he is suspicious: "I don't believe in it, and I'm afraid that all this heap of clemency points to that cruelty we feared" (25 Feb. 49, *Att.* 8.9a.2). But it is the association of Pompey with Sulla that seems to grow, perhaps fostered by memories of Pompey's early career, which included a marriage connection with Sulla and executions of men proscribed by Sulla, as well as the label "teenage butcher" (*adulescens carnufex*).³ Pompey himself helps by saying, "Will I not be able to do what Sulla could?" (18 March 49, *Att.* 9.10.2). In the same letter Cicero claims that for two years "Pompey's soul has been inclining toward Sulla and proscriptions" (*Att.* 9.10.6). A week later we hear that whole towns are afraid of Pompey's "cruelty and anger" (25 March 49, *Att.* 9.15.3). When Cicero summarizes events after Caesar's trip to Rome, he reports with approval Servius's remark that "the victory of either is a horrible prospect, both because one [Pompey] was cruel and the other [Caesar] unrestrained and because both needed money" (8 May 49, *Att.* 9.14.1). The reference to money alludes to proscription and memories of Sulla.

1b Naming names

What can we say so far about the audience Caesar imagines? It is one that, like Cicero, feared the cruelty of civil war and hoped for reconciliation, one that wanted to assign blame both for the failure to reconcile and for the failure to prepare, and one that resented the coercion under which the Senate acted in January of 49. He writes for those who wanted peace and who would have kept trying to reach terms of peace, which is to say, for a large majority of the prewar Senate: on 1 December 50 the vote was 370 to 22 in favor of a motion (proposed by Caesar's supporter Curio) to have both Caesar and Pompey disband their armies (Appian, *Civil War* 2.30).

It is striking how few warmongers there are in Caesar's narrative. By the time the "final decree" is passed (1.5.3), we have seen in Caesar's narrative only three anti-Caesarians in addition to Pompey himself: Metellus Scipio, father of Pompey's wife, who was Pompey's consular colleague in 52 and seemed to speak for Pompey in the Senate in early January; Lentulus Crus, consul in 49 and hard-line opponent of Caesar, who according to Hirtius was one of a pair of consuls elected to ruin Caesar's standing and honor (*Gallic War* 8.50.3); and Cato, a conservative and Stoic who had long opposed Caesar (see Epilogue). Even when the Pompeian forces are being mobilized and provinces assigned (1.6), we get no comprehensive list of Caesar's enemies. Caesar names Faustus Sulla, son of "cruel Sulla" and Pompey's son-in-law; Gaius Marcellus, Lentulus's colleague in the consulship; Philippus, a tribune; and Domitius, Caesar's replacement. But even this brief list is odd: Marcellus is said to have resisted Pompey's plan to form an alliance with the Numidian king, Juba, and Philippus to have vetoed Faustus Sulla's mission. One might even say that Marcellus and Philippus are mentioned because they oppose Pompey, not Caesar.

That is, despite the fact that Caesar says that "Pompey himself was provoked by Caesar's enemies" and that "he had wholly turned away from friendship with Caesar and returned into the good favor of their common enemies" (1.4.4), he does not list these enemies. The implication seems to be that in some fundamental way most of those who opposed Caesar were not to blame. If the Senate had been a different institution in late 50 and early 49—if senators had not been intimidated by Pompeian threats, if Sulla and his proscriptions were not always lurking in the background—perhaps they would have been different men and taken different decisions. In effect, Caesar's refusal to name any but the most egregious opponents allows all who were in the Senate on the day when the "final decree" was passed to become, after the war's conclusion, who they want to be.

2 | Redeeming Curio

Some of the issues we have just been considering also govern Caesar's characterization of participants in the conflict. That Caesar was interested in how his contemporaries judged men on both sides is evident from a letter written in March of 49, where he invites a comparison. Concerning the ingratitude of the men he released at Corfinium but who continue to fight against him, he says that he wants nothing more than that both he and they continue to act in character.[4] Actions speak, obviously, and these Pompeian actions, in Caesar's view, spoke ill of their actors. In the next three sections of this chapter we consider his descriptions of five men whose actions speak loudly in the *Civil War*, beginning with supporters of Pompey and Caesar in sections 2a and 2b, followed, in section 3, by Pompey himself. In section 4 we look at Caesar's portraits of two Pompeians who led the fight against him after the battle of Pharsalus. Caesar on Caesar we reserve for chapter 4.

2a Marcus Terentius Varro

This polymath author of nearly five hundred volumes of Latin prose, friend of Cicero and Atticus, and post-Pharsalus Caesarian, was Pompey's legate in Further Spain at the beginning of 49. Caesar's military campaign in that province was a minor affair won without a single battle. Dio accordingly allots Varro a scant half-sentence reference (41.23.2), Appian and Plutarch nothing at all. Caesar, however, lavishes five long paragraphs on him (2.17–21). The narrative of Varro's failure as a legate serves as foil to the adjacent portrait of Curio, a man emblematic of a quality crucial, as we will see, to Caesar's success.

Varro's command in Further Spain is noted at 1.38.1 but is apparently irrelevant—never mentioned, anyway—to Caesar's hard-fought contest with the Pompeians in Nearer Spain. When Varro moves into the limelight, at 2.17, in a passage that takes the narrative back from August to the first weeks of 49, he is visibly disheartened by Pompey's withdrawal from Italy and speaking "in a very friendly fashion" about Caesar. On every possible occasion and to anyone who cared to listen, says Caesar, Varro states that, although as legate he has a duty to Pompey (literally, he is "constrained by [Pompey's] trust [*fides*]"), his personal ties with Caesar are no less strong. He claims, too, that his responsibilities as legate oblige him to know the temper of his province, and that this is altogether favorable to Caesar. In short, he avoids taking a side himself and makes no attempt to counter the prevailing pro-Caesarian sentiment (2.17.1–3).

When the military situation of the Pompeians elsewhere improved, however, particularly in Nearer Spain, Varro strengthened his own military situation with new levies, new stockpiles of grain, new ships, new monetary requisitions (2.17.4–18.5). Varro then signaled Pompeian allegiance by announcing in public assemblies that he had heard from reliable authorities that Caesar had suffered reverses and that a large number of his troops had deserted (2.18.3),[5] by treating with particular severity cities and individuals who favored Caesar (2.18.5: the former get garrisons, the latter, "for having spoken against the republic," have their private property confiscated), and by compelling his province to swear an oath "to abide by his commands and Pompey's" (2.18.5). He was, says Caesar, "preparing war"; indeed "[Varro] thought that with provisions and ships collected on an island it would not be difficult for the war to be prolonged" (2.18.6; for the theme of Pompeian prolongation of the war see sec. 5 in chap. 2).

When Caesar arrives, however, the provincials respond with the enthusiasm Varro had earlier sensed. As had happened in Italy before and would be happening soon in Greece (as Caesar tells it), town after town closed its gates to the Pompeians in order to welcome Caesar the better (2.19, Carmona; 2.20, Cadiz, Hispalis, Italica; cf. sec. 3a in chap. 2). Not only that, but Pompeian troops, too, declare for Caesar (2.20.2). Indeed one of Varro's legions offers its services to Caesar while its commander looks on, helpless to stop the desertion (2.20.4).[6] Whereupon Varro, for all his talk about his governorship being "a task entrusted to him" (2.17.2) and his "being constrained by [Pompey's] trust," and for all his confidence in his ability to wage war against Caesar, promptly surrenders his other legion and informs Caesar of the whereabouts of his provisions and ships (2.20.7–8). He also gives Caesar the money he had with him, along with the accounts of public funds, which he had kept—and here Caesar gently taunts Varro—"in a trustworthy manner" (2.20.8, *cum fide*). Varro may have taken Pompey's side, but, as Caesar shows in this episode, loyalty to Pompey does not last.

Caesar's verdict on Varro is captured in a memorable phrase— "he began to move to the movements of Fortune" (2.17.4)—that yields an image of Varro dancing with Dame Fortune. Varro danced his way to Pharsalus after his defeat in Spain, and back into Caesar's favor after the Pompeian defeat at Pharsalus. Dame Fortune was less kind to Curio, to whom we turn next, but Caesar redressed the balance handsomely.

2b Gaius Scribonius Curio

Juxtaposed in book 2 to the cameo of the inadequate Pompeian legate Varro is that of the Caesarian commander responsible for one of Caesar's worst defeats, Gaius Scribonius Curio. Curio's expedition, which was supposed to secure the coast and harvests of North Africa for Caesar, was a costly failure. Two legions were lost, Curio himself died, and the opponents of Caesar retained a territory from which they could threaten Italy's food supply and in which they regrouped after Pharsalus. Pompeian resistance in North Africa prolonged the civil war for nearly two years; Caesar himself finished at the battle of Thapsus (6 April 46) the task that Curio's failure left undone. Caesar devotes to that failure twenty-two paragraphs, half of book 2 (2.23–44). What is more, he uses direct quotation lavishly in these paragraphs, employing in aid of this story a powerful element of style used sparingly elsewhere in the *commentarii*. Curio is brought to life in two long speeches—one of them the longest Caesar wrote for any character—and there are also brief first-person utterances spoken by and to Curio. For Curio's story illustrates particularly well something more important to Caesar's cause than the outcome of any single military campaign, namely, the relationship between Caesar and his supporters.

Curio began the civil war at Caesar's side (1.12.1); the fact that his allegiance went back less than a year is not so much as hinted.[7] He participated in the invasion of Italy in early 49, meeting with an easy military success at Iguvium (1.12.3). He was in charge of one of Caesar's two camps at Corfinium (1.18.5), after which he was sent to Sicily with four legions, two of them formerly Pompeian. The Pompeian commander abandons the island to him (1.30.4–31.1). So far Curio's civil war has been a string of easy successes.

While still in Sicily, however, he fails to prevent (or even notice) Pompeian reinforcements en route to Marseilles via the strait of Sicily (2.3.1–2). Worse, when he crosses to North Africa as ordered (1.30.2), he takes only two legions, and those the former Pompeians, on the grounds that he does not anticipate serious resistance from the Pompeian commander, Attius Varus.[8]

In North Africa easy successes continue to accrue. Curio's first potential opponent flees, leaving his warship behind; the second force in his path likewise moves off to safety (2.23.3–4). When Curio finally makes contact with the enemy outside of Utica, his cavalry overcomes that of Varus's ally, the Numidian king Juba (2.25.5). He is also successful in commandeering supplies (2.25.6–7). These successes are acclaimed by his troops, who salute him as "victorious commander" (*imperator*, 2.26.1). He then wins another easy cavalry victory (2.26.3–4). But there are also disquieting developments: two of Curio's cavalry commanders desert to Varus (2.27.1), and the first engagement between the legionary troops, though it ends in a military standoff, sows fear and moral dubiety in Curio's men (2.28–29). He responds to these challenges in two speeches, the first, on strategy, to his officers, the second, on loyalty, to his men (2.31–32).

In the council of war two strategies are suggested to him: to attack the Pompeians despite their advantageous position and the uncertain loyalties of his own troops, or to retreat to a position from which he (and they) would be able to flee North Africa if the troops should in fact rejoin the Pompeians. Curio says no to both plans, but dismisses the officers without revealing his own. Instead, he addresses the wavering troops directly with a speech centered on the moment's (and the war's) crucial issue, how to choose your side.

The solution to Curio's immediate military problem and to Caesar's long-term political problem is the same: generating support for Caesar's cause. The speech Caesar writes for Curio here lays out in concentrated form the argument that, as we saw in chapter 2, undergirds book 1, and that, as we will see in chapter 4, dominates the authorial self-portrait.

Since the issue at hand is the choice between sides, Curio begins with contrasts. He tells the former Pompeians that Caesar feels himself in their debt—their choice at Corfinium put all Italy on his side—while the Pompeian leaders are correspondingly resentful (2.32.2). Caesar's actions, he says, indicate no suspicion on his part about the troops' good faith: he entrusts important people and tasks to them (2.32.3–4; cf. 2.31.4, where Curio warned his officers about the danger of letting morally sound soldiers think their loyalty suspect). Where Caesar encourages loyalty by showing trust, the Pompeians, Curio says to his men, are urging you to betray that trust, both for their immediate military advantage and to implicate you in crime (2.32.4). The moral point—that supporting Caesar involves virtuous action, while supporting Pompey involves crime —is reinforced by the practical point that Caesar has already won important (and quick) military victories in Spain (2.32.5; cf. 2.32.13).[9] But Curio returns to the moral argument with his assertion that the actions of the leadership on both sides reflect what he has just said about the choices open to the soldiers. The Pompeians who want the soldiers to betray Caesar's trust have themselves betrayed their soldiers' trust, whereas Caesar has offered safety (at Corfinium) and an opportunity for virtue (here and now in North Africa) (2.32.7–10). Moreover, Caesar's supporter Curio, like Caesar himself, is successful, and promises to show his gratitude in material form (2.32.11–13). And unlike the Pompeians his motivation is not self-interest. Curio's final move is to show what a loyal Caesarian will do for his leader: if his being in command is, for whatever reason, interfering with their allegiance to Caesar, he will, he says, stand aside, relinquish command (2.32.14).

The speech is an immediate success. When he has finished, the soldiers clamor for him to test their good faith, *fides*, in battle (2.33.1). As Caesar tells the story, they manifest their eagerness to live up to Caesar's expectations and to show that the Pompeian expectation of disloyalty does them an injustice.

Caesar's Curio is an apt spokesperson for loyalty, as we will see. And Caesar repays his devotion with a narrative that clothes Curio

—impetuous, overconfident, and ultimately unsuccessful though he was—in his leader's understanding and affection.

Curio's success in activating the loyalty of Caesar's soldiers does not translate into success on the battlefield. His own sterling loyalty is, as Caesar explains, complicated by other characteristics: "Urging him on were his youth, his aspirations, his recent successes, and his confidence in achieving a victory" (2.38.2).[10] The defeat occurs in painful stages, as confidence changes to hope (2.39.5, 6, 2.40.3), then to exhortation (2.41.3), and finally to despair (2.41.8) and pleas (2.42.1). When his army's defeat is inevitable Curio is urged by one of his officers to save himself (2.42.3), but this Curio will not do: "Never, Curio asserts, will he return to Caesar's presence having lost the army that he accepted as a trust from Caesar. Fighting on, he is killed" (2.42.4). With his death he demonstrates his commitment to the army Caesar placed in his trust (*fides*) and to Caesar's trust in him. Hence Curio's value to Caesar's narrative; in subordinates loyalty meant more to Caesar than success.

3 | Undressing Pompey

Caesar set these portraits of declared partisans side by side in book 2. Pompey's inability to retain the loyalty of his legate Varro makes the devotion Caesar inspires and admires in Curio the more striking. The contrast between their superiors will emerge from Caesar's account of the campaign in Greece, where he and Pompey faced one another in 48.

The essential features of Caesar's portrait of Pompey in book 1, discussed in chapter 2, were political and personal: his refusal to discuss policy and negotiate a peaceful solution, his overconfidence, his cruelty. Military actions—Corfinium, Ilerda—were commanded by supporters and legates. Surrogates also dominate book 2: these include, in addition to Varro in Further Spain and Curio's opponents Varus and Juba in North Africa, Domitius and the besieged citizens of Marseilles (on this episode see sec. 2a in chap. 5). In the present discussion of Pompey we focus on book 3, which covers the period when Caesar and Pompey are both in Greece and offers a long buildup to the battle of Pharsalus.

Pompey's record as a commander is mixed in book 3. At the beginning of the book, after his fleet fails to prevent Caesar's crossing to Greece (3.6.3; cf. 3.5.2 for the task), Pompey himself fails to prevent Caesar from gaining control of coastal towns (3.12; cf. 3.11.2 for the objective). Similarly, when Antony brings a second army across in the spring, Pompey fails to prevent the conjunction of his opponent's forces. His inability to stop Caesar is simultaneously a Caesarian success: when Antony lands north of Pompey while Caesar himself is based south of him, Caesar's objective is "to effect a conjunction with Antony as soon as possible" (3.30.2), Pompey's to prevent him from doing so (3.30.2: "in order to block the approaching forces on their journey"). The outcome? "The next day Caesar reached [Antony]" (3.30.6).

On the other hand, Pompey is long successful in avoiding the battle Caesar wants to fight. He disengages his army from the combined forces of Caesar and Antony at 3.30.7, refuses to be drawn when Caesar lines up his troops for battle at Asparagium (3.41.2), and endures a months-long siege just south of Dyrrachium rather than fight a decisive battle (3.43–72).[11]

The months near Dyrrachium yielded successes for both generals. Caesar gloried in having undertaken a "new and unprecedented type of warfare" (3.47.1), and demonstrated superior generalship in the numerous skirmishes that punctuated the hard slog of fortification.[12] Pompey, however, emerged victorious from the siege.

But not from the narrative of the siege. At 3.45–46 Caesar offers "as an example" of his generalship a battle for a single hill. At 3.45.2, Caesar's 9th legion takes a hill and begins to fortify it, Pompey takes one nearby and does likewise. Moreover, "sending archers, slingers, and light-armed troops across, he interrupts Caesar's fortifying" (3.45.3). Caesar, recognizing the difficulty of fortifying and fighting simultaneously, and concerned about his men's vulnerability, orders a retreat (3.45.4). Pompey, however, preens: "It is said that at that time Pompey, swaggering [*glorians*] among his associates, asserted that he was not unwilling to be considered a commander of no use if Caesar's legions did not withdraw with huge losses from a place to which they had rashly advanced" (3.45.6). As we saw above in the story of Curio, words that characterize their speaker with particular clarity are "quoted" in full.

Meanwhile Caesar, "fearing for the retreat of his soldiers" (3.46.1, *timens*), has them construct a barricade-and-ditch obstruction and stations slingers of his own "to be a defense for our men as they pull back" (3.46.2). To no avail, at first, since the Pompeians push the wooden barricade into the ditch to cross (3.46.3). Realizing that the safety of his soldiers depends on a show of bravery, Caesar orders an attack, whereupon "the soldiers of the 9th legion quickly took heart and hurled their javelins. Running up the slope from below they drove the Pompeians headlong and forced them to turn back" (3.46.4–5). The barricade and ditch now impede the fleeing Pompeians (3.46.5).

Against a general endowed with tactical skill, disciplined troops, and luck, it is Pompey who has rashly advanced. He eventually suffers the damage he had intended to inflict: there were "many killed" on Pompey's side, five on Caesar's (3.46.6). At a minimum, in this "exemplary" skirmish, Pompey failed in his boast about inflicting "huge losses." How useful he was as a commander is a question that readers may ask as they continue through book 3.

The physical distress of his besieged troops finally forces Pompey onto the offensive at 3.62.1. But he wins little credit from Caesar for the ensuing victory (on which see sec. 2 in chap. 4), which, says Caesar, came about contrary to Pompey's expectation (3.70.1) and with a helping hand from Fortune (3.68.1)—considerations that do not temper the Pompeian reaction to victory: "they were no longer thinking about fighting the war but seemed to themselves already to have won it" (3.72.1). If there is any good to be found in the loss, Caesar tells his men, it lies precisely in this overconfidence: the enemy, which had earlier been afraid to fight, might now be willing to venture a battle (3.73.6). When Pompey himself voices the post-Dyrrachium confidence as he welcomes the troops from

Syria (3.82.1)—"they should be willing to have a share in the booty and rewards of a victory that was already in hand"—Caesar's long-desired battle seems (and is) within reach.

When the two armies meet in Thessaly, Pompey yields to the aggressive strategy of his supporters, just as Caesar had hoped: Pompey, despite his considered policy of avoiding a potentially decisive confrontation, "had decided to fight it out, at the urging of everyone on his side" (3.86.1). He explains his plan in direct speech, and in some detail:

> I know that I am promising something nearly unbelievable. But hear the reasoning underlying my plan, so that you may go forth to battle with stouter heart. I have persuaded our cavalry (and they have assured me that they will do this) to attack Caesar's right wing on its open flank when the two armies have drawn near one another. When Caesar's line is surrounded, they are to drive off his disheartened army before we throw a weapon at the enemy. In this manner we will finish off the war without danger to the legions and practically without a wound. It isn't a difficult matter, since we are so dominant in cavalry. (3.86.2–4)

As a battle plan this has several odd features, including the relationship between commander and troops implied in the phrase "I persuaded the cavalry," the confidence in numbers alone ("we are so dominant in cavalry"), and the fact that the plan depends on Caesar's army losing heart ("his disheartened army").[13] It is dominated by wishful thinking ("without damage to the legions," "practically without a wound," and especially "it is not a difficult matter"), and acquires a darker tint in the closing allusion, now in paraphrase form, to the possibility of failure, specifically, to the possibility that leading supporters might fail their side: "[he said that] they should be mentally ready for the following day, and now that the battle opportunity they had often demanded was at hand, they should not fail either his or others' expectation" (3.86.5). (On quotation and paraphrase see sec. 2c in chap. 5.)

The narrative of the battle of Pharsalus takes place on this carefully prepared ground. Caesar gets the opportunity for battle he has been pressing for since his arrival in Greece, Pompey forsakes his successful policy of avoiding battle. Before laying out the disposition of the troops on both sides (3.88–89), however, Caesar puts one last preparatory detail in place: an oath sworn by the Pompeian leadership, Pompey included, that they would not return from the field unless victorious (3.87.5–6).

The battle itself goes as Caesar, not Pompey, expected. Pompey starts out badly by keeping his men from charging at the enemy (3.92.2–3). In this he followed the advice of one Gaius Triarius, a fleet commander (3.5.3). He wanted to preserve the men's orderly ranks and to reduce the impact of weapons thrown at them, as well as to give them an advantage over men tired and disorganized after an unusually long charge. But instead he damped their spirits, to his cost: "to us, anyway," says Caesar, "this seems to have been done by Pompey senselessly" (3.92.4). When the two lines do meet, Caesar's strategy for coping with the threat posed by Pompey's vaunted advantage in cavalry (3.89.4) works as planned (3.93.5–94.4) and quickly produces a rout.[14]

As Caesar tells it, the overwhelming defeat of the Pompeians at Pharsalus—fifteen thousand Pompeian soldiers dead on the field, twenty-four thousand surrendering (3.99)—resulted from a combination of poor tactics and the moral collapse of the Pompeian leadership. For when Pompey saw "that he had been in effect betrayed by a category of men from whom he had expected victory" (3.96.4), he resorted to betrayal himself. Returning to his camp in defeat—something he swore not to do—he urges centurions and men to fight on: "Guard the camp," he said, "and defend it attentively if anything unpleasant happens. I am making a circuit of the other gates and strengthening the defense of the camp" (3.96.5–6). But his statement is as empty as his oath, for instead of visiting the other gates Pompey hides in his tent until Caesar's men enter his camp. And then he leaves Thessaly altogether (3.96.3–4), next appearing on shipboard bound for Amphipolis and points east (3.102).

To facilitate his flight from Pharsalus, Pompey removes the insignia that mark him as the commander (3.96.3; quoted in sec. 2 of chap. 2). In so doing he gives physical expression to the characterization Caesar has been developing in book 3. A commander who fails to achieve his objectives (indeed who suffers the very harm he had hoped to inflict), who becomes so overconfident that he engages in a decisive battle inconsistent with his own strategy, and who abandons those who trust their lives and cause to him forfeits the title and insignia of a commander. The logic of this characterization reaches its culmination in the death scene Caesar writes for Pompey (see sec. 2b in chap. 1): down to his last companion, Pompey meets an ignominious death in an Egyptian rowboat at the hands of a former beneficiary and a former soldier (3.104). The man who fails his supporters is in the end betrayed by them.

4 | Fighting back

If the war had ended at Pharsalus, as Caesar and many in his audience hoped (see section 5), the characterizations of Varro, Curio, and Pompey might have been enough to help readers decide who they want to be (see section 1). But some of the aristocrats and officers who abandoned eleven legions to Caesar's mercy (fortunately forthcoming) at Pharsalus kept fighting even after Pompey's death. Two are portrayed in the *Civil War*. Caesar goes to unusual lengths to make these portraits unflattering; his Labienus and Metellus Scipio call forth resources of style rare elsewhere in the work.

4a Titus Labienus

Labienus was Caesar's most trusted officer in Gaul, the one with responsibility for the largest number of legions and the greatest freedom for independent action. He figures frequently in the pages of the *Gallic War*.[15] The association between the two men went back at least to 63.[16] From Hirtius we know that in 50 Caesar wanted Labienus as his consular colleague for 48.[17] Yet early on in the *Civil War* Labienus is registered, without explanation, on Pompey's side.

The general topic of the passage is the welcoming reception that Caesar says his forces received in parts of Italy where one might not have expected it. First mentioned is the territory around Picenum, Pompey's home ground (1.15.1). Next Caesar says that "even from Cingulum" he got support and obedience (1.15.2). Why "even"? Because, he explains, Cingulum was a town that Labienus had founded and built with his own money. Underlying this simple statement is a desertion that, according to Cicero, "made [Caesar] smart" (*dedit illi dolorem*).[18] Caesar avenged himself amply in the *Civil War*. In the narrative of the fighting in Greece, in particular, Caesar repeatedly brings Labienus front and center.

Labienus enters the *Civil War* promising that he will not desert Pompey and will suffer whatever fate the future has in store for Pompey (3.13.3). The oath rings rather hollow in the mouth of a man who, the reader knows, deserted Caesar for Pompey and did not, in fact, suffer Pompey's fate.[19]

Labienus next appears on the banks of a river that flows between the rival camps (3.19). The soldiers had gotten in the habit of making temporary truces to discuss how to end the war. Labienus, like Petreius in Spain, interrupts the processes that might lead to peace: "There will be no peace," he says, "until we have Caesar's head" (3.19.8).

After Dyrrachium Labienus demonstrates again his hostility to former associates when he gains control of men who had fought under his command in Gaul: "With Pompey's permission Labienus ordered that the captives be turned over to him. He apparently wanted to make a spectacle of them, in order to increase [Pompeian] confidence in a traitor. He called them his "comrades in arms" and asked, most insultingly, whether veterans were in the habit of turning tail. Then he killed them in view of everyone" (3.71.4). The quiet oxymoron "confidence in a traitor" (*perfugae fides*) captures the fundamental impossibility of Labienus's aim. How could anyone trust a legate who betrayed his commander and a general who killed his men?

Yet in Labienus's next (and last) appearance in the *Civil War* he is taken to be a credible authority on the weakness of Caesar's troops. The passage in question, part of Pompey's council of war before Pharsalus, is a collage of the ills besetting the Pompeian party even before they reach the field of battle. Pompey's concluding words have a peculiar resonance when ushering in a traitor: Pompey urges his officers "not to fail either his own or others' expectation of them" (3.86.5). Enter Labienus:

> Don't think, Pompey, that this is the army that conquered Gaul and Germany. I took part in every battle and I am not talking rashly about something of which I have no knowledge. A very tiny fraction of that army survives today. The majority has perished utterly—as was inevitable given the number of battles. Many men the pestilence took in Italy, many have departed for home, many were left behind in Italy. Or have you not heard that entire cohorts have been mustered at Brindisi from men who stayed behind in Italy because of ill health? These forces that you are looking at were restocked by recruitment drives in recent years in Cisalpine Gaul, and many of the men are from colonies across the Po. Whatever was sound was lost in the two battles at Dyrrachium. (3.87.1–4)

This is a long speech—at eighty-eight words, it is the longest in the *Civil War* apart from Curio's, and, like Curio's and several others considered in this chapter, it is a "quotation" rather than the normal paraphrase. Labienus overstates both his role in Gaul[20] and the weakness of Caesar's army. His statement that the majority of that army had perished in battle is countered by Caesar's own references to the war in Gaul as an experience he and his troops share (3.73.6; cf. 3.47.5, 3.64.3); even if the legions' numbers are low, as he says at 3.2.3, they feel themselves to be Caesar's Gallic legions. The reader has heard nothing about departures or "entire cohorts" being mustered from the men left behind in Italy. As for losses at Dyrrachium, Labienus's claim is challenged by the casualty figure: "Caesar lost 960 men from his legions" (3.71.1). This is a high number—Gergovia, where Caesar lost "just under seven hundred men" (*Gallic War* 7.51.4), is the next highest—but perhaps less devastating than Labienus makes it out to be, since Caesar put twenty-two thousand men in the line at Pharsalus (3.89.2). Not, therefore, a convincing speech. And yet, incredibly, it convinces his audience: "The council broke up with everyone feeling great hope and expectation. In their imaginations they already had hold of victory, because none of the assurances of so experienced a commander on so important a subject seemed to have been made in vain" (3.87.7). The irony of "so experienced a commander on so important a subject" is palpable.[21] The council scene goes on to show Labienus and the rest swearing "not to return to camp unless victorious" (3.87.5). But at Pharsalus Labienus, like Pompey, found neither victory nor death.

If in creating his portrait of Labienus Caesar had in mind the desertion with which Labienus began the civil war, he succeeded in drawing a man who continued "to act in character" (see on Cic. *Att.* 9.16.2 above). Caesar's Labienus is fundamentally unreliable. He makes empty promises and empty threats, kills men who fought under him, goes back on his sworn word. That he seems to Pompey's council of war a witness capable of "making no assurances in vain" is a symptom of their weakness, not his virtue. The people of Cingulum, the town he founded, who abandoned his cause for Caesar's, showed him as much loyalty as he deserved.

4b Quintus Caecilius Metellus Pius Scipio Nasica

We turn next to Caesar's depiction of Pompey's fourth father-in-law (Caesar was the third), Metellus Scipio.[22] At the time when Caesar was writing the *Civil War*, Scipio was commanding the opposition to him in North Africa.

Scipio first appears in the *Civil War* as the mouthpiece for the ultimatum from Pompey that forced the majority of senators, who wanted peace, to move toward war (1.5.6; cf. 1.2.1 with discussion in chap. 2). Caesar explains at some length the factors motivating Scipio to oppose the will of the Senate: Scipio desires provinces and armies, as do other leading Pompeians, but he also fears prosecution, wants to make a splash, and toadies up to powerful men (1.4.3).[23] One of his hopes is realized in short order, for to him falls the first provincial assignment in the new dispensation, Syria with its two legions (1.6.5, 3.4.2).

Scipio's actions as governor, general, and member of Pompey's inner circle between January 49 and August 48 occupy some eleven paragraphs of book 3 (31–33, 36–38, 57, 80–83). Caesar opens his report on Scipio's provincial command with a telling incident: Scipio suffered some losses and proclaimed himself *imperator*, "victorious general" (3.31.1). The paradoxical conjunction of loss and victory is reinforced by the procedural anomaly: the proclamation ought to have come from his soldiers, as it did for Curio, who "was proclaimed 'victorious general' by the shouts of his whole army" (2.26.1).

This travesty of military honor is followed by more serious failures on the part of Syria's governor. Despite being responsible for defending Roman territory against the Parthians, who had inflicted damaging losses—Caesar mentions two—in recent years, Scipio strips Syria of its troops when he moves against Caesar (3.31.3). His troops, apparently more conscious of the empire's interest than their commander is, threaten to mutiny, whereupon Scipio offers them "extremely lavish gifts of money" and the profitable pleasure of "pillaging cities" within the empire (3.31.4). A governor, then, who neither defends his province nor maintains discipline in his army, and who is prepared to pillage where he should protect.

Scipio's record in the financial sphere is equally disturbing. In a paragraph replete with stylistic special effects, Caesar shows Scipio's innovations in avarice and cruelty (3.32). Taxes were levied on the persons of slaves and freedmen, as well as on columns and the entrances to private houses, measures obviously instituted to extract wealth from those who possessed it in the greatest concentration. Contributions in kind, of many kinds, were ordered: grain, soldiers, weapons, rowers, artillery, vehicles. In short, Caesar generalizes, anything you could give a name to was turned to profit (3.32.2). From this hyperbolic expression as to sources of income Caesar turns to methods of exaction. Scipio sent his agents, backed up by soldiers, to every city, village, and outpost. Paradox is called into service: "whoever did his job with the greatest harshness and cruelty was considered the best man and citizen" (3.32.3). Sound effects, sentence structure, and metaphor are deployed the better to describe the terrible situation: "the province was full of flunkies [*lictorum*] and functionaries [*imperiorum*], crammed [*differta*] with agents and enforcers" (3.32.4: Caesar's rhymes are here represented by English alliteration; the parallel English phrases modifying "province" and the food metaphor are also present in Caesar's Latin). Metaphor also conveys the affliction added by the personal initiative of Scipio's agents: "they slaved away for their own profit" (ibid.). The excuses offered—"they kept saying that having been driven from home and country they lacked all necessities"—are deemed by Caesar insufficient: "covering an utterly shameful practice with an honorable pretext" (ibid.). Sound effects are again pressed into service to highlight the sarcasm of Caesar's comment on the high interest rates that accompanied Scipio's widespread requisitioning of instantaneous cash: Scipio's agents, he said, "called a grant of more time to pay, a gift" (3.32.5; the key words in the Latin, *prolationem* and *donationem*, rhyme).

Bad as his record as governor was, Scipio's record as a military man was worse. The self-proclaimed "victorious general" of Syria proves overzealous, insecure, and unsuccessful in Greece. Paragraphs 36–38 of book 3 describe a series of reciprocal maneuvers in Macedonia and Thessaly by Scipio and the Caesarian general Calvinus.[24] Their principals are absent. Scipio charges into action (3.36: "in a great hurry," "suddenly," "quickly," "hurrying," "journeying day and night"), impressive at first (3.36.5). But when the two forces finally come face to face it is Calvinus's men who are eager to fight, while Scipio hangs back (3.37.3). In fact, to escape a situation in which he will either have to fight unwillingly or stay shamefully in camp, he sneaks away by night. Caesar's verdict is unsparing: "having advanced rashly he made a disgraceful exit" (3.37.4). The ignominy that Scipio feared incurring by staying in camp Caesar awards him for running away. When instead of a pitched battle

Scipio opts for an ambush, he fails miserably even at this, losing some eighty men to Calvinus's two (3.37.5–7). Further losses ensue in the next paragraph (3.38.4).

With these as his military laurels it is startling to see Scipio accorded deference by Pompey, who is fresh from his biggest victory over Caesar when they meet. Pompey merges Scipio's army and his own in one camp, but "shares command with Scipio," who gets a trumpeter and commander's quarters (3.82.1). In the next paragraph this same Scipio is shown squabbling with Pompey's other noble adherents over postwar rewards; Scipio trusts in his kinship with Pompey (3.83.1; cf. 1.4.3) but not, Caesar implies, in his merits. Certainly Caesar credits him with no merits at Pharsalus, where Scipio commands the center of Pompey's line with his best troops (3.88.3), but disappears unmentioned from Greece.

Even more surprising than Pompey's deference, however, is Caesar's. For Caesar seeks Scipio's aid in the last of his attempts to negotiate a peace with Pompey. Caesar woos Scipio by sending to him a mutual friend and indulging him with praise—Scipio, as was mentioned earlier, was inclined to attach himself to powerful men (1.4.3). Caesar's message is as follows:

> Scipio's position enabled him not only to explain freely what he recommended, but also to restrain and overrule someone who was making a mistake. He commanded an army in his own name, so that in addition to authority he had the forces to compel compliance. If he should do so, everyone would credit him alone with having given calm to Italy, peace to the provinces, and salvation to the empire. (3.57.3–4)

Strong stuff for someone with no reputable successes so far, but a correspondingly powerful indicator of Caesar's desire to be seen as pursuing peace. But in this task too Scipio fails, a victim of his own fundamental insecurity: when a subordinate chides him for having listened to Caesar's message, Scipio refuses further communication and the mutual friend goes away with his task undone (3.57.5).

Caesar's Scipio got the power he wanted, but misused it in Syria and turned it to no account either militarily or politically in the war. The dominant features of his portrait are selfishness and a failure to comprehend the nature and purpose of military command. Such is the man in whose hands, while Caesar is writing the *Civil War*, lies the direction of the forces gathering against him in North Africa.

5 | Post-Pharsalus views

By the time Caesar stops writing, he has shown his audience a variety of problematic Pompeians and one particularly meritorious Caesarian. We now turn to the retrospective view of the war offered by Cicero and his correspondents, which offers a good picture of how the Pompeian cause and leaders were viewed by Caesar's contemporaries after Pharsalus and shows how these men wanted their own actions to be understood.

More than a year ensued after Pharsalus (August 48) before Rome saw Caesar. These were anxious months, with Caesar facing foreign enemies while the threat from fellow Romans, particularly those based in North Africa, grew stronger by the day.[25] Individual pardons and public policy alike awaited his return; nothing could be done in the absence of the newly unique authority figure. In this period of political limbo Cicero and his correspondents, especially those who hoped after Pharsalus to be reconciled to Caesar, began to assess Pompey's leadership and to develop an argument as to why continued resistance to Caesar was wrong. Not just impractical in view of Caesar's military successes, although that was part of their argument, but wrong for a right-minded citizen.

Criticism of Pompey—crying over spilt milk, really—was a less urgent topic than criticism of his still living supporters. He is said, for example, to have relied on associates who were unreliable (*Fam.* 9.1.2, late 47 or early 46) or "by no means conspicuous for their good sense" (*Fam.* 4.9.2, Sept. 46). These men were eager for war (*Fam.* 9.6.2, Jun. 46) and motivated by hope of personal gain, either avoidance of debt (*Fam.* 7.3.2, April 46; *Fam.* 6.6.6, Oct.? 46) or acquisition of property and priesthoods (*Att.* 11.6.6, Nov. 48).

Criticisms of the continuing resistance to Caesar are more fully developed still. As early as November of 48, Cicero, having abandoned resistance to but not yet pardoned by Caesar, ventures a first explanation of his decision to his most trusted correspondent, Atticus, mentioning, in addition to the cruelty that was a concern earlier, some new worries:

> I have never regretted quitting the war. There was so much cruelty in those men, so close a connection with barbarian peoples, that proscription—not of individuals but of whole classes—had been planned, and it had been agreed by universal consent that the possessions of all of you should be booty in that victory. I mean "you" literally; for with respect to you personally there were never any but the cruelest intentions. (*Att.* 11.6.2)

All of the themes sounded here—the cruelty feared in the event of a victory for the Pompeians, the prospect of proscription, the involvement of "barbarian peoples" (by which Cicero means principally Juba, the king of Numidia, who gave important support to the Pompeians in Africa and committed suicide together with one of Pompey's most devoted officers after Caesar's victory at Thapsus)[26]—recur in other letters by and to Cicero. This list is a kind of self-defense offered by Cicero to Atticus, of whose approval he has already been assured, presumably for transmission to others, whose approval he craves (*Att.* 11.6.1). Three weeks later he restates his fear of Pompeian reprisals, amplifies his comment about the barbarian allies ("I did not consider it right to defend the state with the barbarian auxiliaries of a treacherous nation"), and adds another argument: resistance is a lost cause, he says, since Caesar, as he proved at Pharsalus, has "an army accustomed to victory" (*Att.* 11.7.3, Dec. 48). After more time has passed he frames his reasoning more positively. Writing in August of 47 to Gaius Cassius Longinus (later one of Caesar's assassins), who not only abandoned the Pompeians after Pharsalus but put himself at Caesar's service, Cicero reviews their "common reasoning" after the battle of Pharsalus:

> Each of us, hoping for peace and hating civil bloodshed, wanted to avoid persistence in an unnecessary war, . . . and, as I am often in the habit of reminding myself, my discussions with you and yours with me brought us both to the plan, to the idea that it was appropriate for our verdict, at least, if not the whole cause, to be decided by a single battle. No one has ever really blamed our decision, except those who thought it better for the republic to be entirely destroyed than for it to survive lessened and weakened. (*Fam.* 15.15.1, 3)

Here Cicero is writing to someone with whom he can profess a cozy companionship in virtue, rather than addressing a potentially hostile audience. Accordingly we hear of hopes for peace, hatred of civil bloodshed, and a desire to save the republic from complete annihilation. Both saving citizen lives and saving the state (albeit in its weakened form) are powerful moral imperatives encouraging the view that after Pharsalus war was no longer right.

By the time Caesar returned to Rome in July of 46, after his victory over Metellus Scipio and Juba at Thapsus, Cicero and his correspondents had worked out a retrospective view of the civil war and the leading Pompeians that agreed to a remarkable degree with the account Caesar gave of them in his *Civil War*. They agree that Pharsalus should have been the end of the fighting, that the question of military superiority had been decided irrevocably in Greece. They agree that the men who had been Pompey's most prominent supporters did not deserve the kind of loyalty that had drawn Cicero's correspondents to Pompey in the first place. And not even Pompey escapes the general verdict that the leading Pompeians "died shamefully."[27]

On the other hand, there is only a feeble echo in the post-Pharsalus correspondence of Caesar's characterization of his own side. Cicero and his friends say rather little about the virtues—political or moral—of Caesar's cause. To some extent this is only to be expected: the practical advantages of siding with Caesar after

Pharsalus were so obvious as to make reasons (such as the desire to help rebuild the republic) read like rationalizations. As we will see in the Epilogue, not even Caesar's leniency sufficed to make people fully his. But this, we will argue in the next chapter, was the long-term objective of his self-portrait in the *Civil War*, an objective central, in his view, to mastering victory.

·4·

Mastering Victory

> Caesar was sober when he went to overthrow the republic.
> —CATO, quoted by Quintilian, *Education of an Orator* 8.2.9

The three preceding chapters explored Caesar's literary achievement in the *Civil War* in terms of genre, structure, and characterization, and began to place the work in its contexts both literary and political. This chapter looks at how Caesar presents himself to his contemporaries through his text. The focus is not on what he says about himself and his virtues—his superiority to Pompey as general, for example, which was treated in chapter 3—but on the self he reveals to his readers by his authorial choices.

At first glance, the *Civil War* seems to be structured around the contest for primacy between Pompey and Caesar. It begins with Pompey's assumption of leadership in the opposition to Caesar (1.1) and builds to their military confrontation in Greece (3.6–96). But neither Pompey's flight from Pharsalus (3.96.4) nor his death at Alexandria (3.104.3) is the end of the work. Pompey's defeat was, Caesar and others hoped, the end of a war (see sec. 5 in chap. 3), but the narrative carries Caesar on into another war, a "foreign" war this time, one fought to impose a Roman settlement on the Egyptian kingdom of the Ptolemies (3.107.2). The *Civil War* breaks off incomplete before the end of the resulting war.[1] The trajectory of the narrative thus indicates that for Caesar the contest with

Pompey had become part of a larger story, a story of Rome. That story, however, Caesar eventually abandoned.

A preliminary indication that Caesar was after more than military victory can be found in a letter he wrote to his supporters Oppius and Balbus just after Corfinium: "Let this be our new policy for maintaining the victory: to strengthen our position with mercy and generosity" (*Att.* 9.7C.1, early March 49). The letter continues with news of Caesar's capture and release of three Pompeian officers. Caesar hopes they will requite the benefit: "If they want to be grateful, they will have to urge Pompey to prefer to be a friend to me than to the men who have always been extremely hostile to both him and me, by whose machinations the republic has been brought to its current state" (*Att.* 9.7C.2). A "lasting victory" is the goal here (*Att.* 9.7C.1; quoted in sec. 2c in chap. 2) and the paired policies of mercy and generosity are means to this end.[2] Beneficiaries can be expected to show proper gratitude by putting pressure on Pompey (this is what Caesar hopes for from the released Pompeians) or by publicizing and developing Caesar's policies (this is what he hopes for from Oppius, Balbus, and Cicero). Lasting victory will depend on the creation of active relationships of mutual obligation and friendship. In this letter of March 49, less than three months into a civil war that would last five years, Caesar is already pondering the foundations of future stability.

In the end, Caesar did not use the *Civil War*; the exigencies of the continuing conflict and, even more, of victory changed Rome more than he anticipated. But the objective of establishing and developing ties with contemporaries is evident in the *Civil War*, where Caesar, in a variety of ways, shows himself as a participant in relationships.

The tone of Caesar's *commentarii*, with their everyday diction, plain style, and arm's-length third-person references to "Caesar," is often pronounced impersonal. But readers also note over the course of the ten Caesarian books a perceptible development, one element of which is the increased access he provides to an "authorial personality." In the first section of this chapter we explore the techniques by which Caesar makes himself present to the reader;

in the second and third, the personality that emerges. Section 4 looks at the argument implicit in Caesar's self-presentation: how the values he espouses in the narrative and the narrating of the civil war convey his aspirations for post-Pharsalus Rome.

1 | Common ground

Throughout the *Civil War*, Caesar creates a sense of intimacy with his reader by assuming that the reader and he have things in common. A common understanding of the nature of pre-battle exhortations, for example, allows him to say that before Pharsalus he addressed his army "according to military custom" (3.90.1). Since he then gives a résumé of the key points of his speech (see sec. 2c in chap. 5), the reference to what was customary is not meant to supply information but to appeal to a shared understanding. Similarly, Caesar refers to "the manner of pirates" (3.112.3) and "the sort of thing said by well-educated men"(2.12.4; see sec. 2c in chap. 5).

Another type of expression for which he expects a nod of recognition is the generalization, as, for example, in his conciliatory address to defeated Pompeian soldiers in Spain: "what befell their leaders was the sort of thing that generally befalls men as a result of excessive stubbornness and arrogance" (1.85.4). For the most part, Caesar's generalizations are offered directly to the reader in the present tense: "in novel circumstances rumor generally anticipates event" (3.36.1); "as often happens" (1.44.2); "inasmuch as experience is a universal teacher" (2.8.3). The connection established between author and reader by such phrases is particularly intimate when couched in the first-person plural, as at 2.27.2: "We eagerly believe what we want to believe and we hope that others feel what we ourselves feel."

Similarly, Caesar's concern with duty and what "ought" (*debere*) to happen reinforces shared values. Forms of *debere* are particularly frequent in passages of quoted speech, passages, that is, where a connection has already been established between speaker and addressee(s), and it is especially apt in attempts to reinforce connections. Caesar uses it to propose peace to Pompey (3.10.3: "each of us ought to put an end to his stubbornness," and 3.10.8: "peace terms ought to be sought in Rome"), to persuade Marseilles to remain neutral (1.35.1: "they ought to follow the lead of all Italy," and 1.35.4: "they ought to show equal favor"), and to urge his soldiers to take heart (3.73.3: "they ought to remember").

"Ought" can also help present an exchange as a contest for the moral high ground. Thus Pompey uses it in his one private message to Caesar: "Caesar too, being a man of standing, <u>ought</u> on the republic's behalf to let go of his grievance and his anger and <u>ought</u> not to feel so weighty an ire against his enemies as to let his hopes of harming them lead him to harm the state" (1.8.3). In the exchange that follows, Caesar suggests mutual disarmament, and, when Pompey refuses, demanding *fides* (proof of good faith) without offering any himself, Caesar's comment is "unfair terms," an evaluation that challenges Pompey's commitment to what ought to happen.

Caesar's "oughts" become more frequent in the third book. Occurring five times in the first book, "ought" generally refers to the particular obligations of specific circumstances—the sole exception being Pompey's misappropriation of the term (see above). In the second book it occurs three times and refers to rewards that are "due," either as bribes or as obligations. But in the third book we find ten occurrences, most of them articulating general principles: restitution ought to come from Rome, not from Caesar (3.1.5); Pompey and Caesar ought to seek peace and ought to turn to Rome and the Roman People (3.10.3, 3.10.8; both quoted above); a general's duty ought to be different from that of an officer (3.51.4), and a general ought to increase his soldiers' innate alacrity and ardor (3.92.4); the Pompeians ought to think about how to use victory, not about their self-interest (3.92.4). In all of these instances, Caesar offers a bond of shared understanding with his reader, just as he distinguishes his (and their) understanding of duty and obligation from that of the Pompeians. "Ought" is an appeal as well as an argument.

Another stylistic element, the rhetorical question, works similarly. Toward the end of the first book, Caesar explains his strategy of starving the Pompeians in Spain into surrender rather than fighting a decisive battle: "Even if he won the battle, why should he lose some of his men? Why should he suffer soldiers who had earned his best thanks to be wounded? Why should he take a chance on fortune?" (1.72.2). Since Caesar begins paragraph 72 with a reference to his hopes, the reader has the impression of overhearing Caesar's internal dialogue.[3] It is a moment of remarkable intimacy.

The same stylistic device is turned against those who would unsettle the republic by taking advantage of the Pompeian Caelius's revolutionary cancellation of debts in 48: "But to insist on holding onto one's possessions when one admits to owing a debt—what kind of person, what kind of impudence is that?" (3.20.3).

Another way of cultivating a common understanding between writer and audience is the rejected negative. Like the rhetorical question, it appeals to what is expected, but does so by recalling the norm in order to reject it. In Caesar's long address to the defeated Pompeians in Spain (1.85), for example, he uses no fewer than twelve such negatives.[4] He had not been willing to fight, he says, even when everything was in his favor (yet one would expect him to be); his opponents had respected the rules neither of negotiation nor of truce (one would expect decent men to do so); he intended to profit neither from their defeat nor from his favorable circumstances (as an ordinary general would); the Pompeian army in Spain had no other purpose than to oppose Caesar (Roman armies were supposed to conduct the business of the state); for no other reason were so many auxiliaries and such experienced generals sent there (ditto); none of these forces was there to pacify the Spanish provinces, none to further provincial affairs (the normal tasks of provincial garrisons). And so on. The process is clear: Caesar puts his own actions in a favorable light by saying that he did not do what an ordinary (shortsighted, greedy) commander would have done in his circumstances, and those of his political enemies in an unfavorable light by saying that they did not do what an ordinary (honorable, traditional) policy would require. The bond with the reader here is strengthened by the fact that the reader must fill in important information, as we have done in the parentheses above.

Sometimes, however, Caesar supplies the knowledge that he wants his reader to use in evaluating events. Hence the contextualization in his critique of the Pompeian commanders' hasty departure for their armies at the outset of the war: "nor did they wait, <u>as had been done in previous years</u>, for their commands to be voted by the people" (1.6.6).

As is obvious from this last example, the rejected negative can be tendentious. In characterizing Pompey's men in Spain, for example, Caesar says that "no one was so sluggish and averse to effort as not to think that they had better leave camp immediately and hurry to block Caesar" (1.69.3). By book 3, Caesar's tendentious negatives can be downright contemptuous: "nor were the Pompeians inadequate in this matter" (3.93.2); "Pompey did not delay his pursuit at all" (3.75.3). That is, Pompeians are expected to be inadequate and Pompey reluctant to move.[5] The trait in Caesar himself that such negatives convey is intelligence. Circumstances that might be meaningless or misleading to others are easy fare for Caesar: "nor was his initial opinion mistaken"; "nor did it escape his notice."[6]

Besides opening up a world common to Caesar the author and his reader, the *Civil War* also constitutes, by its narrative, a guarantee by Caesar of his desirability as an associate, the topic, variously considered, of the chapter's remaining three sections.

2 | Imperturbable Caesar

Setbacks are inevitable in war, or so Caesar puts it to Pompey in one of his attempts to stop the fighting:

> [He said that] each of them ought to put an end to his stubbornness and relinquish his arms. They ought to tempt fortune no longer. Both sides have suffered significant setbacks, which they can take as a lesson and a warning to fear future eventualities: [Pompey], driven out of Italy, in the loss of Sicily and Sardinia and the two Spanish provinces; Caesar himself, in the death of Curio and the awful loss of his African

army and the capitulation of his soldiers at Curicta. They should therefore spare themselves and the state, since they were themselves, in their own setbacks, sufficient proof of how powerful fortune is in war. (3.10.3–6)

Caesar's language is tactful here: the failures of major military efforts such as Pompey's attempt to hold Spain and Caesar's to gain Africa are called "setbacks" (*incommoda*) and attributed to fortune. His focus is on the future: the sensible thing to do is to learn from these setbacks, whose like must eventually befall their armies again, and lay down arms immediately. This offer, like all of his others, gets a cold reception from Pompey (3.18.4, quoted in n. 31), but throughout the *Civil War* Caesar makes it clear how learned he is in the lessons taught by war's setbacks.

2a Fear

Perhaps the most interesting setbacks, and certainly the most numerous, are those that arise from fear. Most of the fear in the *Civil War* is on Caesar's side, but the author is never perturbed by his soldiers' fear or the resulting setbacks, nor does he blame it.[7] He looks for its causes, understanding that it is a fact of war.

Typical is the account of a costly and ultimately unsuccessful day of fighting soon after Caesar's arrival in Spain (1.43–47). Caesar leads out three legions and orders an elite unit to take control of a hill that dominates the supply route (1.43.1–3). After a brief battle, the Pompeian forces take the hill, while Caesar's elite troops retreat to the legions (1.43.4–5). Caesar explains to his reader how his men were worsted. The enemy's tactics, he says, were like those of the barbarian tribes they had been facing for so many years in Spain: their impetuous and incautious advance frightened our men, who were unaccustomed to this kind of fighting and thought they would be surrounded (1.44.1–3). That is, the fear of the advance unit, although unwarranted, is understandable. When it communicates itself to Caesar's whole force the author is equally understanding: they hadn't expected and weren't used to failure, he says (1.45.1).

Elsewhere, when a ship full of novice soldiers surrenders to the enemy, Caesar explains their decision (which cost them their lives) as follows: "terrified by the number of [enemy] ships and exhausted by the sea and seasickness, they believed the promise that the enemy would not harm them and handed themselves over to Otacilius" (3.28.4). Their subsequent execution and the parallel example of the ship full of veteran soldiers who fought their way back to safety show that they made the wrong decision, but the fear that prompted it was not, as Caesar tells it, unwarranted (3.28.5–6; see sec. 1c in chap. 5).

Sometimes the only justification offered is the contagiousness of fear. When five cohorts of the 9th legion are attacked on the beach at Dyrrachium, the first reinforcements sent to help the cohorts on the beach, seeing them routed, themselves panic and flee (3.64.1). As Caesar puts it, "whatever was sent as help became infected by the fear of the men in flight and increased both the terror and the danger" (3.64.2). Even worse is the conduct of his troops later in that long day at Dyrrachium, when the cavalry, anxious about its escape route, initiated a retreat, frightening thereby the infantry cohorts of the right wing, whose subsequent panic-stricken flight prompted the retreat of the left wing (3.69.2–4). "Then everything," says an unusually impressionistic Caesar, "was full of confusion, fear, and flight" (3.69.4). Again style communicates his feeling that the soldiers ought to have been able to fight the contagion. But he does not make his feeling policy: the only soldiers who are punished after the battle of Dyrrachium are the standard bearers who disobeyed Caesar's direct order to stop or abandoned their standards (3.74.1 for the punishment, 3.69.4 for the incidents).

In short, the author understands the reality of fear in soldiers, even if he does not condone all of its manifestations. He shows himself equally understanding of fear in political life under the sway of Pompey. An ex-consul, Marcus Marcellus, was frightened into changing his vote in the Senate by the reproaches of Caesar's enemies (1.2.5), and the Senate as a whole was frightened by the proximity of Pompey's army (1.2.6) and by the declarations and unanimity of those hostile to Caesar (1.3.5) into acceding to Pompey's wishes. Even the senators who are too frightened to undertake a peace mission voted by the Senate—"it was principally owing to fear that each man refused the role of emissary for himself"—have Caesar's understanding: "Pompey," he reports, "had said when leaving the city that he would rate equally (i.e., equally badly) those who stayed in the city and those who were in Caesar's camp" (1.33.1–2). That is, Caesar shows himself understanding, despite the fact that the senators' fear closed off an avenue of negotiation he himself had proposed opening (1.32.8).

2b Error

The second source of setbacks cited by Caesar at 3.73.5 was "some error." We have seen the error made by his 9th legion in their excessive zeal to undo a defeat (1.45.2). Another costly error was his right wing's "ignorance of the terrain" at Dyrrachium (3.68.2), which led them to follow a misidentified fortification wall into tight quarters where they panicked and fled over the corpses of their fellows. In his account of Dyrrachium, Caesar goes into considerable detail about the many fortification walls that were built or begun and abandoned there during the months-long siege, preparing the narrative ground, so to speak, for his men's error.[8]

Ignorance of military discipline is the implicit explanation for another error that cost him lives. Early in 48, Caesar's campaign against Pompey in Greece was hampered by the fact that a substantial portion of his forces was still in Brindisi. He needed them as soon as possible (cf. 3.8.2), but stopped a crossing already in progress by warning the officer in charge, Calenus, that the landing sites were held by the enemy (3.14.1). The ships were recalled to Brindisi, but one "continued on its way and did not obey Calenus's order" (3.14.2). Why? "Because it was without soldiers and was run on civilian advice" (ibid.). That ship was captured, everyone aboard killed (3.14.3). Regrettable, but not blameworthy, as Caesar tells it, since civilians can't be expected to behave like soldiers.

The reality of error as an important feature of battle is stated programmatically in Caesar's critique of Pompeian confidence after

Dyrrachium. Among their many errors of judgment, according to Caesar, is the fact that "they did not remember the everyday incidents of war . . . sudden fear . . . the shortcomings of a leader or the mistake of a tribune" (3.72.4).

2c Fortune

Only in these three passages does Caesar ascribe setbacks to error. Fear was, as we saw above, responsible for considerably more setbacks, and the same is true of Caesar's third source, fortune. *Fortuna*, as befits the blind goddess, is responsible for favorable as well as detrimental turns of events. In the narrative she generally takes the form of weather events or accidents of timing. For Caesar, as we will see, adverse fortune requires a response.

Early in the Spanish campaign, a flood proved good for the Pompeians and bad for Caesar's troops. Two of Caesar's legions were cut off from the main Caesarian camp and his cavalry when a bridge over the Segre river was washed away "by a sudden storm of wind and mass of water" (1.40.3). Pompey's generals took advantage of this "gift of fortune" (1.40.7) and attacked with superior numbers. Annihilation was prevented by the foresight of Caesar's legate and by the fact that he had built two bridges, over the second of which he sent reinforcements (1.40.7; cf. 1.40.1).

Shortly thereafter the river flooded again, destroying both bridges this time. The bad weather continued for some time (1.50, 1.51.3, 1.54.1); again the cause is fortune (1.52.2). But Caesar builds boats of a type he had encountered in Britain and gets troops across, establishes a bridgehead, and has a bridge in place two days later (1.54.2–4). Similarly at Marseilles, "sudden misfortune" (2.14.3) destroyed many months' effort but did not end the siege: "by the ingenuity and valor of the soldiers the loss was quickly made good" (2.15.4).

Accidents of timing are another challenge. In fact, fortune gets some of the credit for Pompey's victory at Dyrrachium, since it was an accident of timing, as Caesar describes it, that prevented the right wing lost in the maze of fortifications from undoing its error: "<u>Meanwhile</u> Pompey . . . brought up five legions as reinforcements. At <u>one and the same moment</u> his cavalry neared ours and his legions were spotted by our men. . . . Everything was <u>suddenly</u> changed" (3.69.1). The temporal expressions (underlined above) insist on coincidence, and the whole panic-driven scene is said to manifest the effect of fortune, "which has very great power . . . especially in war" (3.68.1).

In general, Caesar's response to fortune is vigorous action. Understanding that plans can be foiled by bad weather or accidents of timing is no grounds for congratulation, nor is it material for a laudatory self-portrait; you have to insist that you won't be stopped, that either your virtues or your enemy's faults will remedy the situation. At Dyrrachium, for example, when Caesar has suffered his most dangerous defeat, he turns to his men to say, "Whether it was their own frightened disarray or some error or even fortune that interrupted the victory already present and at hand, they must all strive to repair with their courage the damage done" (3.73.5).

It also helps, of course, to show that when weather and timing are on your side, for a change, your opponents are helpless (good weather: 3.26.4, 3.26.5, 3.27.1; opportune timing: 3.14.3, 3.101.4).

2d Human nature

Besides these three sources of setbacks, Caesar's narrative shows him making allowances for a fourth, human nature. Like fear and error, it can be understood but not avoided. At Marseilles, word of the arrival of a few ships sent by Pompey to support the city caused a self-destructive "hope and enthusiasm" (2.4.4) after an initial defeat at sea. Caesar explains: "For it happens by a defect of our human nature that in the face of unprecedented and unfamiliar circumstances our confidence grows too great and our fears too strong" (ibid.). The citizens rebuild their fleet only to suffer a second defeat (2.5–7). Since the Pompeian ships contributed nothing to the battle (2.7.1), the confidence in Marseilles was indeed "too great." The gesture of understanding in Caesar's generalization is part of his remarkably favorable depiction of a city that reneged on a promise of neutrality (1.35.4–5) and attacked during a truce (2.14.1), a depiction that is consonant with his (as he tells it) remarkably lenient treatment of the city when it did finally capitulate: "preserving the city more out of respect for its fame and antiquity than on account of any favors it had done him" (2.22.6).[9]

Observation of human credulity prompts two other generalizations in book 2. In the first instance, Varus, the Pompeian commander, believes what deserters from Curio's army tell him about the low morale of Curio's troops and the possibility of winning them over without a fight. Caesar knows that the deserters might have been telling Varus what he wanted to hear, "for we willingly believe what we want, and we hope that others feel what we ourselves feel" (2.27.2). Unlike the people of Marseilles, Varus does not get a favorable portrait from Caesar. In fact, credulity of this sort is a characteristic of Pompey himself in the opening chapters of the first book (see sec. 2 in chap. 2).

When a similar credulity is shown by Varus's opponent Curio, by contrast, Caesar pulls his punches. A fatal decision is based on Curio's belief in what his cavalry tells him about a fight they had won: "But their deeds were reported by them with some exaggeration, so inclined are men to boast about their own successes. Moreover, there was a large amount of booty on show and captives from both infantry and cavalry were displayed. In the end, every passing moment seemed but a delay of victory" (2.39.2). Curio's ignorance of human nature and his consequent failure to distrust the self-promoting report are almost lost in the evidence for why it would have been believable.

The last setback connected with human nature in the *Civil War* is the assassination of Pompey, although human nature is only one of two possible causes suggested by Caesar for this unnecessary (as Caesar tells it) death (see sec. 3 in chap. 1). Those who planned the assassination "were either motivated by fear . . . or else they scorned him in his misfortune." For the latter explanation Caesar's reasoning is as follows: "It generally happens in a calamity that enemies arise from among one's friends" (3.104.1). Both explanations, the political and the human, depict the author as someone who can muse upon a setback that affected him directly (in denying him an opportunity to pardon Pompey) with a sad shaking of his head at humankind in general.

One feels in this passage and in the author's reaction to the other setbacks examined in this section the force of Caesar's pragmatism. He understands that human nature is frail, that soldiers panic, officers make mistakes, and people lose their moral bearings in matters closely connected to themselves. Where he can, he takes precautions against these liabilities,[10] but when setbacks occur he explains and moves on. Fortune sometimes shows him favor, but when she is averse he and his men fall back on reserves of character and intellect. In short, he never seems to lose his balance.[11] He creates a world where his virtue and understanding are equal to the setbacks. It is this world and his role in it that Caesar shares with his readers in the *Civil War*.

3 | "I" and "we," not "Caesar"

The self-consciousness of Caesar's narrative increases over the course of the *Civil War*. In book 1 he refers back just once in the first person to antecedent events as already narrated (1.31.2: "as we showed above"). Twice in book 2 he muses in the first-person plural about human nature (2.27.2; quoted in section 2d above). But in book 3 he refers to his own narrative fourteen times, to his conclusions twice, and once to himself as a post-Pharsalus writer. We begin our consideration of these passages with the only one in which Caesar speaks in the first-person singular. When the situation at Dyrrachium is at its most dire, help unlooked-for prevents the utter destruction of Caesar's army. Caesar reflects on the outcome:

> In these terrible difficulties two factors provided aid: that Pompey, fearing an ambush, did not dare approach the walls for some little time—because, I believe [*credo*], events were turning out contrary to the expectation of a man who a little earlier had seen his men fleeing from the fort—and that his

cavalry was delayed in its pursuit by the narrow gap between the walls and by the fact that our cavalry was in possession of it. (3.70.1)

In this long and complex sentence, the statement "I believe" introduces an apparently minor point. It is not a sign of authorial reluctance to assert outright what can be no more than speculation; neither here nor elsewhere does Caesar hesitate to tell the reader what was going through Pompey's mind. Nor is he characterizing Pompey as fearful. Fear in a general is no bad thing, as its association with Caesar shows (see n. 7). So, why the unique "I believe"? In context it gives appropriate emphasis to the instance of fear that had the most far-reaching consequences. But it is not just a stylistic marker. It makes explicit what is implicit in the entire work, that after the war Caesar felt the need to look back and assess what had happened. Victory was not enough.

Other passages in book 3 make the same important point. At 3.17.1, after saying that at the time he did not think some arguments in support of an improbable peace proposal made by probably deceitful Pompeians deserved a response, he says "nor do we now think it worthwhile to put one on record." He has looked back, weighed his silence, and decided that it was justified.[12] At 3.51.3 he gives an equally favorable verdict to a decision made by his legate Publius Sulla: "it does not seem to merit reproach." Pompey's decision to keep his line of battle stationary at Pharsalus, however, does merit reproach: "to us, anyway, this seems to have been done by Pompey senselessly" (3.92.4). Caesar's assessment of another Pompeian blunder—Pompey's declaration that he was willing to be considered a general of no use if he did not inflict a stinging defeat on Caesar (3.45.6; see sec. 3 in chap. 3)—is expressed less directly, but still in the present tense: "It is said that at that time Pompey. . . . " With his "it is said," Caesar evokes others who are also at present reviewing the war's events. And the cumulative effect of these evocations of the postwar review is amplified by references to information that reached Caesar "after the war was finished."[13]

Another setback, the disloyalty of men who (in Caesar's view) owed everything to him, undermined the foundations Caesar was trying to establish after his victory, and it elicits a telling use of the first person: "they decided to depart from us and to try a new fortune and to test new friendships" (3.60.3). The crucial word is "us," which collapses the distinction, established by all of Caesar's references to "Caesar," between the general of the civil war and the author of the *Civil War* (see sec. 1 in chap. 5). Unlike the first-person references considered above, where "I" or "we" referred to the author, this "us" is both the benefactor who was betrayed by his beneficiaries and the author who records that betrayal. As we will see in the next section, loyalty, like fear, occupies the pen of Caesar constantly in the *Civil War*. Both are topics that bring out the "personality" of the author, topics in connection with which he is willing to reveal himself to (or construct himself for) his reader.

4 | Caesar's *fides*

More than once Caesar lays claim to the virtue of forbearance in the face of injury, but his narrative shows an increasing interest in the moral implications of trust and betrayal.[14] The central importance of *fides* in Caesar's account of Curio's African expedition was explored in chapter 3, as was the general lack of trustworthiness on the Pompeian side. Here we examine Caesar's presentation of his relationships with individuals and communities that had harmed or served him, with particular attention to the personal dimension imparted by his treatment of the mutual obligations involved.[15]

Caesar introduces the personal dimension of his role as a political actor in his first speech in the *Civil War*. After six chapters set in Rome detailing the moves of his opponents, the narrative follows the flight of the tribunes from Rome to Caesar, whereupon Caesar takes his case to his soldiers. His speech begins with the injuries he has suffered at the hands of his political enemies (1.7.1) and ends with his desire that his soldiers should protect him from such harm:

"Given that under his leadership over nine years in Gaul they had conducted the state's business with great success, experienced a favorable outcome in a great number of battles, and pacified all Gaul and Germany, they ought to protect his reputation and standing from his enemies" (1.7.7). The logic is simple: the soldiers should repay the successes they gained through his effort with their efforts on his behalf.[16] The argument implies that his men had a stake in the winning of military campaigns and, more generally, in the conduct of public business, and that this was somehow commensurate with the stake Caesar himself has in his reputation and standing. In this speech he complains both about the suppression of the tribunician veto and about the Senate's "final decree," but he does not ask his men to uphold the majesty of the law (e.g., the law, passed in 52, that permitted him to be an absentee candidate for a second consulship, which would have solved his political difficulties in the short and long term), or the sovereignty of the Roman People (which had voted him a governorship that was now being cut short by the Senate), or any other such public good. These wrongs are mentioned elsewhere in the *Civil War* (e.g., 1.9.2, 1.22.5, 1.32.2–3), but here, at the outset of the contest, the relationship on which his future will depend is a relationship of mutual advantage between commander and soldier.[17] That such was the reality of the situation will not surprise any student of late republican history. But that Caesar should so baldly state it in the opening salvo in a self-justifying narrative is a sign that the terms of political engagement are changing.

The old patriotic terms appear in Pompey's mission to Caesar, which Caesar calls a mission concerning "private business" and describes as an effort on Pompey's part to excuse himself to Caesar. Pompey's argument, on the other hand, is that he acted for the good of the republic and that "he had always considered the advantage of the republic more important than his private relationships" (1.8.3). Caesar, he says, should do likewise: "Caesar, too, being a man of standing, ought on the republic's behalf to let go of his grievance and his anger and ought not to feel so weighty an ire against his enemies as to let his hopes of harming them lead him to harm the state" (1.8.3). The language is a typically Roman conflation of the political and the personal. But it is vague and Caesar dismisses it: "these points seemed irrelevant to repairing the harm suffered" (1.9.1). The message Caesar sends back to Pompey joins his own success to the good of the body politic (1.9.2–6; see sec. 2b.ii in chap. 2). He, too, is willing "to endure anything for the sake of the republic." But, in place of self-sacrifice, he speaks of his dignity and its recognition by the Roman People in the form of a special provision for his election, and of his pursuit of compromise, all of which, like his personal safety, are threatened by the treachery of his enemies. The underlying principle here is one of mutually beneficial action: just rewards for services, and good faith in obligations. For Caesar, this is the republic, not some abstract idea of self-sacrifice. In this section we look at how Caesar presents the mutual obligations of *fides*-based relationships.

4a Punishments and rewards

Caesar's interest in obligations and recompense changes over the course of the *Civil War*. In book 1, he is concerned with the political implications of Pompeian bad faith. Toward the end of the Spanish campaign, when troops on both sides take advantage of a temporary absence of the Pompeian commanders to mingle with one another (1.74.1), the Pompeians express their gratitude to Caesar's men for their restraint in a recent victory: "thanks to them, they are still alive" (1.74.2). They then ask about Caesar's trustworthiness, his *fides*; and they seek a pledge (in Latin, *fides*) that their commanders will not be harmed, "lest they seem . . . to have betrayed their own" (1.74.3). *Fides* requires *fides*, it seems. *Fides* also generates *fides*. Receiving sufficient assurances, the Pompeian soldiers proceed with the planned capitulation (1.74.4–7). But when Petreius returns, he starts a bloody reprisal, killing all of the Caesarian soldiers he finds in his camp (1.75–76).[18] The Pompeian soldiers protect and hide Caesar's men (another instance of *fides*); Pompeians in Caesar's camp are sent back unharmed or choose to remain with Caesar. This story shows how good faith works and how it lays the foundation for peace, and it shows that when good faith is broken by Pompeian leaders, Roman soldiers and citizens are killed.

Books 2 and 3 shift the emphasis from analysis to compensation. In fact, much of book 2 can be read as Curio's posthumous reward for exemplary loyalty, despite his ultimate failure (see sec. 2b in chap. 3). In book 3 we again see Caesar repaying loyalty, and also betrayal.

The city of Gomphi, which like other Greek cities (3.79.5) had declared for Caesar, changed its allegiance to Pompey after hearing news of the defeat at Dyrrachium (3.80.1–2). The betrayal was initiated by a single prominent individual, Androsthenes, whose role allows Caesar to focus on the personal dimension of Roman foreign relations: Androsthenes "preferred to be a companion of Pompey's victory than an ally of Caesar when he had suffered a reverse" (3.80.3). But Androsthenes' personal connections had public consequences. He persuaded the citizens to close the city to Caesar. Requests for assistance were sent to nearby Pompeian forces (3.80.3), but Caesar (as usual) arrived first. Before nightfall he had stormed the city and handed it over to his soldiers for pillaging (3.80.5–7). Caesar made an example of Gomphi, and he recorded it without making excuses for the brutality of the punishment. It was warranted, the bald narrative implies, and it was also effective in reminding neighboring cities of which man's friendship was to be preferred in the choice between Pompey and Caesar (3.81.2).

Those who supported his cause, on the other hand, receive public and material expressions of gratitude:

> At a public meeting in Corduba Caesar thanked everyone, group by group. The Roman citizens, because they had exerted themselves to keep the town in their control, the Spaniards [of Carmona], because they had driven out the garrison, the people of Cadiz, because they had foiled the plans of his adversaries and asserted their own freedom, the [Pompeian] military tribunes and centurions who had come to garrison Cadiz, because they had assisted the townsfolk's undertaking with their courage.[19] The money that

the Roman citizens had promised to [Pompey's legate] Varro for public uses he remitted. He restored the confiscated possessions of those who, he learned, had spoken too freely and been punished in this fashion. (2.21.1–3)

Caesar's rewards not only made manifest his sense of obligation to those who had aided him, they also undid harm inflicted by the Pompeians.[20] Neither point would have been lost on residents of the empire.[21] After Pompey was dead, the choice facing contemporaries was not between Caesar and Pompey but between supporting and resisting Caesar. This may help explain the very large number of passages in which the author Caesar pays his debts, mostly of gratitude, to individuals and communities through the events he narrates in the *Civil War*.

4b "General, I shall make you grateful"

Many of his debts were owed to his soldiers. Both individual and collective valor contributed to the victory of Caesar the general, and he recognizes this in a unique passage—the only passage where Caesar quotes his own words directly—in which he uses the first-person plural to mark his sense of cohesion with his men: "We must put off our journey for the present and turn our thoughts to fighting, as we have always desired. Let us be ready in spirit for the battle, an opportunity we will not easily find hereafter" (3.85.4). Caesar's sense of cohesiveness finds a response in his soldiers—both when they shout out that they are ready to defend their general's reputation (1.7.8; see sec. 2b in chap. 2) and when they display to Caesar the evidence of their efforts: "They counted out for Caesar some 30,000 arrows that had been fired into their position, and brought him the shield of a centurion named Scaeva, in which there were found to be 120 perforations" (3.53.4). Caesar's gratitude results in a promotion and a gift of money for Scaeva. He also doubled the pay of Scaeva's unit and provided other benefits "on a most generous scale" (3.53.5). These material rewards are, of course, supplemented by the narrative's testimonial.[22] And Caesar adds a telling explanation for his generosity: the promotion was "as [Scaeva] deserved from Caesar and the republic." As with Caesar's presentation of his role in Gaul (see sec. 1a in chap. 2), so here Caesar's role and that of the republic are indistinguishable.

That Caesar pays attention to what his men deserve from him (and the republic) is perhaps clearest in the cameo of an ex-centurion named Crastinus, which occupies two brief but stylistically highlighted episodes in the narrative of the battle of Pharsalus.[23] The first episode, Crastinus's exhortation to the 120 men under his command, shows the tight nexus between Caesar, Crastinus, and soldiers as this final battle begins: "'Follow me, you who used to be members of my unit, and assist the general you have made victorious. This one battle remains. When it is over he will regain his standing and we our freedom.' With a glance at Caesar he continued, 'General, I will make you grateful to me today, alive or dead'" (3.91). The exchange proposed is simple. Crastinus offers a service that will be repaid with gratitude. The service is both personal ("his standing") and political ("our freedom"), and for Crastinus the outcome ("alive or dead") is less important than the loyalty ("I will make you grateful to me"). Ultimately, Caesar's gratitude will be the guarantee of freedom.

In the second Crastinus passage, the immediate debt of gratitude is paid: "Killed fighting with extreme bravery was Crastinus, whom I mentioned above; he took a sword in the face. Nor was it false, what he said as he entered the battle. As Crastinus had predicted, Caesar deemed his bravery outstanding in that battle and judged that Crastinus had done his best for him" (3.99.2–3). Caesar puts his gratitude on record, and pays his debt by according Crastinus distinction and renown, the only coin he has for the dead.[24] The promise of freedom is redeemed by the rhetoric of the *Civil War* as a whole (see chap. 2).

4c "Trying new friendships"

Caesar's narrative also repays betrayal. To be sure, he depicts more failures of *fides* on the Pompeian side than on his own,[25] but he does devote one extended passage to an occasion when the fabric of his army was deliberately rent by men he considered his. This long story from book 3 illustrates particularly well the growing importance of *fides* in Caesar's account of the civil war.

The narrative starts with a flashback: "There were in the cavalry of Caesar's army two brothers, Roucillus and Egus" (3.59.1). Caesar explains his long-standing relationship with them: he knew their father, a Gallic dignitary; they fought for him in all of his Gallic campaigns; he lent his support to their political careers in Gaul; and, finally, "made poor men rich" (3.59.1–2). Not only rich, but influential, since the esteem in which they were held by Caesar "made them popular in the army" (3.59.3). This is how *fides* is supposed to work. But these officers misunderstand the obligations they become subject to as the beneficiaries of Caesar's good will and *fides*: "Counting on their friendship with Caesar, and beside themselves with foolish and barbarian arrogance, they paid no heed to their own men, but defrauded the cavalry of its pay and took for themselves every bit of booty" (3.59.3). When the cavalry soldiers seek redress (3.59.4), Caesar remains loyal to the brothers:

> Caesar, thinking that this was not the moment for punishments and making numerous concessions to them on account of their courage, deferred the whole business. He scolded them in private for having made a profit at their men's expense, and he advised them that there was nothing they could not expect from his friendship and that they should base their hopes for the future on his past services to them. (3.60.1–2)

Caesar's characterization—quite exceptional for him—of the motivation of these men as "foolish and barbarian arrogance" suggests that his personal feelings may not have been entirely generous.[26] In any event, the brothers soon reveal that their misunderstanding of *fides* is incorrigible. Determined to "try new friendships" (3.60.3), they desert to Pompey. Later their companions boast of a Pompeian success to some of Calvinus's scouts and in so doing reveal troop movements (3.79.6). Caesar expresses his sardonic gratitude: "by the good offices of the enemy" the Caesarians are saved (3.79.7).

Then, in reporting the death of one of the brothers (unnamed) in battle he takes, uniquely, direct credit for it: "In that same period [Caesar] was victorious in a cavalry battle and killed one of the two Allobroges whose flight to Pompey we recorded earlier, along with some others" (3.84.5). For a military account, much of this is irrelevant, but that is what makes the moral and exemplary value of the narrative stand out. Caesar may have been wrong to think that Roucillus and Egus would change, but he was right to handle the situation as he did, "making concessions to them on account of their courage" (3.60.1). And, in the end, they got what they deserved.

Civilians who had served Caesar during the war also get their reward or punishment in the narrative. Four Greek aristocrats, for example, are named as supporters of Pompey or Caesar. We met Androsthenes in the narrative of the punishment of Gomphi; his fate is not reported, but his name is forever associated with betrayal. Of Macedonia's Menedemus and Thessaly's Hegesaratus and Petraeus, Caesar reports only their standing and their allegiance (3.34.4, 3.35.2). The association of Roman citizens in the Dalmatian port city of Salonae, however, gets a significant tribute. When a Pompeian fleet commander, having won over the nearby island of Issa (3.9.1), turns his attention to Salonae, "he was able to shake its allegiance neither by promises nor by threatening harm," despite the fact that the site was vulnerable (3.9.2). The citizens prepared a vigorous defense involving the construction of fortifications, the manumission of slaves of fighting age, the manufacture of artillery rope from their women's hair, and the deployment of women and children on the walls (3.9.3–6). After enduring a long siege, the men of the city, joining forces with their former slaves, sally forth and drive off the Pompeians for good (3.9.6–8). Caesar does not comment on the strategic significance of this action; the passage's sole function is as a testimonial.

4d "Avoid Caesar's gift"

Apart from Curio, the people concerned in Caesar's loyalty stories are beneath him in the social and military hierarchies. Caesar's record in winning the loyalty of men of his own class gets little play in the

Civil War. There was in fact little success to report.[27] *Fides* was not something his fellow aristocrats expected to be praised for by someone like Caesar. A (small) number of senators served Caesar's side in the civil war well, but of these only the now-dead Curio is praised for his loyalty in the *Civil War*. When Caesar's highest ranking legate, Calvinus, achieves military successes against Metellus Scipio in Macedonia—his *res gestae* (3.38.1)—the virtue Caesar singles out for praise is "diligence" (3.36.8).[28] And in a revealing passage at 3.26.1, the Caesarian legates Antony and Calenus, who commanded the legions waiting in Brindisi to cross to Greece, are praised for "boldness" and "courage," while their troops are shown declaring themselves willing to risk everything to help Caesar; such devotion is apparently more suited to the men than the officers.

Caesar's policy of pardoning those who had opposed him, once they had been neutralized by capture or defeat, represented a fundamental change in the terms of political engagement.[29] The reference point was no longer the state, but Caesar. We saw in chapter 1 that imperial-age authors writing about the capture of Corfinium emphasize, as Caesar's own narrative does not, the ingratitude of the men pardoned there. In the world of these authors the reference point for political virtue is indeed an individual, the emperor; "ingratitude" is a political as well as a personal failing. But one can see this focus on a single political center emerging already in Caesar's narrative.

The longest episode in the Corfinium narrative illustrates the point. Caesar's men are poised to enter Corfinium on the evening of 20 February (1.21). Instead of attacking, Caesar has them make a cordon around the city. Just before morning, an ex-consul, Lentulus Spinther, requests and receives permission to speak with Caesar:

> With him he discussed his personal safety. He begged and besought Caesar to spare him, mentioned their long-standing friendship, and listed the favors Caesar had done him, which were quite substantial: thanks to Caesar he was a member of the Board of Pontiffs, he received Spain as a province after his praetorship, and he was assisted in his candidacy for the

Mastering Victory | 139

consulship. Caesar interrupted mid-speech: he had not left his province to cause harm, he said, but to protect himself from the insults of his enemies, to restore to their proper standing the tribunes of the people, who had been driven from the republic because of their defense of Caesar, and to liberate the Roman People, who had been made subject to a small faction. Heartened by this statement, Lentulus asked permission to return to Corfinium. The concession of safety made to him, he said, would offer solace to the rest about their own prospects; some were so terrified that they were driven to make unduly harsh plans about their lives. (1.22.3–6)

The topic of conversation is Spinther's personal safety, to which he is entitled, he argues, on the grounds of a long-standing friendship with and past benefits from Caesar. These benefits were political, but the relationship under which Caesar subsumes them is that of "friendship"—another term that straddles the line between the personal and the political. Here we see "personal safety" resulting from "favors" and "friendship" and issuing in "safety" and "solace."

The virtue that secures the kind of mutual obligations Caesar hopes to establish with his peers via the pardons at Corfinium, *fides*, is central to the picture Caesar creates of himself in the *Civil War*. He is concerned with its proper cultivation, its obligations, rewards, and risks. According to the argument of the *Civil War*, when the old sources of cohesion failed, or rather were destroyed by the faithless enmity of Pompey and others, the new source of cohesion lay in the qualities and capacities of one person, Caesar, and *fides* is what he offers as the virtue constitutive of a newly cohesive state.

As Caesar tells the story of his conversation with Spinther (and he is the only author who does tell it), there appears to be no reason why the besieged senators should not be glad of the safety and solace he offers. All accept his pardon, and Spinther, at least, is grateful enough to praise Caesar's actions to his peers.[30] But such a pardon can be the kind of favor that is hard to take.[31] Lucan's description of the pardon scene, and particularly of the reaction of Domitius to Caesar's offer, supplies something of what Caesar leaves out (2.511–25):

> Caesar knows that punishment is sought and forgiveness feared.
> "Live on, however unwilling, and by my gift," he said, "see the sun . . ."
> . . . [Domitius], unafraid, suppressed harsh anger
> and to himself said, "Will you go to Rome and the retreats of peace,
> you coward? Are you not at last preparing to enter the furious heart of war,
> since die you must? Onward, boldly;
> shatter all of life's delays and avoid Caesar's gift."

Cato's quip (quoted in the chapter epigraph) that "Caesar was sober when he went to overthrow the republic" was meant as a paradox: no one in his right mind would attempt to overthrow the republic (*ad evertendam rem publicam*—literally, "to turn the public thing upside down"). But Caesar's *Civil War* challenges both parts of the charge. It presents a man who aimed, not to overthrow the republic, but rather to reclaim the "public thing" from the grasp of those who would turn it to their own private ends, and to reestablish the republic's moral foundations. With the uncanny logic of politics, however, this effort to reclaim the "public thing" turned out, over the course of the *Civil War*, to depend more and more upon the willingness of individuals to remain loyal to their personal obligations. And, with a logic both deeply Roman and deeply offensive to Caesar's peers, the rewards and punishments that those personal obligations entailed were dispensed by an individual— "Caesar's gift."

Both the general who responds to setbacks with understanding, ingenuity, and steadfast purpose, and the author who weighs the war's events to assess the rewards and punishments due, are manifestly in their right minds. Indeed Caesar's very confidence in the power of his mind, in the logic of his argument, may have blinded him to the possibility of passionate resistance to him and his logic on the part of those who, while they may not have had a tenable argument themselves, said no to his and meant it.

We will return to the fate of Caesar and his argument in the Epilogue, but in chapter 5 we conclude our literary study of the *Civil War* with a closer look at Caesar's unqualified success, his style.

· 5 ·

Writing Fighting War

> Is mastery of easy, everyday language now to be neglected?
> —CAESAR, quoted by Cicero, *Brutus* 253

Cicero, discussing Caesar's *Gallic War* commentaries in a work on rhetoric and Latin style, made the general comment, "They really must be thought excellent. For they are naked and lovely, with every oratorical ornament stripped away like clothing. . . . For in history nothing is sweeter than a pure and clear brevity" (*Brutus* 262). In the preceding chapters we have seen Caesar's style at work constructing arguments and offering an interpretation of people and events that served Caesar's needs. Here we concentrate on features of Caesar's style that facilitate his presentation.[1] We will see that in the *Civil War*, at least, the general impression Caesar gives of an unornamented plainness is effective in itself and also serves as a foil that allows his occasional ornaments to shine. Everywhere Caesar shows both his "mastery of easy, everyday language" and his sensitivity to the effects produced by variation.

1 | Words

1a "Caesar" and "our men"

At its most basic level, Caesar's narrative deploys two striking strategies. First, he regularly uses the third-person "Caesar" in referring to himself.[2] For instance, the *Civil War* begins, "When the letter of Gaius Caesar was delivered to the consuls. . . ." Second, he consistently uses the first-person plural possessive adjective "our," particularly in the expression "our men" (*nostri*), to refer to his army. The overall effect of this story of "Caesar and our men" is to align Caesar's cause with the Roman reader's interests. Let us see how this works.

1A.1 The third-person narrative: "Caesar"

There is no real precedent that we know of for the use of the third person in place of "I" in a work that is primarily about the author. Xenophon, a Greek historian, writing under the pen name Themistogenes, refers to himself as "Xenophon," and Plutarch notes that this allows more scope for self-praise and self-justification, but Xenophon's practice is a consequence of his pen name. In other words, once he chose to pretend to be Themistogenes, the only way he could refer to himself was as "Xenophon."[3] Caesar's use of the third person does not depend on this sort of pretense. Before Xenophon, the great Greek historian Thucydides, when he spoke of his military actions, in book 4 of his *History of the Peloponnesian War*, referred to himself in the third person, while using the first person for his authorial efforts. But his work is a history of an entire war, in which the part he played was small. To personalize the reporting of those few actions would disturb the surface of objectivity that he had created from the beginning of the work.

The effects of Caesar's "Caesars" are several. First, the story that he tells seems to be told from an impersonal perspective. While his name is repeated throughout the text[4]—something that accrues to Caesar's fame and glory—he seems within the narrative like all the other named participants. This facilitates comparison of all the third-person actors without any overt pressure to align the authority of the text with one particular actor.[5] This apparent objectivity is, of course, a rhetorical pretense, but it is one that has its effect over the course of the work.[6] If we compare this to Thucydidean objectivity, we may say that, while Thucydides does not allow a personal narrative to disrupt the apparent objectivity of the overall narrative, Caesar uses the third person to turn a predominantly personal narrative into an apparently objective history.

Caesar's use of the third person may also be seen to construct and enjoy the opportunities Xenophon found for self-praise and self-justification. Consider the sentence whose beginning was quoted above: "When the letter of Gaius Caesar was delivered to the consuls, it was only through the greatest struggle by the tribunes of the people that it was reluctantly allowed that the letter be read out in the Senate" (1.1.1). Here, third-person forms are used for everyone, but Caesar stands out because only he is named; for the others their offices suffice. Further, Caesar introduces himself into the narrative, as he does others, with two names, "Gaius Caesar," but does not supply an identifying tag, such as that in "Lucius Lentulus, the consul" two sentences on. And, finally, Caesar is named in a context where he is not physically present (he is in Cisalpine Gaul while the Senate meets in Rome). In fact, he is named at least three times in each of the first five paragraphs of the work, which makes him the dominant presence in the text here: dominant in the minds and in the deliberations of others. Only Pompey is similarly, albeit not so consistently, present[7]—and yet the comparison is striking. Caesar presents himself to the Senate in a letter that the consuls resist reading and refuse to debate, while Pompey is present in the devious and duplicitous words of others who seem to speak for him. The *Civil War* begins, then, as a contrast and even a contest in representation and presence, an opening that depends in part, at least, on Caesar's use of names.

Caesar's sensitivity to names and naming has come up in every chapter so far, in reference to the *commentarius* genre, his contemporaries' fears of proscription, Caesar's audience, and the demonstration of *fides*. A summary of the names in this opening panel of the *Civil War* (1.1–5) will reinforce our earlier points. In this narrative, where the Senate is named fifteen times, Caesar specifies the following actors: Caesar (sixteen times), Pompey (twelve times), Lentulus (five times), Metellus Scipio (five times), Calidius (three times), Marcus Marcellus (twice), Cato (twice), Caelius (once), Antony (once), Cassius (once), Lucius Piso (once), Lucius Roscius (once).

What is remarkable here is the political affiliation of those named. If we remove those who made more lenient proposals (Calidius, Marcellus, Caelius), the office-holders who offered to meet with Caesar (Piso, Roscius), the tribunes who fled to Caesar (Antony, Cassius), and Caesar himself, we are left with the men whom Caesar wished to make responsible for the war: Pompey, Lentulus, Metellus Scipio, Cato. These four men stand out from the anonymity of "the friends of Pompey," "the enemies of Caesar," and "the Senate." Clearly, Caesar is not "taking names." Among this company only one other name is cited (twice)—that of a figure who is absent, but whose presence is felt: Sulla, the man known for cruel proscriptions and the precedent for Pompeian activities (see sec. 1a in chap. 3).

"Caesar" is everywhere in the *Civil War*. In fact, only three times do we read more than three paragraphs without encountering a reference to Caesar.[8] He is most frequently the subject of verbs (42% of the time) or he is in the possessive case (28% of the time, frequently in expressions such as "at the arrival of Caesar" or "Caesar's cavalry"). Often, by a kind of shorthand common in other historical narratives, "Caesar" refers to Caesar's army: "Caesar" "fortifies a camp" (1.42.4), "crushes the enemy" and "forces it to retreat" (1.45.1), and "completes a bridge" (1.54.4). In this regard, Caesar's use of "Caesar" is no different from his use of the names of other generals or from the usage of other authors. The general is always more than the individual actor. But, as we have seen, Caesar becomes Rome's might and virtue personified.

The point was taken by the Roman historian Dio. He reports Caesar's response to the German leader Ariovistus, whose tribe made incursions into the Roman province of Gaul, as follows: "Do not regard it as a slight matter and of little moment that he failed to obey me, Caesar, or that he summoned me, Caesar. For it was not I who summoned him, but the Roman, the proconsul, the fasces, the authority, the legions . . . " (38.43.3). In an imperialistic war in Gaul it was relatively easy for "Caesar" to be the virtual presence of Rome.[9] In the *Civil War*, the alignment of "Caesar" with Rome and Roman authority is facilitated by the possessive adjective "our," to which we now turn.

1A.11 The first-person possessive adjective: "our"

It was standard practice in Roman histories written in Latin to use "our" in reference to the Roman army.[10] In a civil war, this use becomes tendentious while seeming merely to participate in tradition. Thus, when Caesar refers to "our men" and "our standards," he broadcasts an image of "Caesar" as the representative of what is truly Roman and republican. In Gaul, when "Caesar" led "our men," Caesar the Roman general was leading a Roman army. When the same "Caesar" leads "our men" against a Roman army, the continuity of language suggests, first of all, that Caesar's army is still "our" army, though aligned against that of Pompey and the Senate. And, if the army is "our men," then the general "Caesar" must be "our general." Thus, the literal truth (that Caesar's army is a Roman army) and the political argument (that Caesar's army is the army of the Roman reader and so its leader is "our general") are united whenever Caesar refers to his army in this way. As he does 115 times in the *Civil War*.

Of the many examples one might choose to illustrate how this works, we look at the first instance of "our" in the *Civil War*. Caesar has crossed the Rubicon; a series of towns along the eastern coast of Italy have willingly surrendered. He hears that Sulmo, a small town near Corfinium, wants to place itself in his hands but is prevented by Pompeians from doing so. He sends Antony with five cohorts. The townspeople took courage "as soon as they saw our standards" (1.18.2). Here the meaning of "our" seems to shuttle back and forth between "representing Caesar and his army" and "representing Rome and our interests." In both meanings it clearly marks the Pompeian commanders Lucretius and Varus as being outside the community of "both townspeople and soldiers" who align themselves with "our standards": "The people of Sulmo, as soon as they saw our standards, open the gates and, all of them cheering, both townspeople and [Pompeian] soldiers come out to meet Antony. Lucretius and Attius [Varus] hurled themselves from the wall."

Caesar's use of the third and first persons produces its effects on every page of the *Civil War*. We now turn to some other equally prevalent features of his style, beginning with the words he selected for his narrative, selection being, in his own words, "the foundation of eloquence."[11]

1b Adjectives

One of the simplest ways to add color or ornament to prose is with adjectives. From Cicero's characterization of Caesarian *commentarii* as unadorned, one might suppose that Caesar avoids adjectives. He doesn't.

The striking thing about Caesar's adjectives is not so much their presence, however, but rather their function. They are rarely ornamental or rhetorical; they rarely play to emotions or add local color. The overwhelming majority of his adjectives function in one of three ways: they label, they arrange, or they assess. In general, they manifest a perspective that stands back from the personal and serves the explanatory function that Hirtius so admired in Caesar's writings (*Gallic War* 8 preface 7).

Among the labels we find many that identify military units either broadly ("auxiliary," "legionary," "attached to the commander") or more narrowly ("cavalry," "equipped with light shields," "light-armed"). Sometimes labels indicate temporary, not permanent, troop conditions ("without baggage," "rear-guard," "in support," "inactive"). Other military labels refer to provisions ("grain-related"), routes ("direct"), transport ("baggage-related"), and topography ("neighboring").[12] Name-based labels such as "Fabian" (i.e., "under Fabius's command") and "Afranian" ("under Afranius's command") are efficient designations for rival forces.

Labels can, however, be used for tendentious purposes, and sometimes are. The adjective "Gallic," for instance, may be a simple identifier ("Gallic ships," 3.29.3) or a disparaging qualifier ("Gallic style," 1.51.1, of the disorganized style of march used by auxiliaries from Gaul). Similarly, a term like "barbarian" can refer to peoples at the fringes of the Roman empire (e.g., 1.38.3: "the Cantabrians and all the barbarians that live on the coast") or describe a non-Roman want of military discipline: in 1.44.2 Roman troops have been infected by the "barbarian manner of battle." The term "Pompeian" is often prejudicial (and we recall that for the corresponding term "Caesarian" Caesar substitutes "our"): Caesar speaks of "Pompeian levies" and "a Pompeian legion," when both levies and legions should be Roman, not Pompeian. But that is the point: even at the level of adjectives Caesar insists that what is "Roman" and "our" possession, like the republic itself, is becoming a private Pompeian possession. The threat to "the public thing" is particularly clear when "Pompeians" and "our men" are juxtaposed, as they are at 3.46.3, for example: "The Pompeians began to press and advance against our men more insolently and boldly."[13]

Our second group of adjectives includes those by means of which substantives are arranged. Temporal adjectives arrange events in time, either ordinally ("first," "second,") or with reference to other markers ("former," "future," "midday"). Orientation adjectives ("left," "middle") arrange troops in battle formations. Comparative and superlative adjectives create spatial series ("far," "farther," "farthest") frequently used to describe places and hierarchies. But what all of these "arranging" adjectives have in common is clarity: they dispose of events in ways that make them easier to understand.

Assessment can be as simple as counting (numbers are adjectives in Latin), but more common are adjectives that imply a norm: "easy," "difficult," "sudden," and, most common of all, "large." Another much-used group assesses the outcomes of military conflicts: soldiers are "unharmed," battle outcomes are "favorable," retreats are "rapid." Similarly, adjectives describe terrain with an eye to its strategic potential: places are "level" or "mountainous," "open" or "narrow," "suitable" or "disadvantageous."[14] Winds are "favorable" or "adverse," "light" or "strong." All such descriptions have strategic consequences. Rivers, if their flow is mentioned, are "rushing"; when they aren't rushing they aren't worth mentioning (see the discussion of the Segre below).[15]

Like places, people in the *Civil War* frequently attract adjectives that assess them in strategic terms. When soldiers are "frightened," this affects battle strategy (or it should), just as when they are "tired" or "inexperienced" or "scattered." Similarly, there is an advantage in soldiers who are "reliable" or "experienced" or "fresh." The common thread among these modifiers is their contingency: soldiers are not always "tired" or "ready." But, when they are, it matters, and Caesar mentions the fact.[16]

The functional role of Caesar's adjectives comes more clearly into focus when a Caesarian description is set beside one by Lucan, whose epic poem on this civil war includes ornament and sentiment in abundance. Here, for example, are two descriptions of the site of Ilerda, in the vicinity of which the crucial battles of the Spanish campaign were fought.

Lucan, *Civil War* 4.11–15 (35 words, 10 Latin adjectives):

On a <u>modest</u> hill there swells <u>rich</u> soil; it has grown into the air with a <u>gentle</u> mound. On this rises Ilerda, founded by an <u>ancient</u> hand. The Segre with its <u>placid</u> waters glides by, not the <u>least</u> of <u>Spanish</u> rivers. A <u>stone</u> bridge embraces it with a <u>huge</u> arch; the bridge will survive <u>wintry</u> waters.

Caesar, *Civil War* 1.45.2–4 (54 words; 6 Latin adjectives):

They arrived beneath the hill on which the town of Ilerda was set. . . . The terrain was <u>broken, sheer-cliffed</u> on either side, and had so little width that <u>three</u> cohorts filled it once drawn up, with the result that support could not be sent from the sides and the cavalry could not be of assistance to men in difficulty. From the town, however, <u>downward-sloping</u> terrain extended with a <u>gentle</u> slope for about <u>four hundred</u> paces.

Lucan's description sets the scene for the coming conflict by creating an emotional contrast with the violence of war. Caesar, by contrast, describes the site only when its particulars are relevant to the battle at hand. Lucan gives more than is needed for a military narrative: the soil was rich, the city old, the river not insignificant. Something is happening in the world, and Lucan wants to suggest that it is momentous: the river's quiet waters will soon be a flood (4.50–120). Caesar does not mention the Segre until its floodwaters render his troops' position perilous (1.48.1–3). What interests him in the topography of Ilerda are its implications for deployment: the nature and dimensions of the access route and the constraints on troop movements.

But Caesar has many styles, and it would be a mistake to think that his only interest is in troop movements, strategic topography, and military analysis. Although he never lavishes as much attention on the human implications of a scene as Lucan does, he can deploy symbol and imagery for emotional effect. At Dyrrachium in book 3, when Caesar's army is short of food while Pompey's army is well supplied and "daily a large number of ships arrived bearing provisions, and no wind could blow that was not favorable for some supply route" (3.47.3), Caesar's men are forced to eat barley and pulses and roots while being taunted by the enemy. But then things begin to change. Caesar begins the narrative of reversal almost poetically, with a suggestion of the pathetic fallacy, a figure of speech in which natural processes are made to reflect human behavior: "And now already the crops were beginning to ripen and hope herself began to sustain their deficiencies . . . " (3.49.1). Caesar had performed the incredible feat of blockading the river and diverting Pompey's water, with the result that Pompey's men were forced to kill their animals and to dig wells or hunt for water in the marshes (3.49.2–3). His own men "heard with delight from deserters . . . that [the Pompeians] were put into no good state of health, being affected by the narrowness of the place, the foul smell from the multitude of dead bodies, and the daily labor—unaccustomed as they were to work—and also by the huge shortage of water." In this passage, smell is "foul," work is "daily," men are "unaccustomed" to work, the shortage is "huge." Thereafter "they began to see that daily the passing of time was bringing them help and that with the ripening of the crops their hopes were growing greater." While this is nothing like Lucan, still it creates an affective and coherent picture, not just of actions and strategies but of how people felt, and it makes vivid the suggestion that Caesar himself is aligned with the forces of nature that ripen the crops.

Finally we come to the explicitly tendentious adjectives. We have seen that labels can perform that function, but we will focus here on moral and political terms. Caesar's use of the superlative "best" (*optimus*) can introduce this group. "Best" is the superlative form of "good." It has a clear moral component, and, since Rome's political conservatives liked to think of themselves as the "best men," the "optimates," it often has political content as well. This means that the word itself is a site for contesting whether optimates are really the best. For instance, as Caesar marches toward Rome, the Italian towns declare for Caesar one after another. First is Iguvium, whose residents, he says, felt toward him "the best goodwill" (1.12.1, *optima voluntas*).[17] The optimate praetor abandons the town and is deserted by his soldiers, which leaves the adjective *optimus* in Caesar's camp.

"Best" also illustrates the tendency of superlatives and other moral terms to cluster—this is probably because moral evaluation requires other evaluative terms. Among Caesar's criticisms of the provincial administration of Metellus Scipio (on whom see sec. 4b in chap. 3), is the fact that the harshest and cruelest (*acerbissime crudelissimeque*) agents of public extortion were treated as the best men and citizens (3.32.3, *et vir et civis optimus*).[18] In addition to "best" in this passage Caesar uses "harshest" (twice), "cruelest," "most shameful," and "most burdensome." Here, the superlatives themselves carry an argument: the incommensurability of "harshest" and "cruelest" and "most shameful" with "best man and citizen" marks the inequity of Scipio's administration. The same kind of argument is carried out in Caesar's account of the two Allobroges who betrayed him to Pompey (see sec. 4c in chap. 4). These men had given Caesar "the best and bravest assistance" in Gaul; consequently they had been raised by him to the "highest public offices." But this community of virtue and reward is undermined by their greed and injustice: "they were beside themselves with foolish and barbarian arrogance" and they cheated and defrauded their own men. Soon, they desert out of fear and bad conscience. The story, with its superlatives, characterizes the deserters' inequity in contrast with Caesar's ability to see Roman virtue and reward it. Pompey, of course, is glad to receive these barbarian men and display them to his troops.

"Shameful" (*turpis*), mentioned above in connection with Metellus Scipio, occurs more often in reported speech or thought than in the narrative proper: it is not a quality Caesar presents as inherent in events so much as inherent in the perspective of observers. The Pompeian soldiers who had become habituated to native fighting tactics during their long stay in Spain, for example, "did not think it shameful" to yield ground (1.44.1). Curio, when arguing against a proposition to separate his demoralized army from that of the enemy, speaks of "shameful flight," indeed of "most shameful flight" (2.31.1). It is striking that five of the seven occurrences of this term refer to flight or retreat. The other two usages refer to financial abuse (cf. on Scipio above). In other words, while "the best" challenges conservative politicians in terms of their own self-evaluation, "shameful" challenges the enemy in terms of military virtue (literally, "manliness," *virtus*) and financial responsibility. This alignment of money, virtue, and masculinity is still with us today.

Like "shameful," sensory words such as "foul" and "pleasant" are generally used by actors, not the author himself, as in the passage quoted above on the "foul" smell reported by deserters from Pompey's water-starved camp. They are, however, rare, as are adjectives that indicate color. In the narrative of the Spanish campaign, for example, the only color-based modifier occurs in the phrase "when the sky was white," which does not paint a landscape but rather specifies a time of day (i.e., "in full daylight"; 1.69.1).[19] Similarly, adjectives associated with the emotions are rare. But this is not to say that emotion is absent from the *Civil War*. The narrative is full of people who are happy, hopeful, eager, fearful, grieving, and more. But Caesar does not use adjectives to depict them. For this he uses other kinds of words, particularly abstract nouns, to which we turn below.

What all of this means is that readers should pay attention to Caesar's adjectives. Most will help the reader to understand strategy and troop movements. They are essential to the military narrative and they in no way contradict Cicero's sense that Caesar's style was naked and unadorned. On the other hand, in this plain context of narrative efficiency, some adjectives are particularly striking and effective. It is for this reason that the relatively simple characterization of the Senate's decree against Caesar on 7 January has such power: "Recourse was had to <u>that last and final</u> decree of the Senate." The adjectives do not name the decree but stigmatize it and its use.

1c Abstract nouns

We said above that people in the *Civil War* experience emotions, but that they are not usually described by adjectives when they do. Instead, Caesar prefers abstract nouns, adverbs, and verbs: for instance, men are never "fearful" (*timidus*), although "fear" (*timor*) appears thirty-six times. This preference is partly a feature of the Latin language, which sometimes lacks the appropriate adjective, but Caesar prefers the noun even when there are good adjectives, as in the case of fearfulness. This preference aligns itself with a strategic preference for the general or abstract over the particular and concrete.

A passage from book 3 illustrates Caesar's strategic and conceptual interests. When Antony crosses to Greece, two ships get separated from the rest and face attack. The new recruits on one ship surrendered while the veterans on the other refused to yield. Caesar's language explains why: "the recruits were . . . undone by the <u>sea</u> and <u>seasickness</u>," while "the veterans were likewise distressed by <u>problems</u> of weather and bilge" (3.28.4). The new recruits are caught up in the particulars of their situation: seasickness and the overwhelming presence of the sea. By contrast, the veterans, though in a like predicament, have a general category, "problems," to which they can assimilate the weather and the bilge water. In other words, the abstract noun "problems" provides the veterans with access to their own experience, and there is all the difference in the world between facing "the sea" and facing "problems." [20] The general category is the difference that experience makes, and it allows the veterans to develop a strategy.

Throughout Caesar's narrative, people are aligned with abstract traits and events are seen in terms of strategy. One sees "retreat" (*receptus*, fifteen times) rather than confusion and fear. A general maneuver is observed—"advance" (*progressus*, fourteen times), "siege" (*oppugnatio*, fourteen times), "truce" (*indutiae*, seven times), "ambush" (*insidiae*, six times)—not the movements of individual men. Purposes are explicit: cavalry is sent "as <u>support</u>" or "as an <u>obstacle</u>," legionary cohorts are sent "as <u>reinforcement</u>." Caesar presents war as a series of strategic moves by rival commanders. Thus, the Pompeian Metellus Scipio observes "<u>enthusiasm</u> and <u>eagerness</u> for battle" in his opponents. When he withdraws, his cavalry escapes ambush because of "the <u>noise</u> of horses" (3.38.3); the kind of noise doesn't matter. Similarly, in the phrase "horses ruined by <u>emaciation</u>" (3.58.5), emaciation is not something seen and suffered but something considered by Pompey in assessing the tenability of his situation.

Since these abstract nouns assess situations and influence strategies, it is not surprising to find that Caesar frequently says that "there was so much X that Y happened."[21] Thus, "there was so great a <u>shortage</u> of fodder that they fed their horses with leaves stripped from trees" (3.58.3), and "everything was so full of <u>confusion, fear</u>, and <u>flight</u> that when Caesar . . . ordered them to make a stand . . . not a single man halted" (3.69.4).

But the good general also knows when abstracts do not tell the whole story. After the defeat at Dyrrachium, Caesar's reading of the morale of his soldiers is particularly elaborate: "There accrued so much <u>grief</u> from the setback and so much <u>enthusiasm</u> for repairing the damage to their <u>reputation</u> that no one waited for an order from a centurion or tribune but each, as <u>punishment</u>, imposed heavier <u>tasks</u> on himself and all burned with *desire* for battle" (3.74.2). This description presents the elements that Caesar must evaluate: grief and enthusiasm, punishment and tasks, <u>desire</u>—how does it add up? Some of his officers read this situation as favorable to immediate reengagement with the enemy, but Caesar puts the details together differently, and this time with an eye precisely on the particulars: "But Caesar, on the other hand, did not have much confidence in his demoralized <u>soldiers</u> and was thinking that they needed some time to regain their 'heart'; the <u>fortifications</u> had been abandoned and he was very concerned about <u>food supplies</u>" (3.74.3). Caesar not only knows what qualities and forces are at work in a situation, but keeps track of the details and the context as well.

Finally, we may note Caesar's attention to abstracts as a rhetorically tendentious device. In the midst of the siege at Dyrrachium, Caesar tries again to obtain peace. He sends a letter to Metellus Scipio asking him to discuss peace terms with Pompey: "if he should do so, everyone would credit him alone with having given <u>calm</u> to Italy, <u>peace</u> to the provinces, and <u>salvation</u> to the empire" (3.57.4). The abstract nouns are like little prizes that Caesar offers to Scipio's self-regard. This flattery is not offered by Caesar the author, but by the Caesar of the text. The author, however, also has a tendentious purpose: the terms "peace" and "salvation" were thematic in book 1, where they defined the Caesarian goals that were always subverted by Pompeian arrogance and violence. Here, Scipio cowers at the criticism of a subordinate, and as a result Caesar again accomplishes nothing for peace.

1d Ornaments

"Naked" is how Cicero described Caesar's *Gallic War*, "with every oratorical ornament stripped away like clothing." Though he praised Caesar's work in this famous passage, Cicero was no fan of the style; indeed, even in describing it he employs colors—a metaphorical adjective and a simile—from his own box of paints. In the *Civil War* passages examined so far we have seen what Caesar can do with simple materials, but we conclude this section with a few Caesarian special effects, passages where Caesar's ordinarily naked narrative is dressed up to confront the enemy.

Even so simple a word as "large" (*magnus*) becomes an ornament when deployed to magnify the forces arrayed against Caesar in Greece:

Pompey, having gained a year's time—free from war and by enemies untroubled—in which to muster forces, put together a large fleet from Asia Minor and the Cyclades islands, from Corcyra, Athens, Pontus, Bithynia, Syria, Cilicia, Phoenicia, and Egypt, and ensured that a large one was built everywhere. He exacted a large sum of money from Asia Minor, Syria, every king, dynast, tetrarch and free city in Greece, and compelled the tax-collection companies from his own provinces to count out for him a large sum. (3.3.1–2)

Caesar's insistence on "large" is clear even in translation. In the Latin the effect is stronger still, since the adjective is the first word in each of its clauses.[22] The rhetorical figure, anaphora, cooperates with the ornamental (and repetitive) chiasmus of "free from war and by enemies untroubled" and the long list of place names to give Caesar's enemies an imposing front.

Similes are infrequent in Caesar's *commentarii*, but all the more striking when they do occur, as in the following passage on the outrageousness of Pompey's treatment of an allied people, the Parthini: "In the preceding days Pompey had treated the Parthini as booty" (3.42.5). What "as booty" means is spelled out in the next sentence: "He had searched out all the grain and, having stripped and gouged all of their houses, brought it back to Petra by means of his cavalry." The second sentence alone would have sufficed to convey the facts. And even the simile-free version is strongly worded, with its participles ("stripped and gouged") personifying the houses as victims of Pompey's search.

A final passage where Caesar needs more than easy, everyday language for the enemy is his description of what his men found upon entering the Pompeian camp after their victory at Pharsalus:

> It was possible to see that *cabañas* had been built, a great weight of silver tableware set out, tents floored with fresh turf, the tents of Lucius Lentulus, in fact, and some others bowered with ivy. [They saw] these and many other things that indicated to them excessive luxury and confidence in victory, so that it was easy to form the opinion that they

[the Pompeians] had had no worries about the day's outcome, since they were searching out unnecessary pleasures. (3.96.1)

The discoveries followed fast upon one another, so fast that Caesar omits connectives (the technical name for this ornament is asyndeton). He lingers, however, over the alliterative name of Lucius Lentulus, who had appeared many times earlier in the narrative and did not need to be identified with two parts of his name here.[23] What the soldiers saw they interpreted with abstract nouns, including one, "luxury" (*luxuria*), with a distinctly negative moral component.[24] And what they saw was unfamiliar enough to require a Greek word (*trichilae*, "gazebos," represented by the Spanish *cabañas* in the translation); apparently no Latin word or institution would serve. Caesar generally abides by his own dictum that one should "avoid the novel and unfamiliar word as you would a reef," but here *cabañas* is a striking novelty.[25] Still, even a prudent sailor will approach a reef, if the stakes are high enough and he is confidently in control of his craft.

2 | Structures

2a Sentences

Turning now to verbs, we also turn to larger structures, since verbs organize clauses and sentences. As one might expect, verbs in Caesar are typically practical rather than colorful. They represent war's *res gestae*: troop movement (approach, reach, depart, cross, turn, send), military endeavor (surround, seize, block, pursue, fortify, explore, fight, wound, kill), communication (report, order, demand), and planning (notice, think, decide), as well as the different stages of these actions (begin, finish, attempt). Few are metaphorical; few have moral resonance.

To see how Caesar's verbs contribute to the literary achievement of the *Civil War*, consider a brief episode from the siege of Marseilles (2.11). Caesarian troops have just moved a siege tower up to the walls of the city. In two sentences, the problem that the town faces is set forth: "The inhabitants are terrified by this sudden problem and move forward rocks—as big as they can manage—with crowbars and roll them off the wall straight down onto our 'gallery.'"[26] The strength of the timber sustains the blow and whatever hits it rolls off the roof of the gallery. Then, the enemy's frantic realization of the failure of their initial response is presented in a sentence of twenty-two words, of which nine are verbs or verbals:

> When they <u>see</u> this, they <u>change</u> their plan: they <u>stuff</u> barrels with pitch and pine, <u>set</u> fire to them, and <u>roll</u> them off the wall onto the gallery; when they <u>roll</u> onto the gallery, they <u>fall</u> off; when they <u>fall</u> they are <u>moved</u> away from the structure with poles and pitchforks.

Then, Caesar turns to his men:

> Meanwhile, under the gallery the soldiers use crowbars to <u>remove</u> the rocks at the base of the enemy's tower, the rocks that <u>formed</u> the foundation. From a brick siege tower, the gallery is <u>protected</u> by our men with javelins and missiles; the enemy is <u>moved</u> back from their wall and towers; no unhampered opportunity for <u>protecting</u> the walls is <u>granted</u>.

There are more nouns and adjectives now, and in thirty-four words we find six verbs or verbals. Caesar brings the event to a close in one long sentence of thirty-nine words with a vivid progressive tense in the middle and a surprise at the end:

> By now a good number of stones are removed from the tower that was close by and with a sudden crash part of the tower falls; the remaining part in consequence <u>was beginning to tilt forward,</u> <u>when</u> the enemy, terrified of a sack of their city, unarmed and with suppliant-ribbons, altogether rushes forward from out of the gate and they extend their hands like suppliants to the officers and army.

After "was beginning to tilt forward"—which uses a tense not hitherto used in the episode—comes a clause that is formally subordinate ("when . . . ") but that contains the most important part of the story, the fact that the assault accomplished its goal. The surprising sentence structure reflects the surprising (and, to Caesar, gratifying) reversal of the situation at the start of the episode: the passage begins with the townspeople in terror moving forward rocks and ends with them in terror rushing forward as supplicants. In this relatively plain passage, every verb is simple and precise: everyday verbs composed for maximum effect.

2b Subordination

The passage discussed in the previous section narrated a sequence of actions and was composed primarily of main clauses. Caesar is not noted for complex sentences with subordinate clauses, but he can use subordination to good effect. In fact, complex sentences are ideally suited for presenting the thought processes that weigh conflicting claims, and that is one of the ways Caesar uses them. Concessive clauses (those that begin "although") in particular report matters that, although important enough to be considered, are in the end disregarded.[27] In Caesar, such concessive clauses generally indicate a rational decision-making process and draw the reader into the mind of the clause's subject. The description of Caesar's response to news that Corfinium was ready to capitulate, for example, is a long and complex sentence in which the reader listens to Caesar's thoughts while the Latin word order separates the subject (Caesar) and the main verb (praised): [28]

> When these things were known, Caesar, although he thought it would be advantageous to seize the town immediately and to bring the town's garrison into his own camp, lest there be a change of heart owing to bribes or renewed courage or false reports—in wartime, after all, large consequences follow from matters of small moment—nevertheless, fearing that the town would be plundered when his soldiers entered, given their generally unruly behavior at night, [Caesar] praised the emissaries and sent them back into the town and ordered a watch kept on the walls and gates. (1.21.1–2)

Here Caesar, as subject, is shown weighing options and in the end opting for order. He recognizes and explains the strategic advantage of seizing the town; then, after a general observation about war, he outlines his other concerns and arrives at his conclusion: he sends the emissaries back and orders his soldiers to keep watch.

There are two things to note in a sentence like this. The first is that Caesar presents himself as the general who, at some strategic risk to himself, decides to avoid the risk of chaos and cruelty. This is a matter of experience and values. But the form that such a sentence takes is also significant. As in English, in Latin a writer may chose between saying, "Caesar, although this was the case, nevertheless did that" and "Although this was the case, Caesar did that." In Latin, where word order is much more expressive than in English, the difference is that the first form makes the concession subordinate to the subject, implying and often even stating that the concession (what is not allowed to determine the outcome) is fully understood. The second form only implies that the actual events could have suggested another course of action.

Caesar frequently says, "Caesar, although . . . " and "Caesar, when . . . ," but he never says "Pompey, although . . . " This means that he never presents Pompey as weighing two alternatives, both of which are compelling, and then opting for a general principle like "protection of the townspeople." In fact, if we turn to the one instance in the *Civil War* in which Pompey is portrayed as conceding an important fact but adopting an unexpected strategy, we find Caesar's style making an important comment: "although Pompey had not decided to blockade Caesar and fight with all his forces, he nevertheless kept sending archers . . . and many of our men were wounded" (3.44.6). The form Caesar chooses suggests that Pompey's decision (or lack of decision) was at odds with his actions, even that Pompey overlooks his own strategy: although he wasn't going to fight, he would still harass Caesar's men. In the event, Caesar, although outnumbered, drives off the Pompeians with a sudden attack and withdraws to finish his fortifications.

2c Speeches

Speech enlivens a narrative, and Caesar includes nearly eighty speeches in the *Civil War*, but most (sixty-six) are indirectly quoted. We have discussed some of the direct speeches, which provide more opportunity for characterization, in chapter 3. Here we focus on the indirect speeches (thirty-seven in book 1, eight in book 2, twenty in book 3).[29] Their length ranges from a single sentence to a substantial harangue, but most are short. In fact, brevity is one of the advantages of the form. In the following passage, envoys from Marseilles plead with Caesar's officers for a truce:

> [They said][30] that they saw that their city was taken, that Caesar's siegeworks were complete, their own tower undermined, and that they were therefore ceasing their defense. [They said] that nothing could happen to hinder Caesar from destroying the city utterly when he arrived, if they did not do exactly what he ordered. They explained that if their tower should collapse completely the soldiers would not be able to be held back from bursting into the city in the hope of booty and destroying it. This and much more of the same type—given that they were educated men—was uttered with great pathos and lamentation. (2.12.3–4)

In the last sentence, Caesar makes a point of trimming back the clever and, as it turned out, deceitful rhetoric that moved his officers to grant a truce (2.13.1) of which the enemy promptly took advantage to make a sortie and burn the Caesarian works to the ground (2.14). Caesar expects that his readers, educated themselves and already aware of the two-facedness of this enemy (illustrated at 1.35), can do without "much more of the same type"—would dismiss it, as he does, as so much hot air.

Indirect speech also allows Caesar to focus. Here he presents his own address to his troops as they move into position at Pharsalus: "Above all he reminded his soldiers that they could themselves bear witness to how diligently he had sought peace, what he had done in his negotiations through Vatinius, what through Aulus Clodius with Scipio, how at Oricum he had discussed with Libo the sending of emissaries. He had never wasted the blood of his soldiers nor wished to deprive the state of one of its two armies" (3.90.1–2). The points did not comprise the whole of Caesar's speech, which was, he tells us, a "customary" battle exhortation (3.90.1), but rather what he later wanted to put on record in connection with what he had mistakenly hoped would be the decisive engagement in the civil war.

In one instance we can see just how Caesar's paraphrase works. We can compare his version of Pompey's response to Domitius before the capitulation of Corfinium with Pompey's own version, which is preserved in Cicero's correspondence. Caesar summarizes: "Pompey had written back that he was not going to put his cause into extreme danger, and that Domitius had concentrated himself in the town of Corfinium contrary to his (Pompey's) plan and wish. Therefore, if it was at all possible, Domitius should come to him with all his forces" (1.19.4). In fact, Pompey had responded over the course of three letters (*Att.* 8.12B, C, and D). He had conveyed his dismay at Domitius's independent decision to resist Caesar in Italy and failure to apprise Pompey thereof directly, Caesar's gathering strength, his own plan of withdrawing further south, and his repeated exhortations that Domitius should join him, along with details about the military situation in Italy. Caesar's paraphrase conveys Pompey's refusal to support Domitius and his plea that Domitius (who had an independent command) join him, but omits the reasons that Pompey gives for both, namely, his distrust of the troops available to him and his knowledge of the forces accruing to Caesar. As a result, it characterizes Pompey as frightened and without a strategy, fundamentally unreliable.

It is clear from these examples that the point of paraphrase is not only efficiency: Caesar can use paraphrase to suggest his own shrewdness and his enemies' bad faith. It can also capture or characterize the style of the "original" utterance. In the threats issued by Lentulus at the beginning of the *Civil War*, the brutal innuendo of the adverbs "boldly and bravely," which was discussed earlier (see sec. 2a.i in chap. 2), gains force from the rhetorical shape of his utterance (A-B-B-A), a figure called chiasmus: "Lucius Lentulus the consul promised the Senate that <u>he would</u> not fail the republic, <u>if</u> they were willing to speak their minds boldly and bravely; but <u>if</u> they kept an eye on Caesar and pursued his favor, as they had done in recent years, <u>he would</u> take counsel in his own interests and would not obey the Senate's authority" (1.1.3).

In another scene, the availability of two registers of reported speech allows Caesar to highlight the faulty reasoning that led to Curio's fatal mistake, and here again another factor—in this case verb tense—adds to the impact:

> When he had marched six miles, he met the cavalry and learned of their accomplishments. He asks the captives who is in command of the camp on the Bagradas River. They reply that Saburra is. The rest he omits to ask, such is his eagerness to complete the march. Looking at the nearby standards he said, "Do you see, soldiers, that the speech of the captives agrees with the fugitives? That the king is absent, that scant forces have been sent, forces that were unable to be a match for just a few horsemen? So hasten toward booty, toward glory, in order that I may be able to think about your rewards and about showing my gratitude to you."
> (2.39.1–2)

The captives' information is presented in indirect quotation: "that Saburra is." It is strikingly brief, a single word in Latin. That is part of the point: Curio's mistake was not getting more—"the rest"—out of them. If he had asked about Juba, the king who sent Saburra to Utica, for example, he would have learned that Juba was six miles away with all of his forces. Curio's response to what he does learn is quoted directly: its faulty logic, its boasting and military bombast, and its empty promises are thereby unsparingly exposed.[31] Because of this mistake, Curio and most of his men perished and Caesar's bid to control North Africa collapsed.

In this chapter we have seen both that Cicero's comment about the "nakedness" of Caesar's *commentarii* is true and that it is not the whole story. Caesar's use of adjectives and verbs is primarily plain and efficient. But against this background he can use a superlative (and frequently several in the same passage) or a stylistic ornament for powerful and damning effect. He likes to use abstract nouns in place of adjectives of emotion, but this is because, as a strategist, he sees forces at work and because he, like his veterans, gathers his experience together and makes it accessible through the application of the right noun. He reports what was said using paraphrases, often for efficiency and to focus on the significant points, but not at the expense of shadowing out the rhetoric of the speaker. His descriptions are simultaneously explanations, sometimes tendentious, and his explanations generalize about war and soldiers and night and fear. He can use simple sentences to create a sense of the rush and chaos of events and long complex sentences to suggest the thought processes that lie behind a decision. In general, every element of Caesar's style rewards close attention. It has been our purpose in this brief overview to show how the reader might begin to appreciate and analyze Caesar's choices. After all, the Roman teacher of rhetoric, Quintilian, said that of all those who lived and spoke while Rome's greatest orator, Cicero, was alive, only Caesar could have successfully competed with him.

Epilogue: Surviving Failure

> If he, with all his genius, never found a way out,
> who will now find one?
> —GAIUS MATIUS, quoted by Cicero, *Letters to Atticus* 14.1.1

1 | *Fides* after Pharsalus

The newly personal terms of political engagement that, in chapter 4, we saw Caesar developing are also visible in the historical record outside his commentaries. From Cicero's correspondence, for example, we know that after Pharsalus Caesar insisted on issuing pardons in person: he wanted to "hear each case" himself (*Att.* 11.7.2, Dec. 48).[1]

One of those whose cases Caesar eventually heard in person was Cicero himself, who, once restored to favor, turned busily to promoting the restoration of others.[2] He tells one anxious petitioner that Caesar favored requests based on personal obligations, requests, that is, made to him by his friends or by those he had already pardoned on behalf of those with whom they themselves had personal relationships:

> I have made your case more openly than my situation really warranted. The circumstance of my weakened influence was overcome by the place you have in my affections and by my long-standing and diligently reciprocated love for you. . . . Conveniently enough, I have all of Caesar's intimates

connected to me by ties of familiarity and goodwill.... This is not at all a matter of yielding to the times; I have long-standing relationships with all of them, and I have not stopped discussing your case with them. Pansa is our chief support; he is eager to serve you and wants my friendship. His influence with Caesar rests as much on personal ties as it does on political clout. Tillius Cimber has also given satisfaction. With Caesar, requests made on behalf of friends are more effective than requests that aim to make friends, and since Cimber's request on your behalf was the former type, it was more effective than it would have been on behalf of anybody else. (*Fam.* 6.12.1–2)

The addressee of this letter, one Ampius Balbus, has appealed to his dear friend Cicero, who has appealed on his behalf to a number of old friends, who in turn appeal to their friend Caesar. All of these relationships stand to be strengthened by the pardon Caesar eventually gives to Ampius Balbus; the more friendships involved the better, perhaps, since Cicero seems to see no reason to choose one string to pull over another.

This pardon is one among many issued by Caesar. But he almost did not pardon Marcus Marcellus at the request of the whole Senate (*Fam.* 4.4.3, Sept./Oct. 46) precisely because he was afraid the pardon would not be counted a favor by Marcellus (*Fam.* 4.7.3, Sept.? 46). When he did grant the pardon, the senators stood up one by one to give him their thanks (*Fam.* 4.4.3); Cicero's thanks survive in the speech *For Marcellus*.

None of this string-pulling is new in Rome, of course. What is new is that there is only one source from which satisfaction for all of these petitions will come.[3] So Caesar's personal ties are not just some of the glue holding the elite to the state, but all of it.[4] Cicero gives expression to the situation in the letter describing the Senate's exchange with Caesar over the pardon for Marcus Marcellus, mentioned above. The friendly relations created by the pardon were construed by Caesar ("to say no would be a bad omen") and seen by Cicero as a first step in the revival of *public* life: "so beautiful a day that I seemed to catch a glimpse of the republic coming back to life" (*Fam.* 4.4.3, Sept./Oct. 46). Also new is the frankness about the situation. The cozy language of some of the passages quoted above is perhaps to be expected in correspondence, but Cicero says much the same thing in his public speeches—for example, "who are more yours than those whom you made safe, little though they expected it?" (*Marc.* 21).

But it was not long before the good omen effected by Marcellus's pardon and the optimism expressed (however sincerely) by Cicero were soured by the practical difficulties of governing on the basis of personal relationships. In the fall of 46, Cicero reports that "many things are happening that don't please Caesar," who is in the position of "having to go along with those through whose assistance he got his victory" (*Fam.* 12.18.2). The "things" alluded to were not likely to go away soon, since Caesar's friends were keeping alive the flames of partisanship.[5] A particularly striking illustration of what it means to run the state "among friends" is given in a bitterly satirical passage from Cicero's correspondence about senatorial decisions made in his name but without his participation:

> Do you think there will be fewer decrees of the Senate if I am in Naples? Even when I'm in Rome and busy about the forum it is in the house of your fan, my friend [Cornelius Balbus], that senatorial decrees get written. Sometimes, if it occurs to him, I am named as "present at the writing," and I learn that a decree of the Senate on Armenia and Syria was passed—one that is said to have been made "as I recommended"—before I even know that the business came up. Don't think I'm joking. In fact, I've received letters from kings thanking me because they had been made kings "at my recommendation," kings about whom I was unaware not only that they had been made kings but even that they had ever been born. (*Fam.* 9.15.4, late 46)

Caesar, faced with the huge task of reconstructing the state and its foreign relations, operates here with no more than a nod to the prewar political system. As we will see in the next section, even those, like Cicero, who seemed to have adapted themselves to the new political reality were eventually moved to open protest. It is ironic, but telling, that the pretext Caesar's assassins—many of whom he counted as his friends—used for clustering about him on the Ides of March was their support for a request by Tillius Cimber for a pardon for his exiled brother, that is, an apparent opportunity for Caesar to make another friend.[6] Writing under the empire, the historian Florus puts it neatly: "his power of conferring favors was intolerable to free men" (2.92).

2 | Saying no and meaning it

Shortly after Caesar's assassination by his fellow senators, one of Caesar's non-senatorial friends, Gaius Matius, told Cicero that in his view the problems of the age were insoluble: "For if [Caesar], with all his genius, never found a way out, who will now find one?" (*Att.* 14.1.1, April 44). Matius was intimately familiar with Caesar's efforts to rebuild politics on personal relationships. He was, for example, someone to whom Cicero appealed when seeking pardons from Caesar for his friends (see Cic. *Fam.* 6.12, 11.27.4–5); Matius asserts proudly that he "worked as hard for pardons for my defeated fellow citizens as I did for my own preservation" (Cic. *Fam.* 11.28.2). This boast is part of a long letter written to Cicero in October of 44 in which Matius justifies his loyalty to the memory of Caesar in the face of attacks from Cicero himself (*Att.* 14.1.1) and others (*Fam.* 9.27–28 passim). In it he raises, only to quash, the argument that the republic takes precedence over a personal relationship; to have agreed, he suggests, would have shown that everything he had done since 49 was motivated by opportunism:

> When our political system came apart it was not Caesar I followed but my friend. Although I made people angry by acting as I did, I nevertheless did not desert him. Not that I ever approved of the civil war or of the cause of the breakdown. This, even as it was coming into being, I did my very

best to stem. Therefore in the victory of a friend I was snared by the sweets neither of office nor of wealth, rewards that other men, although less influential with Caesar than I was, have abused without restraint. . . . Most of those who now rejoice at Caesar's death retained their position in Rome by his favor; I worked as hard for pardons for my defeated fellow citizens as I did for my own preservation. (*Fam.* 11.28.2)

Matius's actions rest on the premise—Caesar's premise, as we have seen—that one need not choose between the republic and friendship: "Why are they angry with me if I desire that they regret their act? Indeed I want Caesar's death to be a bitter thing for everyone. As citizen I should desire the safety of the republic? But I do desire this, though if the life I have led and my remaining hopes don't prove it without me saying anything I don't expect to find the words to persuade you" (*Fam.* 11.28.4). We have no way of judging Matius's sincerity here (or the hypocrisy he faulted in his critics, who profited from Caesar's pardon but felt no real affection for him), but we can see, even before Caesar's death, increasingly outspoken support for the claims of the republic.

This form of resistance to Caesar centered on the figure of Marcus Porcius Cato, who adopted the garb and grooming of a man in mourning after the outbreak of fighting in 49, and killed himself in Utica in April of 46 after Caesar's defeat of the Pompeian forces in Africa at Thapsus.[7] In Plutarch's formulation, Cato was unwilling to be under obligation to Caesar's despotism (*Cat. min.* 66.2).

Cato's resistance to Caesar's new world order quickly gave him iconic status. Two men who capitulated, Cicero and Brutus, wrote laudatory biographies of Cato as early as 46. Cicero's, begun soon after news of Cato's death reached Rome, was complete before the winter but withheld until Caesar went off to Spain in December for his final fight against the Pompeians.[8] Cicero acknowledges to the more conciliatory Atticus that his *Cato* was not something that Atticus's Caesarian friends would want to read: "That man cannot be praised truly unless one displays the fact that he saw our present circumstances coming, exerted himself to prevent them, and left life lest he see them in place" (*Att.* 12.4.2, May? 46). The publication of Cicero's *Cato* during Caesar's absence was meant, and taken, as a protest against Caesar. Caesar responded while still in Spain with the *Anticato*, a text that took the form of a forensic speech ("as if before judges") replying to the "book in which Cicero praised Cato to the skies."[9]

Caesar's *Anticato* is an admission of failure. The work was Caesar's response to a betrayal. As we saw earlier, he put particular stock in winning Cicero's adherence after Pharsalus. But Cicero's *Cato* gave notice that he was not entirely Caesar's creature. A second *Cato*, written by Brutus, whom Caesar had also pardoned and advanced after Pharsalus, added resonance to the rumblings.[10] Caesar's whole system depended on his ability to earn loyalty; these betrayals reveal the weakness of his hold on people whose cooperation he valued.[11] Furthermore, the *Anticato* substitutes an essentially negative program of undermining the opposition for the picture of new possibilities outlined in the *Civil War*, the hoped-for new plan whereby he would "recover everyone's support and experience a lasting victory" (*Att.* 9.7C, early March 49). For the author of the *Anticato*, there was no point in finishing and publishing the *Civil War* or extending its narrative to cover the subsequent wars against Pompeians in Africa and Spain; these would not have happened if Caesar's policy had worked.

In the end both Cato and Caesar survived failure. Cato weathered the military defeat of his political allies and the political revolution directed by Caesar's heir, Augustus, as an image of resistance to tyranny. The Caesar who was murdered by his friends and whose name was once proudly borne by the heads of autocratic, imperialist states (Czar, Kaiser) lives on in the understated brilliance of his prose.

Timeline of the Life of Caesar and the Civil War

100 BCE	birth of Gaius Julius Caesar
mid–late 80s	domination of Sulla
80–78	military service, primarily in the eastern provinces of the empire
77–76	prosecutes powerful ex-Sullan senators in Rome, loses both cases
73	military service in mainland Greece
72	holds first elected office in Rome
69	serves as quaestor (a junior magistracy) in Spain; enters Senate
67	curator of the Appian Way (another junior magistracy); supports Pompey's "province" of eradicating pirates
66	sole senatorial supporter of another extraordinary command for Pompey
65	aedile (another junior magistracy); sponsors lavish shows in Rome
64	judge in charge of murder court

63	elected *pontifex maximus*; leads prosecutions; Catilinarian conspiracy
62	praetor (a senior magistracy); nearly imprisoned for debt
61	military command in Spain; earns triumph
60	forms political coalition with Pompey and Crassus
59	as consul (senior magistracy) passes laws in the interests of coalition partners and himself (command in Gaul for 58–55), as well as legislative reforms; Pompey marries Caesar's daughter, Julia
58	command in Gaul from late March; Caesar's consular legislation declared illegal
57	command in Gaul; enlists two new legions; Senate votes thanksgiving of fifteen days for successful campaign; Pompey granted five-year "province" supervising grain supply to Rome
56	command in Gaul; renewal of alliance with Pompey and Crassus
55	command in Gaul; Pompey and Crassus are consuls; Caesar's command renewed for five years; Senate agrees to pay Caesar's new legions; Pompey and Crassus get five-year commands in Spain and Syria
54	command in Gaul; revolt in Gaul, one legion destroyed, three legions added (one borrowed from Pompey); death of Julia
53	command in Gaul; Crassus defeated and killed in Syria
52	command in Gaul; Pompey sole consul; Roman People gives Caesar privilege of standing for election in absentia; revolt in Gaul

51		command in Gaul; Senate deliberates early termination of Caesar's command
50		command in Gaul; more attempts to terminate Caesar's command
49	1–10 Jan.	Caesar in Cisalpine Gaul
	1–7 Jan.	senatorial debate about Caesar's command
	7 Jan.	Caesar ordered to disband army; tribunes flee Rome
	10 Jan.	Caesar invades Italy with one legion, marches towards Rome
	21 Feb.	defeats Domitius Ahenobarbus at Corfinium
	Mar.	blockade of Pompey at Brindisi
	Mar.–Dec.	Pompey in Greece
	Apr.	Caesar returns to Rome, meets Senate, leaves for Gaul and Spain
	Apr.	Caesar briefly at Marseilles, where siege lasts until October
	Jun.–Aug.	Caesar in Nearer Spain; defeats Pompeian army under Afranius and Petreius
	Aug.–Oct.	Caesar in Further Spain and Marseilles, both capitulate
	Aug.	defeat of Curio in N. Africa
	Dec.	Caesar in Rome as dictator (eleven days), holds elections
48		consul for the second time
	Jan.	conducts state business in Rome
	Jan.	crosses to Greece with part of army
	Jan.–Aug.	Caesar in Greece

Timeline | 175

	Mar.	remainder of army crosses to Greece under Antony, joins Caesar
	Apr.–Jul.	besieges Pompey near Dyrrachium, is defeated in early July
	9 Aug.	defeats Pompey at Pharsalus
	Aug.–Sept.	settles provincial affairs (Greece, Asia Minor)
	late Sept.	Pompey murdered in Alexandria by agents of king Ptolemy
	Oct.–Dec.	Caesar in Alexandria, undertakes to settle dynastic dispute
	Oct.	Cicero returns to Italy
47	dictator (through November)	
	Jan.–Mar.	Caesar in Alexandria, besieged until reinforcements arrive; after his victory and the death of Ptolemy, installs Cleopatra as ruler
	Apr.–May	trip up Nile with Cleopatra
	Jun.–Aug.	settles provincial affairs (Syria, Judaea, Cilicia); fights brief war against Pharnaces, king of Pontus; defeats Pharnaces at Zela; settles provincial affairs (Black Sea area, Asia Minor)
	Aug.–Sept.	travels toward Rome; pardons enemies, including Cicero
	Oct.–Dec.	Caesar in Rome: holds elections, gathers funds, recruits soldiers, pardons enemies
	Jan.–Dec.	Caesar's enemies regroup in Africa and Spain
	late Dec.	Caesar takes army to North Africa

46		consul for the third time; 445-day year owing to calendar reform
	Jan.–Jun.	Caesar in N. Africa
	6 April	battle of Thapsus
	April	Cato's suicide at Utica
	Apr.–Jun.	settles provincial affairs (N. Africa, Sardinia)
	Jul.–Nov.	Caesar in Rome: quadruple triumph (for wars in Gaul, Alexandria, Pontus, and N. Africa); extraordinary honors (e.g., ten-year dictatorship), veteran settlements, pardons, including Marcellus and Ligarius; legislative reforms, including calendar
	Nov.–Dec.	Caesar takes army to Spain
	late 46	publication of Cicero's *Cato*
45		consul for the fourth time
	Jan.–Jun.	Caesar in Spain; writes *Anticato*
	17 March	defeats Pompey's sons at battle of Munda
	Mar.–Jul.	settles provincial affairs (Spain, Gaul)
	Oct.–Dec.	Caesar in Rome: celebrates triumph for civil war victory in Spain; extraordinary honors (e.g., lifetime dictatorship); designates magistrates for future years
44		consul for the fifth time
	Jan.–Mar.	Caesar in Rome
	15 March	assassinated in Senate meeting

Maps

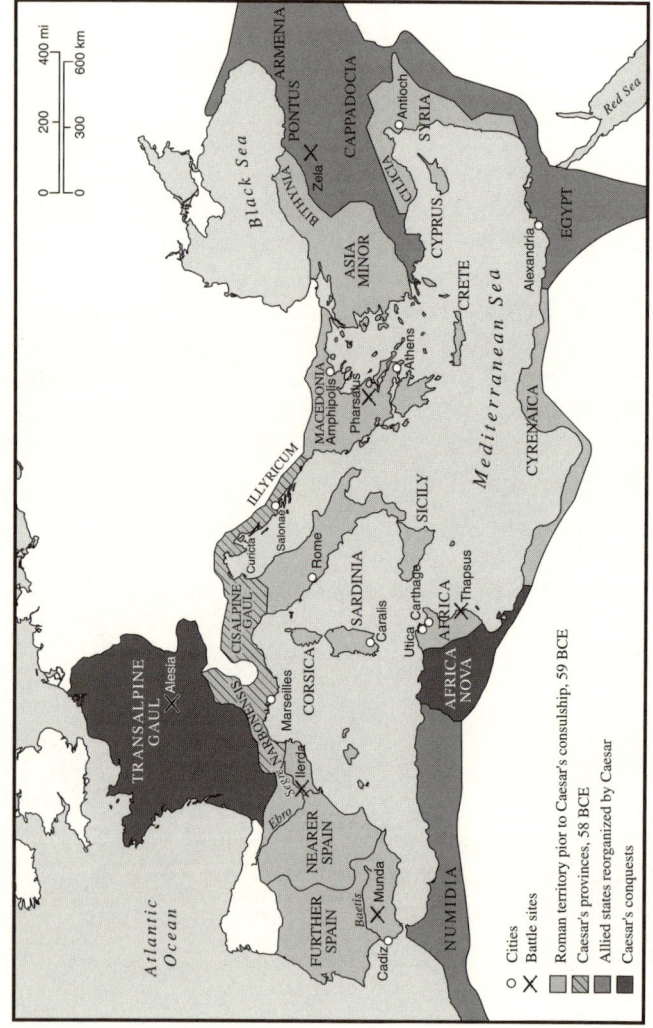

MAP 1

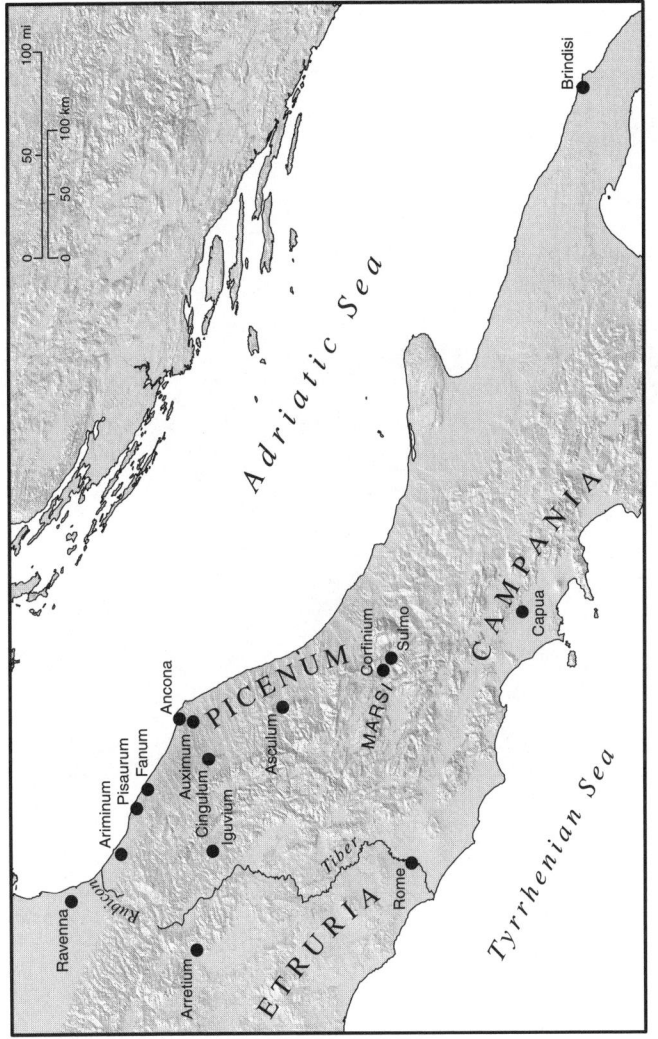

MAP 2

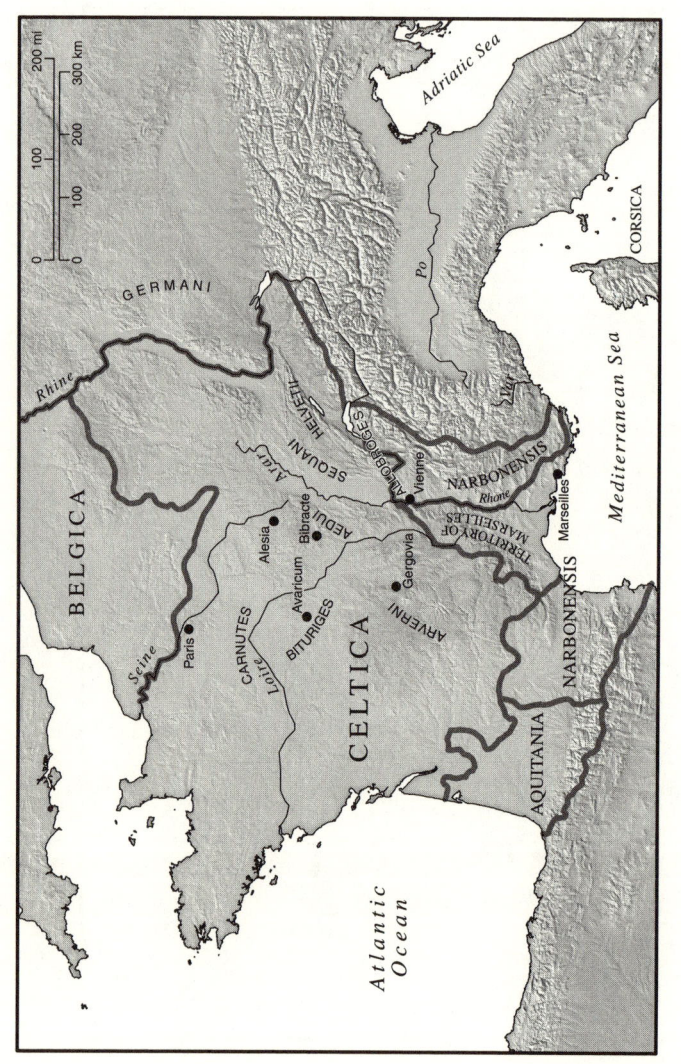

MAP 3

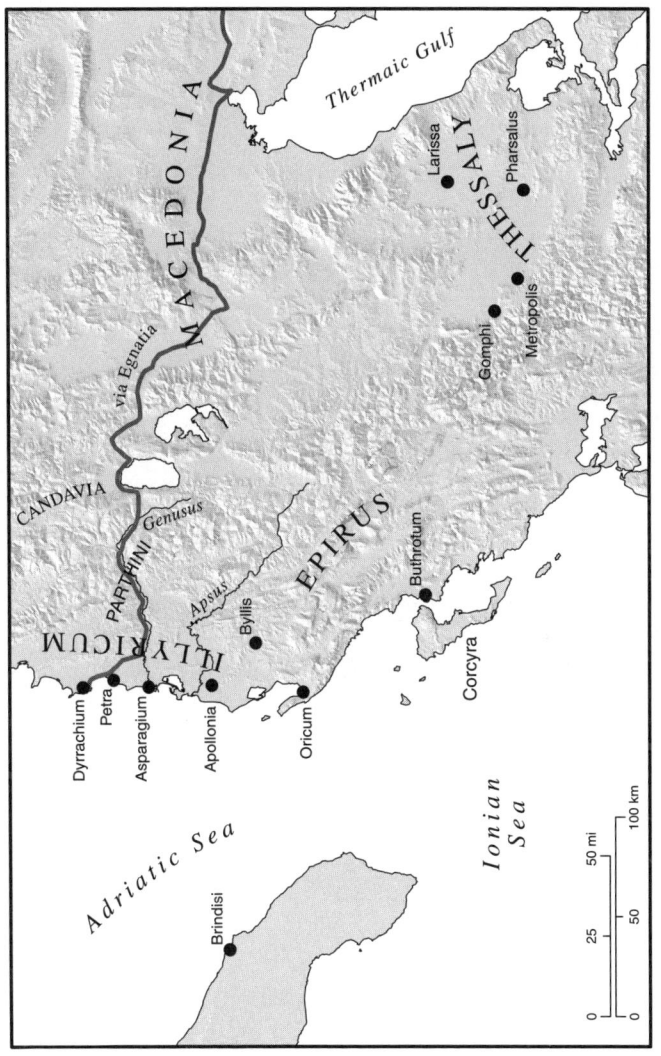

MAP 4

Notes

INTRODUCTION

1. Sulla posted lists of his enemies in the forum. When a man's name appeared on the list (in Latin, he was *proscriptus*, "proscribed"), he lost his citizenship and all legal protections: he could be murdered with impunity and the murderer would receive part of his estate, while the rest would go to Sulla.

CHAPTER 1

1. Hirtius, *Gallic War* 8 preface 2: "our friend Caesar's *commentarii* on his achievements in Gaul"; cf. preface 4: "of those *commentarii*"; Cicero, *Brutus* 262: "*commentarii* on his achievements."
2. *Gallic War* 8.4.3, referring back to 7.90.7; cf. 8.30.1, referring back to 7.5–8, and 8.38.3, referring back to 7.2–3.
3. For a survey see Marincola 180–82, 195–97, and Riggsby chapter 5.
4. See Cic. *Sull.* 67 for reference to the letter and the fact that it was known to others besides the addressee; according to the Bobbio Scholiast it was as long as a book. For the other works see *Att.* 1.19.10 (March 60).
5. Cf. *Att.* 2.1.2 (June 60): Greek writers had been pressing him for something that they could "dress up" (*quod ornarent*).

6. The Latin term *elegans*, which we translate as "elegant," means something like "fastidious in its attention to selecting the right word; precise." For Cicero's "naked" see chapter 5.

7. On book division in the *Civil War* see chapter 2.

8. *Att.* 7.13a.3, 24 January 49; *Att.* 8.5.2, 22 February 49.

9. Other campaigns whose outcomes keep Cicero in unhappy suspense in 49 are those at Brindisi (*Att.* 8.13.1; cf. *Att.* 8.14.1, etc.), in Spain (*Att.* 10.8.1, 10.12A.3), and at Marseilles (*Att.* 10.12A.3). All get detailed narratives from Caesar.

10. By 1 March, Cicero could predict the effect of Caesar's leniency: "If he does not kill anyone, or deprive anyone of property, he will be loved by those who most feared him. I have had many a conversation with men from the towns and countryside around here: they care about nothing but their fields, their country houses, their bank accounts" (*Att.* 8.13.1–2).

11. *Civil War* 1.33.2; cf. Cic. *Marc.* 18, *Lig.* 33, *Att.* 11.6.6, Suet. *DJ* 75.1.

12. The exception is Cleopatra, who is mentioned as a participant in the dynastic struggles in Ptolemaic Egypt (3.103.2, 3.107.2). Her liaison with Caesar (see, e.g., Dio 42.37) is not part of Caesar's narrative.

13. As a consequence, Caesar gives a minimum of background information on the people he names, usually no more than military or political office or social rank. For some striking exceptions see note 24 below.

14. Similarly, although Caesar does not mention the fact that Tullus's father, who was consul in 66, was prominent among the senators conciliatory toward Caesar in early 49, that too may be relevant to his inclusion here: see Cic. *Att.* 7.3.3, 8.1.3, 8.9a.1, etc.

15. For Afranius see Carter's note on *Civil War* 1.38.1; for Fabius see *Gallic War* 5–8 passim.

16. Trebonius was also one of Caesar's assassins . . . but that is another story.

17. Lucius Caesar, 1.8.2; Lucius Roscius, 1.8–10; Numerius Magius, 1.24.4–5; Caninius Rebilus and Scribonius Libo, 1.26.3–6; Lucius Vibullius Rufus, 3.10–11; Marcus Atilius and Staius Murcus, 3.15–17; Aulus Clodius 3.57.

18. For a similar conclusion about the *Gallic War* see Welch 101–2.

19. The Pompeian cause was discredited by its association with Juba (see sec. 5 in chap. 3).

20. *Att.* 9.18.2, 9.19.2, 10.1a, 10.3a.2, 10.14.3, etc. The father wins a pardon and later promotion from Caesar after Pharsalus; he is governor of Achaea in 46.

21. The son survived until 43 at least (Cic. *Phil.* 9.12) and perhaps later (Broughton 3: 203).

22. Damasippus and Scipio died together immediately after their defeat at Thapsus (*African War* 96).

23. R. Brown comments aptly, "The vivid and sarcastic particularities of the sketch are worthy of the finest satire" (344).

24. One may compare two passages where Caesar, contrary to his habit, supplies background information. At 2.28.1, before a discreditable and ineffective rhetorical effort by Sextus Quintilius Varus, Caesar reminds the reader that Varus was one of the senators captured and released at Corfinium. And at 3.67.5, in connection with a defeat inflicted on Titus Pullienus, he reminds the reader that Pullienus had earlier betrayed a Caesarian army (referring back to an episode meant for but absent from book 2; see section 4 of this chapter). The practical failures of these men are in his view connected with their earlier moral lapses.

25. A fragment from an unknown tragedy by Sophocles (Radt 873).

26. Appian names the soldier as Sempronius; all other sources report his name as Septimius.

27. That such an edition was in preparation shortly after Caesar's death is clear from Hirtius's statement that he "wove together" the *Gallic* and *Civil Wars* and carried the narrative on to the end of Caesar's life (*Gallic War* 8 preface 2). The corpus as we have it is not precisely what Hirtius describes here, since its last three works are by three different authors, all anonymous. But our corpus is preserved as a unit in one branch of the manuscript tradition, which suggests that a "collected edition" of the Caesarian wars was eventually made.

28. The story is told by Appian (*Civil War* 2.41, 47), Dio (41.40), and Lucan (4.402–580).

29. Pollio's remark is paraphrased at Suet. *DJ* 56.4; the specific criticism of the Pharsalus narrative is mentioned at Plut. *Caes.* 46.3. For a careful analysis of the context in Suetonius see Lossmann; for the purpose of Pollio's remark see Morgan 55–60.

30. Jehne 168–71 argues that in 47 the potential political utility of the *Civil War* was such as to prompt Caesar to publish it, imperfect as it was. He likens it to a work of journalism, where faults are tolerated so long as publication is timely. Holding up publication for perfection makes sense, he says, for an "ambitious author," but not for a "propagandist working from day to day" (n. 108). It is our contention that Caesar was an ambitious author.

31. See Carter 1991: 216–18.

32. Whether he wrote some of it—say, the campaigns of 49—earlier is impossible to determine and irrelevant to the larger question at issue here. For discussion see MacFarlane.

33. No, according to Boatwright. For the law see Sumner, esp. 265.

34. No, according to Collins 1959: "it is a work *republican* through and through" (117). Caesar's abuse of republican tradition is a topic in Suetonius's biography (see *DJ* 76–77).

35. Raditsa 434.

36. See, e.g., Meier 437–52, and the contemporary views discussed in section 5 of chapter 3.

37. A political argument has also been offered for the absence of a narrative from Caesar's pen on his final two seasons in Gaul, 51–50 BCE; see Welch 86: he "abandoned the account of the Gallic campaigns when they became inconvenient."

CHAPTER 2

1. In Latin, the phrase translated in the epigraph as "take account of" (*rationem habere*) can, depending on context, mean "hold an election," "audit an account," or "consider an argument." Cicero represents Caesar as saying "Hold my election" and himself as responding, in the same words with a different meaning, "Consider our reasoning." The exchange captures the contentiousness of the political issues underlying the war and the need for the argument Caesar makes in the *Civil War*.

2. The book's final battle takes place on 2 August 49. On the division between books 1 and 2 see section 2 of this chapter.

3. This Celtic people was attempting to migrate from its territory in (modern) Switzerland into Gaul.

4. At *Gallic War* 8.48.10 Hirtius defends his decision to record two years in his one book: "I know that Caesar composed the records of individual years in individual books. I didn't think I needed to do this, because the next year [50 BCE] contained no significant achievements [*res gestae*] in Gaul."

5. For the manuscript evidence on book division see V. Brown 82–87. In brief, books 1 and 2 are distinct numbered books in two of the three "branches" generated (by centuries of copying) from the original manuscript "stem."

6. There is some question as to whether Caesar would have begun his commentary without explanation or introduction, and without detailing the contents of his letter, but the letter was delivered to the consuls at the Senate meeting on 1 January, so if there is something missing, as is suggested by the fact that the end of the contiguous *Gallic War* 8 is missing in the manuscript tradition, it is not likely to be very much.

7. Caesar exaggerates in saying "the tribunes of the people," since only two of the ten tribunes supported Caesar's side.

8. Pompey himself could not attend a meeting of the Senate in the city because he held military command and so had to remain outside of the civic boundary. But he was nearby, watching and directing.

9. Caesar had ten legions in Gaul, but evidence as to the number of his legions at the outset of the civil war, after two had been transferred to Pompey, is conflicting (as is often the case with ancient numbers): Hirtius says nine (*Gallic War* 8.54.4), Cicero eleven (*Att.* 7.7.6, mid-December 50), Plutarch ten (*Pomp.* 58).

10. Pompeian confusion becomes thematic: "in haste and confusion" (1.5.1), "in utter confusion" (1.73.1).

11. *hi omnes* convicio *L. Lentuli consulis* correpti *exagitabantur. Lentulus sententiam Calidi pronuntiaturum se omnino negavit, Marcellus* perterritus conviciis *a sua sententia discessit. sic vocibus consulis,* terrore *praesentis exercitus,* minis *amicorum Pompei plerique* compulsi inviti *et* coacti *Scipionis sententiam sequuntur.* The causal clauses ("because of") are parallel in structure, not wording, in the Latin.

12. Pompey was married to Caesar's daughter, Julia, from 59 until her death in 54.

13. Caesar's rhetoric is so effective that a decree of the Senate entrusting the republic to the protection of magistrates and promagistrates is today known as "The Final Decree of the Senate" (*senatus consultum ultimum*, abbreviated *s.c.u.*). In Latin, however, the name appears only here, where Caesar, perhaps with some irony and contempt, calls it "that last and final decree."

14. Ten verbs are not passive, among them the bland "to be," "to happen," and "to have."

15. We paraphrase Carter's text here: "without taking auspices" is an emendation based on Plut. *Caes.* 34.1, *Pomp.* 61.4.

16. This speech, like others in ancient historical texts, is not a verbatim record of what was said at the time but rather a distillation of what suits the present narrative context.

17. *omnium temporum iniurias inimicorum in se commemorat; a quibus* deductum ac depravatum *Pompeium queritur* invidia atque obtrectatione *laudis suae, cuius ipse* honori et dignitati *semper* faverit adiutorque fuerit.

18. Caesar here supplies the argument for his position in the exchange reported by Cicero in the chapter epigraph (see note 1).

19. The following paragraphs are based on Batstone 1991, which provides a more detailed analysis.

20. In this passage we translate Carter's text, which (following one manuscript) reads "will fail" (*defuturum*) where other manuscripts read "will be" (*futurum*).

21. Conducting war: *Gallic War* 5.11; 7.21, 71, 76; *Civil War* 1.25, 36; 2.12; 3.112. Governing the republic: *Gallic War* 6.20; *Civil War* 1.32; 2.18.

22. For how Caesar solves the problem of ending book 2 with Curio's defeat see chapter 3.

23. For the data underlying this survey see the appendix to chapter 2.

CHAPTER 3

1. Numerous letters survive from the period immediately preceding the outbreak of armed conflict (roughly a dozen in the period Oct.–Dec. 50, ninety from Jan. to May 49), even more from the years 47 and 46, when Cicero had left the Pompeian party and moved closer, and finally into, the group of those acquiescing in Caesar's political dominance (roughly a hundred in the period Nov. 48–Dec. 46). There are almost no letters, however, from the period when Cicero was in Greece with Pompey (May 49–Oct. 48; only *Att.* 9.1–4a and *Fam.* 14.6 to his family, *Fam.* 8.17 and 9.9 from friends to Cicero), and there is nothing after February 49 from the diehard Pompeians. We thus have a fairly rich array of Cicero-centered commentary, both prospective and retrospective, on the civil war, but little contemporary with the fighting.

2. Other segments of Caesar's audience—provincials, posterity—needed basic information about the events of the war (see sec. 2a of chap. 1), and Caesar's original partisans needed to see their support rewarded (see sec. 4 of chap. 4).

3. On Pompey's career under Sulla see Seager 196–97. A passage including the names of Pompey's victims and the label is quoted by Valerius Maximus (6.2.8) from a speech from the 50s.

4. Cic. *Att.* 9.16.2, quoted in the chapter epigraph. In this same letter

he says that Cicero's approval of his leniency at Corfinium causes him to "celebrate a triumph of joy" (*Att.* 9.16.2).

5. Here, Caesar's readers will judge Varro credulous, for Caesar has just said that the reports on which Varro relied were letters from Afranius about his meager successes in Nearer Spain, letters whose tone was "rather expansive and exaggerated" (2.17.4; cf. 1.53.1, where the same letters are described as "rather full, even fulsome"). See also n. 10 below on Curio's credulity.

6. Cf. Varro's reference to Caesarian desertions at 2.18.3. As we will see, Caesar looks for opportunities to show the Pompeians suffering setbacks they believed themselves capable of inflicting and doing things they had criticized in Caesar.

7. Before 50 he had been an opponent; his change of allegiance was widely thought to have been bought (see Gelzer 178–79). In the *Civil War* and in Hirtius he appears unheralded on Caesar's side (1.12.1, *Gallic War* 8.52.4–5).

8. Caesar's narrative gives some justification for Curio's contempt: Varus had already suffered humiliation at Caesar's hands (1.13.4), his command in Africa was of dubious legitimacy (1.31.2; cf. Cic. *Lig.* 22), and his two legions were new recruits (1.31.3).

9. The historical Curio is unlikely to have known of these victories at this point: Caesar mentions the arrival of "news and letters about Caesar's successes in Spain" only at 2.37.2, at least two days after the speech. Varro's capitulation in Further Spain, which is mentioned in Curio's speech (2.32.13), occurred after Curio's death (see timeline).

10. Like Varro (see n. 5 above), Curio bases his confidence on exaggerated reports of military success (2.39.4). Caesar knows better: "men are inclined to boast about their own successes" (ibid.).

11. Pompey also avoids opportunities for battle at 3.44, 3.55, 3.73.5, 3.82.2, 3.85.2.

12. The walls eventually reached more than fifteen miles in length and were still incomplete when abandoned (3.63.3).

13. The speech is well discussed by R. Brown 345–48.

14. For other important features of the battle—e.g., the heroics of Caesar's officer Crastinus, and the Pompeian betrayal of their own troops—see section 4b of chapter 4 and section 3 of this chapter.

15. Labienus was a legate throughout Caesar's governorship (58–50) and is mentioned in every book of the *Gallic War*. An extended period of independent command is reported at *Gallic War* 7.57–62.

16. Dio 37.26–27, Suet. *DJ* 12.1. See Syme 1938, esp. 119.

17. *Gallic War* 8.52.2. Textual difficulties complicate the interpretation of this passage; see Gelzer 186 n. 3.

18. Cicero cheered: "I call Labienus a hero," he says on 23 January 49, "it is the finest political action we have seen for a long while. If he has achieved nothing else, he has made Caesar smart" (*Att.* 7.13.1).

19. Labienus met his death in battle in Spain, in the last wave of resistance to Caesar's domination (*Spanish War* 31.9).

20. See Carter 1993: 208: "Labienus often operated quite separately from his commander in Gaul (for example, he was left behind when Caesar crossed to Britain in 54, and he had no part in the fighting at Gergovia in 52), and Caesar surely expected his readers to know this."

21. R. Brown (347) calls the speech "a masterpiece of Caesarian misrepresentation."

22. The full form of his name as given in the heading reflects his retention of the cognomina of his birth family (the Cornelii Scipiones, who also used Nasica) after his adoption into the Caecilii Metelli (who also used Pius).

23. The prosecution Scipio feared may have been for debt; see Cic. *Att.* 9.11.4, March 49.

24. Calvinus was a good status-match for Scipio: praetor in 56 and consul in 53, he held both offices in the years immediately preceding Scipio's tenure. He was one of the highest ranking men to fight for Caesar (see Bruhns 39). He faced Scipio again at the battle of Pharsalus (3.88.3; cf. 3.89.3) and was Caesar's deputy in Asia Minor thereafter (see *Alexandrian War* 34–41).

25. See esp. *Att.* 11.10–15, Jan.–May 47. In July of 47 Cicero says that Caesar's regime seems likely to collapse (*Att.* 11.25).

26. See *African War* 19.3, 25.1, 52.1, 57, 74.2, 85.4 for his influence, 94 for his suicide pact with Petreius.

27. *Fam.* 9.18.2, July 46; Cicero names, besides those whose deaths Caesar recorded in the *Civil War* (Domitius, Pompey, Spinther), those who died in North Africa (Metellus Scipio, Afranius). Only Cato died well (see Epilogue).

CHAPTER 4

1. The balance of the Alexandrian war and the war against Pharnaces in Asia Minor, as well as campaigns in Illyricum and Spain, are narrated in the misleadingly titled *Alexandrian War* in the Caesarian corpus.

2. Caesar, though later famous for his clemency, does not use that term or its cognates for his policies in the *Civil War*. It is first prevalent in Cicero's writings, particularly so in the speech *For Marcellus* (e.g., 1, 9, 12, 18), but also in the correspondence. See Griffin.

3. The technical term for this kind of internal dialogue, which is much discussed by linguists and narratologists, is "free indirect discourse."

4. Our phrasing illustrates the effect: "no fewer than twelve" is an emphatic way of saying "twelve," since it prompts the reader to think that twelve is really quite a lot, that one would have expected fewer.

5. Cf. 2.33.3 on the Pompeian general Varus ("not even Varus hesitated to lead out his troops") and 3.32.6 on a Pompeian fleet commander ("nor did he . . . desist from his attempt").

6. 1.71.1; 3.67.4; 3.94.3.

7. Verbs denoting fear are associated with Caesar twelve times, Caesar's men five times, Pompeians nine times. The two verbs represented by this count, *timeo* and *vereor*, particularly in participial forms, often indicate caution. Terms closer to panic, for example *perterritus*, are applied more often to Pompeians (five times) than to Caesarians (three times), and not at all to Caesar.

8. 3.42.1, 3.43.1–2, 3.44.3–4, 3.54.1, 3.58.1, 3.63.1–4, 3.65.3, 3.66.2.

9. Dio, by contrast, reports a thorough punishment: "At the time [of their capitulation] he took away their weapons and ships and money, and later everything else except the name of freedom" (41.25.3).

10. Caesar and Caesarians take preventive measures against possible fear in their soldiers at, for example, 1.41.4 and 3.84.4.

11. Imperturbability is not a trait assigned to Caesar in the biographical tradition, where he is, if anything, unusually irritable and given to emotional excess. Plutarch, for example, makes Caesar thoroughly despondent after Dyrrachium (*Caes.* 39.9–10).

12. Silence is deemed appropriate again at 3.66.7: "his plans having changed for certain reasons that it is not necessary to mention."

13. At 3.18.5, 3.57.5, 3.60.4, 3.86.1.

14. For forbearance (*patientia*) see 1.32.4, 1.85.11; cf. also 1.9.1, 1.21.1, 1.23.3. Cicero praises Caesar for this virtue at *Lig.* 35: "he is accustomed to forget nothing but injuries."

15. This section has much in common with Wistrand, but our emphasis is on Caesar's presentation of his loyalty-based commonwealth in the *Civil War* rather than on its historicity.

16. Details of their "successes"—an allusion to, among other things, the tangible rewards of victory—are hard to come by, since money is "the great

silence of the 'Bellum Gallicum' (almost nothing is said of that tremendous flow of wealth that Caesar scooped from Gaul and distributed with princely liberality and well-considered selection of recipients)" (Collins 1972: 938). Caesar does tell us of a centurion motivated by his hope of riches from Caesar (*Gallic War* 7.47.1; cf. 7.50.4, 7.52.1), and Hirtius mentions booty on several occasions (*Gallic War* 8.5.9, 8.27.5, 8.36.5). For rewards in the *Civil War* see section 4a.

17. Suetonius summarizes the speech as follows: "he called upon the *fides* of his soldiers" (*DJ* 33). Cf. Wistrand 39: "the moral backbone of the Caesarians is their personal loyalty to Caesar." See Wistrand 39–43 for further appeals to this ideology.

18. According to Lucan, Petreius's action gave Caesar a moral edge over his opponents (4.258–59).

19. See the narratives at 2.19.3 (Corduba), 2.19.4 (Carmona), 2.20.1–4 (Cadiz), 2.20.2 (tribunes and centurions).

20. Similarly at 3.1.4–5, where Caesar reports his active support for a law recalling citizens who had been convicted and exiled in the anomalous judicial conditions of the year 52, when Pompey was sole consul. The exiles had offered their services to him early in the war, and when he is in Rome late in 49 he returns the favor "as if he had taken up their offer," though he hadn't.

21. For other collective testimonials see 1.13.5, where Caesar thanks "the soldiers of Attius" and "the citizens of Auximum," and 3.13.5, where he mentions "cities that have deserved well of me."

22. The only time Pompey is shown giving thanks is in connection with the battle of Dyrrachium (3.82.1), for which, according to Caesar's analysis (see sec. 2), his men did not deserve it.

23. The episode is well discussed at R. Brown 350–52.

24. A similar episode, similarly highlighted by direct speech, occurs at 3.64.3. Cf. also Caesar's praise for a centurion who perished in Spain (1.46.4).

25. See n. 6 in chapter 3.

26. Caesar's comment that the military situation made him reluctant to consider punishing the men at that time, his term "deferred," and later his conjecture that the brothers themselves were afraid that punishment might still be in the offing (3.60.3) suggest that his offer is conditional; on the (limited) evidence of the *Civil War*, Caesar gives people a second chance, but not a third. He makes a point of showing that those who betray his trust in some signal fashion commit further misdeeds. In addition to these

brothers (on whom see 3.79.6), there are follow-up stories on a man who betrayed a Caesarian army in Illyricum (3.67.5) and a man who was pardoned at Corfinium but continued to resist Caesar (2.28.1). Similarly, pardons were granted once but not twice. Caesar's policy is illustrated at *African War* 64.1, where Caesar captures a man who had been released in Spain, gone back to Pompey, fled the field at Pharsalus, and continued to resist in Africa: "on account of his false oath and broken promise Caesar ordered him killed."

27. After Pharsalus a number of senators fled rather than accept an offer of safety from Caesar (3.97.5, with 3.98.2 for the offer).

28. For Calvinus's rank see note 24 in chapter 3.

29. See Wistrand 1–26.

30. The evidence survives in the correspondence of Cicero, who in March of 49 communicates Spinther's expressions of gratitude to Atticus (*Att.* 9.11.1, 9.13.7) and Caesar himself (*Att.* 9.11A.3). Despite his gratitude to Caesar, however, Spinther remained Pompeian.

31. Compare Pompey's protest at 3.18.4, "What use to me is either life or citizen status, if I will seem to possess it by Caesar's favor?"

CHAPTER 5

1. Caesar's style has had an abiding fascination; for other, more specialized, approaches, see von Albrecht, Eden, Gotoff. The introduction to Carter 1991 offers a helpful overview. We focus on elements of style that can be observed on virtually every page of the *Civil War* and appreciated in translation.

2. For the exceptions—first-person forms referring to Caesar as author, not participant—see section 3 in chapter 4. Other first-person forms are found only in speeches.

3. For Themistogenes as author see Xenophon, *Hellenica* 3.1.102; for Plutarch's comment see *Moralia* 345E.

4. Caesar is named 402 times, to be precise; Pompey 258 times. The frequency of "Caesar" in Caesar's *commentarii* distinguishes them from the works of Xenophon and Thucydides (and others), in which the author is an occasional third-person actor in the narrative.

5. See Nousek chapter 3 for the argument that Caesar's use of the third person for his own military achievements in Gaul facilitates comparison between "Caesar" and other military leaders in the narrative.

6. This argument is made by (among others) Adcock: "the use of the third person has an air of objectivity, almost of detachment, which may subtly win the reader's assent" (74).

7. The occurrences of "Pompey" by paragraph are: one in 1; five in 2; four in 3; two in 4; none in 5.

8. 2.1–4, 2.6–11, and 2.24–27.

9. This passage is quoted by Lieberg in an excellent discussion of Caesar's use of the third person in the *Gallic War*, 33–34.

10. See Marincola's Appendix 5. Only Caesar uses "our" in a civil war narrative.

11. Quoted by Cicero, *Brutus* 253.

12. Less salient but nevertheless present are the technical terms of Roman politics (e.g., "civil," "tribunician") and the technical terms of finance (e.g., "borrowed," "financial").

13. Similarly at 3.44.3, 3.48.2, 3.63.6, 3.65.1 (twice).

14. Like places, times receive strategic assessments as "advantageous" or "disadvantageous."

15. Rivers in Spain are "in spate" (*rapidus*) and even "in full spate" (*rapidissimus*). By contrast, the river Bagradas (modern Majerda), which is mentioned several times in the account of Curio's North African campaign, is never characterized as to speed by Caesar and is never a factor in the fighting; Lucan describes it as "sluggish" (*lentus*, 4.588). Similarly one-sided attention is given to autumn (if qualified, "severe," 3.2.3) and winter (if qualified, "extremely severe," 3.8.4).

16. Other qualities, like bravery and speed, are not typically found in adjectives. For instance, Caesar never calls his soldiers "speedy," though "speedily" (*celeriter*) is one of his favorite adverbs (thirty-three times in the *Civil War*) and "speed" (*celeritas*) a favorite abstract noun (fourteen times in the *Civil War*). Likewise absent from the *Civil War* is "loyal" (*fidus*), despite the importance of loyalty to the program of the work (see sec. 4 in chap. 4). The virtues underrepresented by adjectives show up more often in adverbs, where they modify actions rather than people. Thus, in addition to "speedily," we find "vigorously," "boldly," "patiently," "very calmly," and "knowledgeably," to name a few. On the blame side, Caesar uses "rashly" and "badly" more than the corresponding adjectives. For abstract nouns ("eagerness," "firmness," etc.) see section 1c.

17. Cf. 1.12.3: "highest goodwill" (*summa voluntas*), again on Iguvium. Other superlatives mark the accession of Auximum (1.15.1: "with most eager enthusiasm") and Cingulum (1.15.2: "most eagerly").

18. One may compare the Pompeians' praise of those who spoke "most harshly and most cruelly" (*acerbissime crudelissimeque*) in the opening chapters of the *Civil War* (1.2.8).

19. For the phrase and its context see Stadter.

20. Other occurrences of the term (*vitia*) refer to problems in fortifications (1.81.3, 3.63.7), leadership (3.57.2, 3.72.4), or human nature (2.4.4).

21. The tactical considerations underlying such expressions emerge from definitions of distance, such as the description of the access route to Ilerda ("only so wide that three cohorts in formation filled it"), and the specification of gaps between combatants (3.51.7: "only so distant from our guardpost that missiles couldn't reach them"; 3.55.1 and 3.92.1 are similar), and the capacity of a fleet (3.2.2: "only so many ships that fifteen thousand legionaries and six hundred cavalry men could at a pinch be transported").

22. Cf. Carter ad loc.: "His purpose is to portray Pompey as a Goliath to his own David." The anaphora of *magnus* here may be a jab at Pompeius Magnus, "Pompey the Great" (Elaine Fantham, in personal communication).

23. In Latin the effect is stronger still, since the word translated by "in fact" is placed between the two parts of Lentulus's name (*Luci etiam Lentuli*).

24. It is clear from the next sentence (3.96.2: "And these men used to reproach Caesar's exceedingly impoverished and patient army with luxury, an army that always lacked every necessity!") that the two sides traded reproaches on this score. See Rossi on the historiographical precedents for this scene, especially Herodotus 9.80, and the argument that Caesar is here likening Pompey to an Oriental potentate, for which see also Tronson passim and Goldsworthy 211–12.

25. The saying is quoted by Aulus Gellius, *Attic Nights* 10.1.4.

26. This was a wooden roof protecting Caesar's soldiers as they undermined the city's fortifications.

27. The following discussion is based on Batstone 1990, which studies Caesar's use of concessive clauses in both *Gallic War* and *Civil War* and discusses examples in greater depth than is possible here.

28. The separation is too great for English, hence the repeated subject in our translation.

29. Figures from Hyart 174–75.

30. The indirect quotation, as often, lacks an initial introductory verb in Caesar's Latin. Word forms indicate that a quotation is indirect even without a Latin equivalent of "they said."

31. Direct quotation is also used to mark a fatal mistake by Caesarian legates in the *Gallic War* (5.30.1–3).

EPILOGUE

1. This was true at least for cases that involved members of Rome's political elite. According to Suetonius, after the battle of Pharsalus Caesar allowed each of his men to save anyone he pleased from the opposite party (Suet. *DJ* 75.2); Caesar is silent on this point.

2. Plut. *Cic.* 39.3–4. Cicero was a prize acquisition for Caesar's party. He boasts at *Fam.* 4.13.2, Aug. 46, "I can't think of anything to desire that Caesar doesn't give me unasked." Two books featuring Cicero were being written by Caesarians or would-be Caesarians in 46: Trebonius compiled a book of Ciceronian *bons mots* (*Fam.* 15.21, Dec. 46), and Aulus Caecina (who was seeking restoration) wrote a tribute to Cicero, perhaps to Cicero as orator (*Fam.* 6.7, late 46 or early 45). Caecina must have thought the work would increase his claim on Caesar.

3. On the resentment of Caesar as sole source see also Nicolaus, *Life of Augustus* 63.

4. "Personal" ties reach beyond the elite: Caesar makes a favorable response to a petition delivered by his friend Cicero on behalf of Cicero's friend Atticus on behalf of the people of Buthrotum, with whom Atticus had a long-standing connection (*Att.* 16.16A.4, July 44).

5. *Fam.* 6.12.3, Aug./Sept. 46. Cf. *Lig.* 15, late 46, where Cicero says (to Caesar) that Caesar's friends want him to be cruel. On resentment harbored by his longtime friends at his good treatment of new friends see also Nicolaus, *Life of Augustus* 62–63.

6. Plut. *Caes.* 66.5, *Brut.* 17.2, App. *Civil War* 2.117. Tillius Cimber was one of the friends Cicero expected to be helpful in winning a pardon for Ampius Balbus (*Fam.* 6.12; see discussion in text).

7. For the mourning see Plut. *Cat. min.* 53.1; cf. 56.4 for additional signs of mourning adopted after Pharsalus. His death scene is written up in Plut. *Cat. min.* 66–70, App. *Civil War* 2.98–99, Dio 43.10–11, and other sources.

8. Cicero's *Cato* was being copied in July 46 (*Fam.* 16.22). Brutus's *Cato* (being copied March 45; see Cic. *Att.* 12.21.1, March 45) added to the betrayal, as did his marriage (June 45) to Cato's daughter Porcia.

9. Description from Tac. *Ann.* 4.34.4. Caesar's *Anticato* was at least in part a deconstruction of Cicero's *Cato* (see Cic. *Top.* 94); Plutarch cites but does not credit the view of unnamed others that the *Anticato* was written not out of hatred, but as a political document (*Caes.* 54.3–4).

10. This suggestion is reinforced by the fact that Cicero credits Brutus in writing for having encouraged him to undertake the *Cato* in the first place (*Orator* 35, published October 46); one of Cicero's correspondents says that Cicero made Brutus his "ally" thereby (*Fam.* 6.7.4, Dec. 46 or early 45). Both Hirtius and later Octavian also wrote replies to the *Cato(nes)* (Hirtius: Cic. *Att.* 12.40.1, 12.41.4, March and May 45; Octavian: Suet. *Aug.* 85.1; perhaps never published?). In 45 Cicero makes Cato a speaker in his treatise on ethics entitled "On the Ends of Goods and Evils."

11. Caesar may have continued to value this cooperation. According to Cicero, Hirtius's response to the *Cato* included lavish praise of Cicero (*Att.* 12.40.1). The opening of Caesar's *Anticato*, too, contains an elaborate show of courtesy to Cicero (frr. 2–4; cf. *Att.* 13.46.2, Aug. 45); the surviving evidence does not permit firm conclusions about its sincerity.

Prominent Persons

A Roman man had two names (the praenomen, a personal name, and the nomen, a family name) or three (praenomen, nomen, and cognomen, a name distinguishing individuals or branches of a family) or even more: Quintus Caecilius Metellus Scipio Pius Nasica used multiple cognomina after his adoption from one proud Roman family into another.

In this book Roman men, once introduced, are generally referred to thereafter by cognomen if they have one (Gaius Julius CAESAR, Marcus Tullius CICERO, Marcus Porcius CATO) or nomen (Lucius AFRANIUS, Gaius PETREIUS); some are referred to by the more familiar Anglicized version of their nomen: ANTONY for Marcus Antonius, POMPEY for Gnaeus Pompeius Magnus, or by two parts of a name where one is insufficiently distinctive (QUINTUS Tullius CICERO, PUBLIUS Cornelius SULLA). Greek and Gallic men are referred to by their single name: PHARNACES, EGUS. Ancient authors are referred to by the familiar forms of their names (APPIAN, DIO, LUCAN). Listed below are names of persons mentioned in more than one section of this book, alphabetized by the capitalized names. For place names and Gallic peoples see maps.

Lucius AFRANIUS: Pompey's legate and Petreius's associate in Nearer Spain in 49. Defeated and pardoned by Caesar in the campaign narrated in *Civil War* 1. Joined Pompey in Greece before Pharsalus. Continued to resist Caesar until his capture and execution after Thapsus.

Gaius ANTONIUS: Caesarian legate, younger brother of Antony.

ANTONY = Marcus Antonius: Caesar's legate during the Gallic and civil wars; in 48 he commanded the forces waiting in Brindisi for their crossing to Greece and fought at Pharsalus. Consul in 44.

APPIAN: author of a history of Rome's civil wars. Active in the second century CE.

ARIOVISTUS: king of a Germanic people in Gaul. Defeated and expelled by Caesar in 58 BCE.

Titus Pomponius ATTICUS: contemporary of Caesar, a rich and influential Roman who avoided direct involvement in politics. Addressee of a large collection of letters from Cicero.

Lucius Cornelius BALBUS: Caesarian agent and correspondent of Cicero. Originally from Spain, he and his nephew (see below) gained Roman citizenship in the 70s BCE.

Lucius Cornelius BALBUS (the younger): Caesarian centurion wounded in Greece. Nephew of Balbus.

Marcus Junius BRUTUS: protégé and political associate of Cato, Pompeian during the civil war. Pardoned and promoted after Pharsalus. He married Cato's daughter in 45. Leader, with Cassius, of Caesar's assassins. Correspondent of Cicero's and dedicatee of his treatise on oratory at Rome, *Brutus*; author of a laudatory biography of Cato.

Marcus CAELIUS Rufus: Caesarian in 49. As praetor in 48, he attempted to undermine Caesar's control of Italy and was killed in a failed insurrection. Correspondent of Cicero's.

Gaius Julius CAESAR (see timeline)

Quintus Fufius CALENUS: Caesarian legate in Spain; commander, with Antony, of the Caesarian force that crossed to Greece in the spring of 48.

Marcus CALIDIUS: praetor in 57. In January of 49 he voiced a compromise position in the Senate. Caesarian legate in Cisalpine Gaul in 48 and 47.

Gnaeus Domitius CALVINUS: consul in 53 and 40. A high-ranking Caesarian legate in Macedonia, at Pharsalus, and later in Asia Minor.

Gaius CASSIUS Longinus: legate of Pompey, later adherent of Caesar, later still a leader, with Brutus, in the assassination of Caesar. Correspondent of Cicero's.

CATILINE = Lucius Sergius Catilina: Roman aristocrat responsible for an armed insurrection in 63, the year of Cicero's consulship. Killed in battle.

Marcus Porcius CATO: praetor in 54. Uncompromising opponent of both Pompey and Caesar during the 50s. Pompeian in the civil war. Appointed by the Senate to govern Sicily in 49, he abandoned the island to Curio. Joined Pompeians in Asia. After Pharsalus, joined resistance to Caesar in Africa. Suicide after Thapsus. Subject of laudatory biographies by Cicero and Brutus. Correspondent of Cicero's.

Marcus Tullius CICERO: consul in 63. Built a political career on oratorical successes. As consul, directed suppression of Catiline's insurrection. During the 50s, his political career suffered from the dominance of Pompey and Caesar, with both of whom he had a complicated relationship. Courted by Caesar in 49, he joined Pompey in Greece. He was reconciled with Caesar after Pharsalus, and worked thereafter for the restoration of former Pompeians. Proscribed and executed at Antony's behest in 43.

Lucius Tillius CIMBER: his record during the civil war is unknown. Held office under Caesar in 45 and 44. Joined the conspiracy to assassinate Caesar.

Marcus Aurelius COTTA: Pompeian appointed by the Senate to governorship of Sardinia in 49. Expelled by populace. Joined Pompeians in Africa.

Gaius Scribonius CURIO: active in support of senatorial authority during the 50s, as tribune of the people in 50 he parried political attacks on Caesar, bribed, it was thought, by Caesar. Commanded Caesarian troops in Italy, Sicily, and Africa. Defeated and killed by Juba in 49.

DECIMUS Junius BRUTUS: Caesarian officer in Gaul and later commanded the naval force attacking Marseilles. Governor of Cisalpine Gaul in 46. Joined conspiracy to assassinate Caesar in 44.

DIO: author of a history of Rome from the foundation to his own day (early third century CE).

Lucius DOMITIUS Ahenobarbus: praetor in 58. Opponent of Caesar during the 50s. Appointed by the Senate to replace Caesar in Gaul in 49. Defeated and pardoned at Corfinium. Joined resistance to Caesar at Marseilles. Later joined Pompey in Greece. Killed at Pharsalus. We follow Caesar's practice in referring to him by his nomen.

EGUS: officer in the Gallic cavalry fighting for Caesar; went over to Pompey before Dyrrachium. His people was the Allobroges. Brother of Roucillus.

Gaius FABIUS: Caesarian legate in Gaul; in 49, he commanded the troops in Spain before Caesar's arrival there.

Lucius Cornelius FAUSTUS SULLA: quaestor in 54. Pompeian in the civil war. Son of the dictator Sulla; son-in-law of Pompey.

GAIUS Claudius MARCELLUS: consul in 49, hard-line opponent of Caesar, commanded a Pompeian fleet in 48. Brother of Marcus Claudius Marcellus.

Aulus HIRTIUS: Caesarian legate in Gaul. Held various political and military posts during and after the civil war (none mentioned by Caesar). After Caesar's assassination he wrote *Gallic War* 8 and other Caesarian *Wars*, as well as an *Anticato*. Died as consul in 43.

ISOCRATES: Athenian author active during the early fourth century BCE and famous for the balanced and ornate style of his oratory.

JUBA: king of Numidia, ally of Pompey. Defeated Curio in North Africa. Supported the Pompeians who continued to resist Caesar after Pharsalus. Suicide after Thapsus.

Titus LABIENUS: Caesarian legate in Gaul 58–51 BCE. Joined Pompey at the outset of the civil war. Fought Caesar at Pharsalus, in Africa, and in Spain. Died at Munda.

Decimus LAELIUS: Pompeian fleet commander in Greece.

Lucius Cornelius LENTULUS Crus: consul in 49. Hard-line opponent of Caesar, appointed by Senate to governorship of Asia Minor. Joined Pompey with two legions in Greece. Assassinated shortly after Pompey in Alexandria. Younger brother of Spinther.

Lucius Scribonius LIBO: Pompeian fleet commander in Greece.

LUCAN: Roman epic poet of the early imperial period; died under Nero. Left a substantial but incomplete epic on the civil war between Pompey and Caesar.

LUCIUS Julius CAESAR: consul in 64. Political associate and distant relative of Caesar. Caesarian legate in Gaul. Father of Lucius Caesar the younger.

LUCIUS Julius CAESAR (the younger): Pompeian. Attempted negotiations between Pompey and Caesar in early 49, without success. After Pompey's death resisted Caesar in Africa. Pardoned after Thapsus. Later killed on Caesar's orders. Son of Lucius Caesar.

LUCIUS Calpurnius PISO: consul in 58, censor 50–49. Father of Caesar's wife.

LUCIUS ROSCIUS Fabatus: praetor in 49. Caesarian officer in Gaul. Attempted negotiations between Pompey and Caesar in early 49, without success.

Numerius MAGIUS: Pompeian officer. Captured by Caesar in 49. Conveyed peace terms between Caesar and Pompey, without result.

MARCUS Claudius MARCELLUS: consul in 51. Political opponent of Caesar during the 50s. Participated in the Senate meetings in January 49, but not in the civil war. Pardoned by Caesar in 46. Subject of Cicero's speech *For Marcellus*. Brother of Gaius Marcellus.

Gaius MATIUS: friend of Caesar and correspondent of Cicero.

Lucius Caecilius METELLUS: tribune of the people in 49. Opposed Caesar's seizure of Treasury funds in Rome, unsuccessfully.

Quintus Caecilius METELLUS SCIPIO Pius Nasica: father of Pompey's fourth wife, Pompey's consular colleague in 52, governor of Syria in 49–48, commander of three legions in civil war. Led resistance to Caesar in Africa after Pharsalus. Defeated at Thapsus, and killed shortly thereafter.

Gaius OPPIUS: friend and agent of Caesar, correspondent of Cicero.

Marcus PETREIUS: Pompey's legate and Afranius's associate in Nearer Spain in 49. Defeated and pardoned by Caesar in the campaign narrated in *Civil War* 1. Continued to resist Caesar until his suicide after Thapsus.

PHARNACES: king of Bosporus. After defeating his father, Mithradates, in 63, Pompey installed Pharnaces as king. During Rome's civil war he took possession of additional territory. Caesar defeated him decisively at the battle of Zela after a rapid campaign in 47.

PLUTARCH: author of the Flavian period. Wrote (among many other works) biographies of famous Romans including Sulla, Cicero, Caesar, and Antony.

Gaius Asinius POLLIO: Caesarian. Curio's legate in North Africa; wrote history of civil wars from 60 BCE.

POMPEY= Gnaeus Pompeius Magnus: after an extraordinarily successful military career and three consulships (70, 55, 52), and a political and personal alliance with Caesar during the 50s BCE (the "First Triumvirate" and marriage to Caesar's daughter), he was leader of the opposition to Caesar in the civil war. Defeated at the battle of Pharsalus in Thessaly in August 48. Assassinated in Alexandria in September.

PUBLIUS Cornelius SULLA: after a political career clouded by indictments, he served as a Caesarian legate in Thessaly. Nephew of Sulla.

QUINTILIAN: teacher of rhetoric during the Flavian period and author of *Education of an Orator*.

Sextus QUINTILIUS VARUS: quaestor in 49. Pompeian captured and pardoned at Corfinium. Joined resistance to Caesar in Africa.

QUINTUS Tullius CICERO: younger brother of Cicero; legate of Pompey, Caesar, and Cicero during the 50s BCE, Pompeian in 49. Proscribed and killed in 43.

ROUCILLUS: officer in the Gallic cavalry fighting for Caesar; went over to Pompey before Dyrrachium. His people was the Allobroges. Brother of Egus.

Publius Cornelius Lentulus SPINTHER: consul in 57. Captured and pardoned at Corfinium, joined Pompey in Greece, fought at Pharsalus. Elder brother of Lentulus Crus.

SUETONIUS: biographer of the imperial period; active under Domitian, Trajan, and Hadrian. Wrote biographies of Rome's rulers from Caesar to Domitian.

Lucius Cornelius SULLA: Roman magistrate and general of the early first century BCE who turned his army on Rome in 88 and 83. Dictator 82–79. Instituted proscription as a political weapon. Author of laws strengthening senatorial dominance. Resigned from public office in 79; died the same year. Author of an autobiography.

Quintus Minucius THERMUS: Pompeian garrison commander in northern Italy in 49.

Gaius TREBONIUS: Caesarian legate in Gaul and later at Marseilles, where he directed the construction of siege works. Consul in 45.

Lucius Aelius TUBERO: appointed by the Senate to governorship of Africa for 49.

Quintus VALERIUS Orca: praetor in 57. Caesarian legate in Sardinia.

Marcus Terentius VARRO: Pompeian legate in Further Spain at the beginning of 49. Survived the civil war and was reconciled with Caesar. A prolific author, most of whose work has been lost.

Publius Attius VARUS: Pompeian commander in North Africa in 49. Died at Munda.

VELLEIUS PATERCULUS: Roman historian from the early imperial period; died under Tiberius. Wrote brief history of Rome from the beginnings to his own day.

VERCINGETORIX: Arvernian leader of the Gallic revolt against Caesar in 52. Defeated Caesar at Gergovia, defeated by him at Alesia. Executed in Caesar's triumph in 46.

Works Cited

Adcock, F. E. 1956. *Caesar as Man of Letters*. Cambridge.
Albrecht, M. von. 1989 (German original 1971). "Caesar." In *Masters of Roman Prose from Cato to Apuleius: Interpretative Studies*. Leeds. 54–67.
Batstone, W. W. 1990. "*Etsi*: A Tendentious Hypotaxis in Caesar's Plain Style." *American Journal of Philology* 111: 348–60.
———. 1991. "A Narrative Gestalt and the Force of Caesar's Style." *Mnemosyne* 44: 126–36.
Boatwright, M. T. 1988. "Caesar's Second Consulship and the Completion and Date of the *Bellum civile*." *Classical Journal* 84: 31–40.
Broughton, T. R. S. 1984–86 (original publication 1951–52, 1960). *The Magistrates of the Roman Republic*. 3 vols. Reprint, with rev. ed. of Supplement volume. Chico.
Brown, R. D. 1999. "Two Caesarian Battle-Descriptions: A Study in Contrast." *Classical Journal* 94: 329–57.
Brown, V. 1972. *The Textual Transmission of Caesar's Civil War*. Leiden.
Bruhns, H. 1978. *Caesar und die römische Oberschicht in den Jahren 49–44 v. Chr.* Göttingen.
Cairns, F., and E. Fantham, eds. 2003. *Caesar against Liberty? Perspectives on His Autocracy*. Papers of the Langford Latin Seminar 11, ARCA 43. Cambridge.
Carter, J. M. 1991. *Julius Caesar. The Civil War, Books I & II*. Warminster.
———. 1993. *Julius Caesar. The Civil War, Book III*. Warminster.

Collins, J. H. 1959. "On the Date and Interpretation of the *Bellum Civile*." *American Journal of Philology* 80: 113–32.

———. 1972. "Caesar as Political Propagandist." *Aufstieg und Niedergang der römischen Welt* I.1: 922–66.

Eden, P. T. 1962. "Caesar's Style: Inheritance versus Intelligence." *Glotta* 90: 74–117.

Gelzer, M. 1968 (German original 1921). *Caesar: Politician and Statesman*. Trans. P. Needham. Cambridge, Mass.

Goldsworthy, A. 1998. "'Instinctive Genius': The Depiction of Caesar the General." In Welch and Powell. 193–219.

Gotoff, H. C. 1984. "Towards a Practical Criticism of Caesar's Prose Style." *Illinois Classical Studies* 9: 1–18.

Griffin, M. 2003. "*Clementia* after Caesar: From Politics to Philosophy." In Cairns and Fantham 2003. 157–82.

Hyart, C. 1953. *Les origines du style indirect latin et son emploi jusqu'à l'époque de César*. Brussels.

Jehne, M. 2000. "Caesar und die Krise von 47 v. Chr." In G. Urso, ed., *L'ultimo Cesare: Scritti, riforme, progetti, poteri, congiure*. Rome. 151–73.

Klotz, A. 1969 (original publication 1950). *C. Iuli Caesaris commentarii: Vol. II, Commentarii belli civilis*. 2nd ed. Reprint. Leipzig.

———. 1982 (original publication 1927). *C. Iuli Caesaris commentarii: Vol. III, Commentarii belli alexandrini, belli africi, belli hispaniensis*. Stuttgart.

Lieberg, G. 1998. *Caesars Politik in Gallien: Interpretationen zum Bellum Gallicum*. Bochum.

Lossmann, F. 1957. "Zur literarischen Kritik Suetons in den Kapiteln 55 und 56 der Caesarvita." *Hermes* 85: 47–58.

MacFarlane, R. T. 1996. "*Ab inimicis incitatus*: On Dating the Composition of Caesar's *Bellum Civile*." *Syllecta classica* 7: 107–32.

Marincola, J. 1997. *Authority and Tradition in Ancient Historiography*. Cambridge.

Meier, C. 1995 (German original 1982). *Caesar*. Trans. D. McLintock. New York.

Morgan, L. 2000. "The Autopsy of C. Asinius Pollio." *Journal of Roman Studies* 90: 51–69.

Nousek, D. 2004. "Narrative Style and Genre in Caesar's *Bellum gallicum*." PhD diss., Rutgers University.

Raditsa, L. 1973. "Julius Caesar and His Writings." *Aufstieg und Niedergang der römischen Welt* I.3: 417–56.

Radt, S. L., ed. 1999 (original edition 1977). *Tragicorum graecorum fragmenta. Vol. 4: Sophocles*. Corr. and exp. ed. Göttingen.

Riggsby, A. 2006. *Caesar in Gaul and Rome: War in Words*. Austin.

Rossi, A. F. 2000. "The Camp of Pompey: Strategy of Representation in Caesar's *Bellum Civile*." *Classical Journal* 95: 239–56.

Seager, R. 1994. "Sulla." In J. A. Crook, A. Lintott, and E. Rawson, eds., *The Cambridge Ancient History, Second Edition, Volume IX: The Last Age of the Roman Republic, 146–43 B.C.* Cambridge. 165–207.

Shackleton Bailey, D. R. 1965–70. *Cicero's Letters to Atticus*. 7 vols. Cambridge.

Stadter, P. A. 1993. "Caesarian Tactics and Caesarian Style: *Bell. Civ.* 1.66–70." *Classical Journal* 88: 217–21.

Sumner, G. V. 1971. "The *Lex annalis* under Caesar." *Phoenix* 25: 246–71.

Syme, R. 1938. "The Allegiance of Labienus." *Journal of Roman Studies* 28: 113–25.

Tronson, A. 2001. "Pompey the Barbarian: Caesar's Presentation of 'The Other' in *Bellum civile* 3." In M. Joyal, ed., *In Altum: Seventy-five Years of Classical Studies in Newfoundland*. St. Johns. 73–104.

Welch, K. 1998. "Caesar and His Officers in the Gallic War Commentaries." In Welch and Powell. 85–110.

Welch, K., and A. Powell, eds. 1998. *Julius Caesar as Artful Reporter: The War Commentaries as Political Instruments*. London.

Wistrand, E. 1979. *Caesar and Contemporary Roman Society*. Göteborg.

Index

General references to Caesar, Pompey, Rome, and the Senate are not indexed; this book is so consistently concerned with these topics that it would be more efficient (if absurd) to cite the pages on which they are not discussed. Personal names are indexed under nomen, where known (see list of prominent persons). The notes are not independently indexed; citations in the notes will be found through references to the text annotated.

Adriatic, 6
Aedui, 36, 39
Aelius Tubero, Lucius, 71–72
Afranius, Lucius, 20, 71, 76–81, 83, 84, 148
Africa. *See* North Africa
Ahenobarbus. *See* Domitius Ahenobarbus, Lucius
Alesia, 39–41, 69
Alexandria, 7, 31, 117
Alexandrian War, 31
Allobroges, 138, 152
Alps, 38
Ampius Balbus, Titus, 167
anaphora, 25
Ancona, 61, 62
Androsthenes, 138

annalistic structure, 38, 75
Anneius, Marcus, 21
antithesis, 25
Antonius, Gaius, 30
Antonius, Marcus, 13, 22, 62, 102, 139, 145–47, 154
Appian, 7, 16–17, 27, 96
  Civil War 2.30, 94
  Civil War 2.38, 17
  Civil War 2.84–86, 27–28
Arar River, 36
Ariminum, 57, 59, 61
Ariovistus, 37, 146
Aristotle, 10
Armenia, 168
Arretium, 62
Arverni, 39–41

Asculum, 63
Asia Minor, 4, 51, 157
Asparagium, 102
Asinius Pollio, Gaius, 30–31
Athens, 157
Atticus. *See* Pomponius Atticus, Titus
Attius Varus, Publius, 62, 66, 71–72, 99, 128, 147
Audience, 90–95
Aurelius Cotta, Marcus, 71
Auximum, 61–63, 66, 71

Bagradas River, 164
Balbus. *See* Cornelius Balbus, Lucius
Belgae, 38
Bibracte, 39–41
Bithynia, 157
Bituriges, 41
Black Sea, 5
Brindisi, 22, 23, 25, 68, 74, 91, 125, 139
Brutus. *See* Junius Brutus, Marcus

Cadiz, 97
Caecilius Metellus, Lucius, 72
Caecilius Metellus Scipio, Quintus, 25–26, 44–46, 48, 50–51, 53, 73, 94, 106, 109–12, 115, 139, 145–46, 152, 153, 155, 156
Caecilius Rufus, Lucius, 24
Caelius Rufus, Marcus, 47–48, 121, 145–46
Caesar. *See* Julius Caesar
Calenus. *See* Fufius Calenus, Quintus

Calidius, Marcus, 47, 48, 145–46
Calpurnius Piso, Lucius, 36–37, 145–46
Calvinus. *See* Domitius Calvinus, Gnaeus
Campania, 12, 91
Capua, 24, 47, 61
Caralis, 71
Carmona, 97
Carnutes, 41
Cassius, Lucius, 36
Cassius Longinus, Gaius, 114, 145–46
Cato. *See* Porcius Cato, Marcus
Celtiberia, 76
Cicero. *See* Tullius Cicero
Cilicia, 14–15, 21, 157
Cimber. *See* Tillius Cimber
Cingulum, 63, 107, 109
Cisalpine Gaul. *See* Gaul
Claudius Marcellus, Gaius, 95
Claudius Marcellus, Marcus, 46–48, 50, 124, 145–46, 167, 168
Cleopatra, 7
closure, 41, 42, 74, 75–84
    argumentative, 80–82
    formal, 83–84
    narrative, 76–80
Comitium, 49
commentarius, 8–11, 27, 30, 34, 98, 118, 145, 148, 157, 165
Corcyra, 22, 157
Corfinium, 6, 16, 17, 23, 24, 64–68, 83, 93, 95, 98, 100, 118, 139, 140, 147, 163
Cornelius Balbus, Lucius, 24, 60, 69, 118, 168
Cornelius Faustus Sulla, Lucius, 95

Cornelius Lentulus Crus, Lucius, 44, 48, 50, 53, 63, 73, 93, 94, 145–46, 158, 163–64
Cornelius Lentulus Spinther, Publius, 17, 24, 25, 63, 67, 139
Cornelius Sulla, Lucius, 5, 6, 50, 56, 60, 93–95, 146
Cotta. *See* Aurelius Cotta, Marcus
Crastinus, 136
Curicta, 30, 31, 123
Curio. *See* Scribonius Curio, Gaius
Cyclades, 157

Damasippus, Lucius, 24–25
Decimus Brutus. *See* Junius Brutus, Decimus
Dio, 7
   38.3.1, 6
   38.43.3, 146
   41.10.2, 16
   41.11.1–3, 16
   41.23.2, 96
Domitius Ahenobarbus, Lucius, 12–14, 16, 17, 24–26, 64, 65, 95, 101, 137, 141, 163
son, 24
Domitius Calvinus, Gnaeus, 111–12, 139
Dyrrachium, 22, 24, 102, 103, 107, 108, 124–27, 129, 151, 156

Ebro River, 77
Egus, 137–38
Egypt, 3, 27, 31, 157
evocati, 49

Fabius, Gaius, 20, 148
Fanum, 61, 62
Faustus Sulla. *See* Cornelius Faustus Sulla, Lucius
Felginas, Gaius, 24
Florus
   2.92, 169
Fortune, 97–98, 103, 122, 127
Fufius Calenus, Quintus, 125, 139
Further Spain. *See* Spain

Gaius Marcellus. *See* Claudius Marcellus, Gaius
Gallic War, 89, 90
Gaul, 4, 6, 8, 10, 12, 20, 34–41, 57, 72, 80, 106, 108, 137, 145, 148
Gergovia, 109
Germany, 57
Gomphi, 134, 138
Granius, Aulus, 24
Greece, 19, 31, 101, 102, 111, 112, 117, 125, 139, 154, 156–57

Hegesaratus, 138
Helvetii, 36
Hispalis, 97
Hirtius, Aulus, 8, 30, 33, 94, 106, 148
   Gallic War 8, 41
   Gallic War 8 preface 2, 30
   Gallic War 8 preface 7, 10, 148
   Gallic War 8.50.3, 95
Homer
   Odyssey 11.964, 92

Ides of March, 32
Iguvium, 61, 62, 152

Ilerda, 42, 70, 74, 76, 80, 81, 83, 150–51 (*see also* Spain)
Illyricum, 30
intercession, 52, 58
Issa, 138
Italian allies, 5
Italica, 97
Italy, 31

Juba, 24, 95, 99, 101, 114, 115, 164
Julius Caesar, Gaius
  addresses Senate, 74
  Anticato, 171
  assassination, 4
  birth, 3
  Cic. *Att.* 9.7C, 18
  Cic. *Att.* 9.7C.1, 60, 118
  Cic. *Att.* 9.7C.2, 118
  Cic. *Att.* 9.7C.6, 45
  Civil War, 90, 106, 107, 109, 113, 115, 117, 119, 122, 123, 128, 129, 131, 133, 135, 136, 139–41, 143, 145–48, 150, 153, 154, 161, 162, 171
  Civil War 1, 34, 56, 91, 99, 101, 129, 133, 156, 162
  Civil War 1.1–5, 145
  Civil War 1.1–6, 72
  Civil War 1.1–11, 80
  Civil War 1.1.1–3, 43
  Civil War 1.1.4, 44–45
  Civil War 1.2.1, 45, 109
  Civil War 1.2.2, 81
  Civil War 1.2.3, 47
  Civil War 1.2.4–6, 48, 80
  Civil War 1.2.5, 81, 124
  Civil War 1.2.6, 124
  Civil War 1.2.8, 45, 81
  Civil War 1.3–4, 49–51
  Civil War 1.3.1–3, 81
  Civil War 1.3.5, 80, 81, 124
  Civil War 1.4.1, 93
  Civil War 1.4.3, 110, 112
  Civil War 1.4.4, 95
  Civil War 1.4.5, 81
  Civil War 1.5, 52
  Civil War 1.5.4, 81
  Civil War 1.5.5, 45, 81
  Civil War 1.5.6, 109
  Civil War 1.6, 53, 95
  Civil War 1.6.5, 81, 110
  Civil War 1.6.6, 122
  Civil War 1.6.8, 51, 74
  Civil War 1.7, 55, 56, 131–32
  Civil War 1.7.3–4, 81
  Civil War 1.7.8, 135
  Civil War 1.8–9, 139
  Civil War 1.8–10, 57
  Civil War 1.8.3, 132–33
  Civil War 1.9, 133
  Civil War 1.9.2, 132
  Civil War 1.9.5, 59, 81
  Civil War 1.9.6, 81
  Civil War 1.10–11, 59
  Civil War 1.11.1, 81
  Civil War 1.11.3, 81
  Civil War 1.11.4, 55
  Civil War 1.12–15, 61
  Civil War 1.12.1, 98
  Civil War 1.12.3, 98
  Civil War 1.13.2, 72
  Civil War 1.14.1, 54
  Civil War 1.14.3, 55
  Civil War 1.15–23, 64
  Civil War 1.15.1, 107, 148
  Civil War 1.15.2, 107

Civil War 1.18.2, 147
Civil War 1.18.5, 98
Civil War 1.19–24, 83
Civil War 1.19.4, 163
Civil War 1.20.5, 17
Civil War 1.21.1–2, 160–61
Civil War 1.22.1–6, 17
Civil War 1.22.3–6, 139
Civil War 1.22.5, 132
Civil War 1.23.1, 17
Civil War 1.23.2, 23–24
Civil War 1.24–28, 70
Civil War 1.25.3, 74
Civil War 1.26, 23
Civil War 1.30–31, 72
Civil War 1.30.2, 99
Civil War 1.30.4–1.31.1, 98
Civil War 1.30.5, 47
Civil War 1.31.2, 129
Civil War 1.32, 70
Civil War 1.32–33, 72, 83
Civil War 1.32.2, 32
Civil War 1.32.2–3, 132
Civil War 1.32.5, 74
Civil War 1.32.8, 125
Civil War 1.32.9–10, 64
Civil War 1.33, 125
Civil War 1.35, 162
Civil War 1.35.1, 120
Civil War 1.35.4–5, 128
Civil War 1.37, 20
Civil War 1.38.1, 96
Civil War 1.38.3, 149
Civil War 1.39–40, 20
Civil War 1.40, 126
Civil War 1.42.4, 146
Civil War 1.43–47, 123
Civil War 1.43–72, 102
Civil War 1.44.1, 153

Civil War 1.44.2, 119, 149
Civil War 1.45–46, 103
Civil War 1.45.1, 146
Civil War 1.45.2, 125
Civil War 1.50, 126
Civil War 1.51, 126
Civil War 1.52.2, 126
Civil War 1.54, 126
Civil War 1.54.4, 146
Civil War 1.64–69, 76–77
Civil War 1.69.3, 122
Civil War 1.71–72, 78, 82
Civil War 1.72, 121
Civil War 1.74, 133
Civil War 1.74–76, 79
Civil War 1.74–85, 83
Civil War 1.74–87, 82
Civil War 1.74.1, 81
Civil War 1.74.7, 45
Civil War 1.75–76, 133–34
Civil War 1.80–83, 110
Civil War 1.80–84, 79
Civil War 1.84–86, 82
Civil War 1.85, 70, 121
Civil War 1.85.2, 83
Civil War 1.85.4, 119
Civil War 1.85.11, 84
Civil War 1.87.2, 80
Civil War 2, 26, 30, 31, 101, 128, 129, 134, 162
Civil War 2.1, 20
Civil War 2.3.1–2, 99
Civil War 2.4.4, 127
Civil War 2.5–7, 127
Civil War 2.8.3, 119
Civil War 2.9, 21
Civil War 2.11, 158–60
Civil War 2.12.3–4, 162
Civil War 2.12.4, 119

Julius Caesar, Gaius (*continued*)
   Civil War 2.13.1, 162
   Civil War 2.14, 162
   Civil War 2.14.1, 128
   Civil War 2.14.3, 126
   Civil War 2.15.4, 126
   Civil War 2.17–21, 96
   Civil War 2.17.4–2.20.8, 97–98
   Civil War 2.21.1–3, 134–35
   Civil War 2.22.6, 128
   Civil War 2.23–44, 98
   Civil War 2.24.3, 45
   Civil War 2.26.1, 110
   Civil War 2.27.2, 119, 128, 129
   Civil War 2.31.1, 153
   Civil War 2.39.1–2, 164
   Civil War 2.39.2, 128
   Civil War 2.44.3, 24
   Civil War 3, 26, 30, 76, 102, 106, 129, 134, 162
   Civil War 3.1.1, 32
   Civil War 3.2.3, 108
   Civil War 3.3.1–2, 157
   Civil War 3.4.2, 30, 110
   Civil War 3.5.2, 102
   Civil War 3.5.3, 105
   Civil War 3.6–96, 117
   Civil War 3.6.3, 102
   Civil War 3.8.2, 125
   Civil War 3.9, 138
   Civil War 3.10.3–6, 30, 122
   Civil War 3.11.2, 102
   Civil War 3.12, 102
   Civil War 3.13.3, 107
   Civil War 3.14, 125
   Civil War 3.14.3, 127
   Civil War 3.17.1, 130
   Civil War 3.18.4, 123
   Civil War 3.19, 107
   Civil War 3.19.7, 24
   Civil War 3.20.3, 121
   Civil War 3.20.3, 120
   Civil War 3.20.8, 120
   Civil War 3.23–24, 22
   Civil War 3.25.2, 45
   Civil War 3.26.1, 139
   Civil War 3.26.4, 127
   Civil War 3.26.5, 127
   Civil War 3.27.1, 127
   Civil War 3.28, 124
   Civil War 3.28.4, 154
   Civil War 3.30.2, 102
   Civil War 3.30.6, 102
   Civil War 3.30.7, 102
   Civil War 3.31–33, 110–11
   Civil War 3.34.4, 138
   Civil War 3.35.2, 138
   Civil War 3.36–38, 110–12
   Civil War 3.36.1, 119
   Civil War 3.36.8, 139
   Civil War 3.38.1, 139
   Civil War 3.38.3, 155
   Civil War 3.41.2, 102
   Civil War 3.42.5, 157
   Civil War 3.44.6, 161
   Civil War 3.45.6, 130
   Civil War 3.46.3, 149
   Civil War 3.47.1, 102
   Civil War 3.47.3, 151
   Civil War 3.47.5, 108
   Civil War 3.49, 151
   Civil War 3.51.3, 130
   Civil War 3.51.4, 120
   Civil War 3.52, 19
   Civil War 3.53.4, 135
   Civil War 3.53.5, 135–36
   Civil War 3.57, 110, 112
   Civil War 3.57.4, 156

Civil War 3.58.3, 155
Civil War 3.58.5, 155
Civil War 3.59–60, 137
Civil War 3.60.1, 138
Civil War 3.60.3, 131
Civil War 3.62.1, 103
Civil War 3.64, 124
Civil War 3.64.3, 108
Civil War 3.67.5, 30
Civil War 3.68.1, 103
Civil War 3.69, 124
Civil War 3.69.4, 155
Civil War 3.70.1, 103, 129–30
Civil War 3.71.1, 24, 108
Civil War 3.71.4, 107
Civil War 3.73.3–4, 120
Civil War 3.73.5, 125, 127
Civil War 3.73.6, 108
Civil War 3.74.1, 124
Civil War 3.74.2, 155
Civil War 3.74.3, 156
Civil War 3.75.3, 122
Civil War 3.79–81, 134
Civil War 3.79.6, 137
Civil War 3.79.7, 137
Civil War 3.82.1, 104
Civil War 3.83.1, 112
Civil War 3.83.1–3, 25
Civil War 3.83.4, 25
Civil War 3.84.5, 138
Civil War 3.85.4, 135
Civil War 3.86, 104
Civil War 3.86.5, 108
Civil War 3.87.1–4, 108
Civil War 3.87.5, 109
Civil War 3.87.5–6, 105
Civil War 3.87.7, 109
Civil War 3.88–89, 105
Civil War 3.89.2, 109

Civil War 3.89.4, 105
Civil War 3.90.1, 119
Civil War 3.90.1–2, 162–63
Civil War 3.91, 136
Civil War 3.92.2–3, 105
Civil War 3.92.4, 105, 130
Civil War 3.93.2, 122
Civil War 3.96, 106
Civil War 3.96.1, 157–58
Civil War 3.96.3, 41
Civil War 3.96.4, 117
Civil War 3.98.2, 45
Civil War 3.99, 105
Civil War 3.99.2–3, 136
Civil War 3.99.5, 26
Civil War 3.100, 22
Civil War 3.101.4, 127
Civil War 3.102, 105
Civil War 3.104.1, 128
Civil War 3.104.2–3, 28
Civil War 3.104.3, 26
Civil War 3.107.2, 117
Civil War 3.112.3, 119
Civil War 3.112.12, 29
consulship, 5–6, 32
duty, 119, 120
engineering, 20–21, 158
Gallic War, 6, 8, 27, 29, 30, 33–35, 42, 51, 57, 80, 82, 106, 156
Gallic War 1, beginning, 37
Gallic War 1.54, 38
Gallic War 2.1, 38
Gallic War 2.35, 38
Gallic War 3.2, 38
Gallic War 3.29, 38
Gallic War 4.1, 38
Gallic War 4.17, 21
Gallic War 4.38, 38

Julius Caesar, Gaius (*continued*)
   Gallic War 5.1, 38
   Gallic War 6.3, 38
   Gallic War 6.44, 38
   Gallic War 7, ending, 38–41
   Gallic War 7.1, 38
   Gallic War 7.51.4, 109
   Gallic War 7.73, 69
   Gallic War 7.90, 38, 43
   leniency, 16, 21, 45, 49, 52, 60, 67, 74, 76, 78, 81, 82, 93, 96, 116, 131, 139, 166
   naming names, 18–27
   oratory, 3
   rhetoric, 17, 25, 29, 36, 48, 52, 54, 56–57, 63, 66, 73, 84, 110, 119–65
   using victory, 14, 18
[Julius Caesar, Gaius]
   African War, 29
   Alexandrian War, 29
   Alexandrian War 1.1, 29
   Spanish War, 29
Julius Caesar, Lucius, 57–58
Junius Brutus, Decimus, 71, 76
Junius Brutus, Marcus, 170

Labienus, Titus, 18, 106–8
Laelius, Decimus, 22, 23
Larisa, 41
Lentulus. *See* Cornelius Lentulus
Libo. *See* Scribonius Libo
Lucan, 7, 141, 150–51
   Civil War 2.511–25, 141
   Civil War 4.11–15, 150–51
Lucretius, 147

Macedonia, 111, 138, 139
Magius, Numerius, 67–69
Marcellus. *See* Claudius Marcellus
Marcius Philippus, Lucius, 95
Marseilles, 6–7, 20, 21, 31, 42, 71, 76, 99, 101, 127, 128, 158–60
Massilia. *See* Marseilles
Matius, Gaius, 166, 169–70
Mediterranean, 4, 6–7, 14
Menedemus, 138
metaphor, 111
Metellus. *See* Caecilius Metellus
metonomy, 34–35
Minucius Thermus, Quintus, 62

Naples, 168
Narbo, 20
Nearer Spain. *See* Spain
North Africa, 4, 5, 6, 25, 31, 42, 71, 75, 98–101, 109, 113, 114, 123, 131, 164, 170, 171
Numidia, 114

Oppius, Gaius, 60, 118
optimates, 152
Otacilius Crassus, 124

Parthians, 110
Parthini, 157
Petraeus, 138
Petreius, Marcus, 71, 76–77, 81, 83, 107
Pharsalus, 6, 22, 25, 26, 27, 31, 41, 90, 92, 96, 98, 102, 105–6, 108–9, 113–17, 119, 129, 136, 157–58, 162–63, 166, 171
Philippus. *See* Marcius Philippus
Phoenicia, 157

Picenum, 63, 107
pietas, 36
Pisaurum, 61, 62
Piso. *See* Calpurnius Piso, Lucius
Placentia, 24
Plutarch, 7, 96, 144
    Caesar 34.6–8, 17
    Cat. min. 66.2, 170
Pindenissum, 21
Plotius, Marcus, 24
polyptoton, 25
Pompeian confidence, 47, 53
Pompeian cruelty, 45, 49, 50, 60, 66, 69, 74, 79, 80, 93, 101, 107, 110, 114, 146, 152, 157
Pompeian duplicity, 44, 47, 48, 49, 56, 65, 79, 80, 81, 93
Pompeian irrationality, 44, 48, 49, 56, 80, 92
Pompeius Magnus, Gnaeus, 5–6, 7, 9, 11, 13, 18–22, 24–26, 30, 31, 41, 45, 47, 50–51, 53–65, 68–70, 73, 76, 81
    assassination, 3, 27–29, 128, 129
    Cic. *Att.* 8.12.B, C, and D, 163
Pomponius Atticus, Titus, 9, 12, 18, 27, 91, 96, 114, 170–71
Pomptinus, Gaius, 21
Pontus, 157
Porcius Cato, Marcus, 6, 14–15, 21, 47, 50, 71–72, 141, 145–46, 170, 171
proscriptions, 5
provinces, 4
Ptolemies, 117
Ptolemy, 7, 27

Puteoli, 24
Pyrenees, 20

Quintilian, 3, 117, 165
Quintilius Varus, Sextus, 24

Ravenna, 6, 52, 55, 57
res gestae, 9, 16, 18, 21, 32
res publica, 41, 44, 49, 51, 54, 57, 58, 60, 65, 68, 69, 73–75, 79, 81, 83, 132–33, 139, 141
Rhine River, 21
Roscius Fabatus, Lucius, 61, 145–46
Roucillus, 137–38
Rubicon River, 6, 12, 55, 57
Rubrius, Lucius, 24

Saburra, 164
Sacrativir, Marcus, 24
Sallust
    Jug. 5.2, 55
Salonae, 138
Sardinia, 70–71, 122
Scaeva, 135–36
Scribonius Curio, Gaius, 13, 31, 62, 70–71, 75, 94, 96, 98–101, 103, 106, 110, 122, 128, 131, 138, 139, 164
Scribonius Libo, Lucius, 22, 23
Segre River, 77, 126, 150–51
Sempronius, 28
Senate, 4, 5, 6, 12, 32, 43–52, 53–56, 61, 64, 69, 70, 71, 82, 84
senatus consultum ultimum, 51, 52, 61, 70, 74, 84, 90, 94, 95, 132, 154

Sequani, 36
Sicily, 6, 70–71, 99, 122
Sophocles, 27, 28
Spain, 5, 6–7, 20, 31, 42, 59, 70–72, 76, 80, 84, 96, 119, 121, 123, 133, 170, 171
speech, 46, 58–59, 65–69, 73, 79, 81–83 (*see also* Ilerda)
Suetonius, 7
   DJ 34.1, 17
   DJ 56.1, 31
Sulla. *See* Cornelius Sulla
Sulmo, 147
Sulpicius, Servius (*filius*), 24–25
Sulpicius, Servius (*pater*), 25, 94
Syria, 5, 51, 104, 110, 111, 157, 168

Temple of Saturn, 54
Terentius Varro, Marcus, 31, 96–98, 101, 106
thanksgiving, 39, 43, 75
Thapsus, 25, 26, 32, 98, 114, 115, 170
Themistogenes. *See* Xenophon
Thermus. *See* Minucius Thermus, Quintus
Thessaly, 22, 111, 138
Thucydides, 144
Tiburtius, Lucius, 24
Tigurinus, 36
Tillius Cimber, Lucius, 167, 169
Transalpine Gaul. *See* Gaul
Trebonius, Gaius, 20, 21, 71
Triarius, Gaius, 105
tribunes of the people, 4, 43, 52, 55–58, 61, 81, 132, 140
Tubero. *See* Aelius Tubero, Lucius

Tullius, Lucius, 21
Tullius Cicero, Marcus, 3, 5, 12, 14, 18, 21, 23, 24, 26, 27, 32, 55, 91–94, 96, 107, 113–15, 154, 165, 170
   Att. 1.20.6, 9
   Att. 2.1.1, 9–10
   Att. 7.3.5, 91
   Att. 7.4.2, 91
   Att. 7.4.3, 91
   Att. 7.5.4, 91, 93
   Att. 7.6.2, 91–92
   Att. 7.7.7, 93
   Att. 7.8.4, 92
   Att. 7.8.4–5, 91
   Att. 7.10.1, 92
   Att. 7.13.2, 47, 54, 92
   Att. 7.13a.3, 18
   Att. 8.3.3, 92
   Att. 8.9.1, 23
   Att. 8.9a.1, 93
   Att. 8.9A.2, 94
   Att. 8.13.1, 23
   Att. 8.15.3, 91
   Att. 9.1.4, 92
   Att. 9.5.1–2, 93
   Att. 9.6.6, 26
   Att. 9.6.7, 9, 23, 93
   Att. 9.6.16, 26
   Att. 9.6A, 26
   Att. 9.7.3, 92
   Att. 9.7C, 171
   Att. 9.10.2, 92–94
   Att. 9.10.3, 93
   Att. 9.10.6, 94
   Att. 9.11.2, 23
   Att. 9.13A.1, 68
   Att. 9.14.1, 94
   Att. 9.14.1–2, 68–69

Att. 9.14.2, 93
Att. 9.15.3, 94
Att. 9.18, 26
Att. 11.6.1, 114
Att. 11.6.2, 114
Att. 11.6.6, 92, 113
Att. 11.7.2, 166
Att. 11.7.3, 114
Att. 12.4.2, 171
Att. 14.1.1, 166, 169
Att. 15.15.1, 3, 115
Brutus 253, 143
Brutus 262, 143
Cato, 171
Fam. 4.4.3, 167, 168
Fam. 4.7.3, 167
Fam. 4.9.2, 113
Fam. 4.9.6, 113
Fam. 6.6.6, 113
Fam. 6.12, 169
Fam. 6.12.1–2, 167
Fam. 7.3.2, 113
Fam. 9.1.2, 113
Fam. 9.15.4, 168
Fam. 9.27–28, 169
Fam. 11.27.4–5, 169
Fam. 11.28.2, 169, 170
Fam. 11.28.4, 170
Fam. 12.18.2, 168
Fam. 15.4.13, 14–16
Fam. 16.12, 18
Marc., 167
Marc., 21, 168
Tullius Cicero, Quintus, 21
Tullus. *See* Volcacius Tullus
Tuticanus Gallus, 24

Utica, 99, 164

Valerius, Quintus, 71
Var River, 80, 84
Varro. *See* Terentius Varro, Marcus
Varus. *See* Attius Varus
Vatinius, Publius, 22
Velleius Paterculus, 3, 7
Vercingetorix, 39–40
Volcacius Tullus, Gaius, 19

Xenophon, 144, 145